SIXTH EDITION

WRITING
WITH A
THESIS

A RHETORIC AND READER

SIXTH EDITION

WRITING WITH A THESIS

A RHETORIC AND READER

DAVID SKWIRE

CUYAHOGA COMMUNITY COLLEGE

HARCOURT BRACE COLLEGE PUBLISHERS

Fort Worth   Philadelphia   San Diego   New York   Orlando   Austin   San Antonio
Toronto   Montreal   London   Sydney   Tokyo

Publisher • Ted Buchholz
Acquisitions Editor • Michael Rosenberg
Developmental Editor • Camille Adkins
Project Editor • Margaret Allyson
Production Manager • Cynthia Young
Senior Book Designer • Don Fujimoto
Permissions Editors • Van Strength/Julia C. Stewart

Printed in the United States of America

ISBN 0-03-079101-4

Library of Congress Number 92-75620

3 4 5 6 7 8 9 0 1 2   090   9 8 7 6 5 4 3 2 1

THIS
BOOK
IS
FOR
MIDGE
WITH
LOVE
AND
GRATITUDE

GUIDE TO
"WHAT ABOUT *YOUR* WRITING?"

As noted in "To the Instructor" (pp. ix-x), "What About *Your* Writing?" entries offer comments and pointers on miscellaneous matters of practical concern to the student writer, as such matters turn up in the readings. For general perspectives and quick references, the following guide is appended.

TO THE INSTRUCTOR

I love the young dogs of this age: they have more wit and humor and knowledge of life than we had; but then the dogs are not so good scholars. Sir, in my early years I read very hard.

SAMUEL JOHNSON

In many respects, *Writing with a Thesis* tries to do a traditional job in a traditional way. Its readings are arranged according to traditional rhetorical patterns, one pattern per chapter. Each group of readings is preceded by a detailed discussion of the writing techniques appropriate to that pattern. Headnotes, explanatory footnotes, and questions on content and style accompany each reading. The book wholeheartedly accepts such traditional ideas about teaching composition as the value of omnivorous reading, the utility of close analysis of individual works, and the salutary influence of models.

In some other respects, *Writing with a Thesis* is less traditional, though its commitment to the job of improving writing skills remains constant.

First, the traditional reader or rhetoric–reader tends to approach each rhetorical pattern as a separate entity requiring the development of a new set of writing skills. Chapter 1 of this book presents what it calls *the persuasive principle:* the development and support of a thesis. It goes on to demonstrate how the persuasive principle underlies almost all good writing, and subsequent chapters show how the persuasive principle functions within each of the rhetorical patterns. A major unifying theme thus runs through the entire book, each pattern being viewed not as a separate entity but as the application of a permanent writing principle to varying subject matter, insights, and purposes. The concept of the persuasive principle has long been stressed in some of the most popular handbooks and rhetorics. It has not ordinarily been the animating force behind a general reader.

Second, in addition to the standard apparatus, the book includes after each selection brief comments titled "What About *Your* Writing?" These comments, directly related to the selection just studied, attempt to teach students something extra, something beyond what they have already learned from the selection as a model for a given rhetorical pattern.

"What About *Your* Writing?" entries offer pointers and tips, quick practical lessons that students can pick up from the reading and apply to their own work. The stress generally is on style because major issues of organization are dealt with in the opening sections of each chapter, but the coverage is wide and by no means confined to style. Topics range all the way from common high school superstitions—"Can I begin a sentence with *and?*"—to such broader issues as topical references and constructive and destructive criticism.

"What About *Your* Writing?" material in no way can substitute for the handbook that will almost certainly accompany *Writing with a Thesis* as a required textbook. "What About Your Writing?" attempts to deal with topics normally ignored or slighted in handbooks; it sometimes also attempts to present familiar topics with a new slant. The entries are not and cannot be systematic because they are directly related to the readings, and no instructor ever assigned all the readings in a text. More important, the entries *should* not be systematic, either.

"What About *Your* Writing?" tries to duplicate in some fashion one of the important ways by which people improve their writing: they read, and they pick things up. What can best be taught systematically must be so taught, of course, but not everything can be. Every instructor knows the benefits that can come when a student raises a hand and says, "This doesn't have anything to do with the subject exactly, but I was just wondering . . . " As an instructor structures a lesson and a course but builds into the structure an atmosphere that welcomes the sudden, just-wondering question, *Writing with a Thesis* uses "What About *Your* Writing?" to complement the rigorously structured elements of the rest of the book.

On page vii, a guide to "What About *Your* Writing?" provides a convenient listing of all topics.

Finally, one of the traditional problems with many traditional textbooks is that they bore and scare too many students. Instructors write them for other instructors, and the students suffer. *Writing with a Thesis,* with all its traditional philosophy, is written in an informal, simple, and, we hope, engaging style. The reading selections themselves, although a few are deliberately long and challenging, are generally short and easy to read. Class time can be devoted primarily to showing not what the readings mean, but what they mean for the student's writing.

ACKNOWLEDGMENTS

This textbook now begins its eighteenth year. Many thanks to the many users who like simple truths simply stated.

I want to express my thanks to Sarah Harrison for all the work she put into the previous edition of *Writing with a Thesis*. While it's good to be back in action, I am forever grateful for her many efforts.

For their help with this edition, I want to thank the whole team at Harcourt Brace—especially Michael Rosenberg, Camille Adkins, and Margaret Allyson—as well as the following reviewers, who offered much good advice: Barbara Brumfield, Louisiana State University, Alexandria; Richard Diamond, Tyler Junior College; Trish Loomis, Jefferson College; and William Wilson, Palm Beach Community College.

Most of all, I want to thank my daughter Sarah, now following in the old man's footsteps as she begins her graduate studies. Her valuable advice, her formidable writing skills, and her incredible tolerance for drudgery were indispensable in creating this textbook. What father wouldn't love her? But I admire her, too.

A Note on the Sixth Edition

The sixth edition of *Writing with a Thesis* is a major revision. An unprecedented number of changes have been made: of ten student essays, nine are new; and of forty-six professional models, twenty-four are new. We can also happily report to those familiar with earlier editions that there is much that is not so new. The reading selections continue to be short, accessible, and lively. The discipline of success and the nearly unanimous message of user surveys not to mess with what works have made it easy to resist indulging in massive overhauls for their own sake and succumbing to every casual brainstorm that comes along. Still the principle of change is an important one. The philosophy suggested in a prefatory note to the second edition continues to make sense: "A good textbook, like any other living thing, either changes or begins to die. We hope that all our changes have been life-giving."

TO THE STUDENT

Buying textbooks is more than the dreariness of waiting in line at the bookstore. It probably also marks the only time in your life when you pay good money for books you know nothing about.

The process isn't quite as outrageous as it might seem. Your instructors already know what your courses are designed to teach and are in a solid position to decide which books will be most helpful. You can safely assume that they've spent a long time wading through piles of texts in order to make their final selections and that you wouldn't have enjoyed taking that drudgery on yourself. Still, in many ways your purchase of this book is an act of faith, and before committing yourself much further, you have a right to some information.

This book is designed to help you in several ways to become a better writer.

First, each section begins with a detailed, practical discussion of how to handle the writing assignments you are likely to get: comparison and contrast, classification, cause and effect, and so on. These assignments are based on highly artificial writing patterns. The patterns often overlap and are rarely encountered in their pure form. A paper devoted primarily to classification, for example, could easily spend a good deal of time comparing and contrasting each class. Most instructors find it valuable, however, to discuss and assign the patterns separately. Nobody ever played a set of tennis using only a forehand drive, but serious players may devote hours at a time to practicing that one shot. Similarly, a substantial piece of writing is likely to demand a combination of patterns, but each pattern is best practiced and mastered by being treated at the start as an independent unit.

Second, each section of the book contains one outlined student essay and a group of readings by professional writers designed to show effective use of the pattern under consideration. These writers had to put ideas together in the same pattern that will be required of you, and they went about their task in such and such a way. Studying the techniques by which they achieved their success can stimulate any writer faced with similar problems—but nobody wants you to write a barren imitation of someone else's work. A tennis player can profit from studying Jim Courier's serve without attempting to duplicate it. The writer, as well as the athlete, uses models to discover the basic principles for shaping individual strengths into an effective force, not to follow blindly some particular conception of good form.

Third, questions on each reading selection are designed to help you look closely at the means by which each writer worked. A vague impression that an essay was competently written will be of little practical benefit to your own efforts.

Fourth, in order to add to the practical emphasis of this book, each reading selection is followed by a brief comment called "What About *Your* Writing?" These comments tend to get away from the presentation of broad principles and deal instead with specific pointers and suggestions, ranging all the way from avoiding overused words like *very* to tips on how to write about controversial subjects.

Fifth, all the readings are designed to drive home a special approach to writing that runs through this book: if writing is thought of, wherever possible, as an attempt to persuade the reader of the validity of a particular point, many common problems virtually disappear or solve themselves. We call this approach "the persuasive principle." Chapter 1 presents this principle in detail; the following chapters show how it can be applied to particular writing assignments.

That's the theory. You and your instructor are the only authorities on whether the theory works for you. If it does, the book was worth the money.

CONTENTS

1

THE PERSUASIVE PRINCIPLE

This book offers you one central piece of advice: *Whenever possible, think of your writing as a form of persuasion.*

Persuasion is traditionally considered a separate branch of writing. When you write what's usually called a persuasion paper, you pick a controversial issue, tell your readers what side you're on, and try to persuade them that you're correct: the defense budget needs to be decreased, handguns should be outlawed, doctors must be protected against frivolous and malicious malpractice suits, required freshman English courses should be abolished. Persuasion is supposed to be based on different principles from those of other kinds of writing—description, narration, exposition, and so forth.

It isn't.

A description of a relative, an account of what you went through to get your first job, a comparison of two makes of dishwashers—if you can approach such assignments as an effort to persuade your reader of the validity of a particular opinion or major point, you're in business as a writer. Your paper's opinion or major point is called its *thesis.* Your thesis may be that your relative is the most boring person you have ever met, that getting your first job was easier than you thought it would be, that a GE dishwasher is likely to last longer than a Whirlpool. If you have a thesis and if you select and organize your material so that it supports the thesis, a number of basic writing problems begin to solve themselves. You have built-in purpose. You have built-in organization. You have the potential of built-in interest. Aside

1

from a few obvious exceptions like newspaper reports, encyclopedia articles, instruction manuals, recipes, and certain types of stories, poems, and plays, *all writing can benefit from a commitment to the persuasive principle: develop a thesis, and then back it up.*

There is no better way to demonstrate the effectiveness of the persuasive principle than to take a close look at what goes on, or ought to go on, as a paper is being planned.

GENERAL SUBJECT

"Write something worth reading about such and such." In essence, all writing assignments—for students, business executives, Nobel Prize-winners, and everyone else—begin this way, though ordinarily the directions aren't that frank.

Let's start from scratch and assume that your instructor has left the choice of subject mostly up to you. You may be entirely on your own, or you may have a list of general subjects from which you must make your selection. Imagine that you have to write something worth reading about one of the following: education, sports, prejudice, politics, television.

You make your choice, if you're like the majority of people, by deciding what you're most interested in and informed about or what will go over best with your audience. Let's say you pick education. You now have a subject, and your troubles have now begun.

You have to write 500 words or so on a subject to which tens of thousands of books have been devoted. Where do you begin? Where do you stop? Will it ever be possible to stop? What's important? What's not important? Until you *limit your subject,* you have no way of answering any of these questions. You are at the mercy of every miscellaneous thought and scrap of information that drifts into your mind.

LIMITED SUBJECT

Narrow down your subject. Then narrow it down some more. Narrow it down until you have a subject that can be treated effectively in the assigned length. In many respects, the narrower your subject, the better off you are, as long as you still have something to say about it. With a properly limited subject, you explore only a small part of your general subject, but you explore it thoroughly.

A paper of 500 words on education is doomed to be superficial at best. It might be possible, however, to write 500 words worth reading on one of your teachers, essay versus objective examinations, reasons for attending college (narrowed down to just one reason if you have enough to say), registration procedures, fraternities, physical education requirements, and so on.

With a sensibly limited subject, you start to have a chance of producing a good paper. You are no longer doomed to superficiality. If you write a description of one of your teachers, for example, you possess immensely more knowledge of your subject than do fellow students who have not taken a course from that teacher. Certainly, you are no longer at the mercy of every thought about education that you have ever had.

General Subject	Limited Subject
Education	Professor X
Prejudice	Interracial marriages
Politics	People who don't vote
Television	Commercials
Sports	Baseball salaries

Your troubles are not over, though. You've limited your subject, and you've done it well, but what now? Look at the most limited of the subjects in the preceding table. You're writing a description of a teacher—Professor X. Do you tell your reader about the teacher's height, weight, age, marital status, clothing, ethnic background, religious background, educational background? Publications? Grading policy? Attendance policy? Lecture techniques? Sense of humor? Handling of difficult classroom situations? Attitude toward audiovisual aids? Knowledge of field? How, in short, do you determine what belongs in your paper and what doesn't?

The truth is that you're still at the mercy of every thought that occurs to you. This time it's every thought about Professor X, not every thought about education in general. But until you find a *thesis,* you still have trouble.

THESIS

Your thesis is the basic stand you take, the opinion you express, the point you make about your limited subject. It's your controlling idea, tying together and giving direction to all other separate elements in your paper. *Your primary purpose is to persuade the reader that your thesis is a valid one.*

You may, and probably should, have secondary purposes; you may want to amuse or alarm or inform or issue a call to action, for instance—but unless the primary purpose is achieved, no secondary purpose stands a chance. If you want to amuse your readers by making fun of inconsistent dress codes at your old high school, there's no way to do it successfully without first convincing them of the validity of your thesis that the dress codes *were* inconsistent and thus *do* deserve to be laughed at.

A thesis, of course, is only a vibration in the brain until it is turned into words. The first step in creating a workable thesis is to write a one-sentence version of the thesis, which is called a *thesis statement.*

Professor X is an incompetent teacher.

Professor X is a classic absentminded professor.

Professor X's sarcasm antagonizes many students.

Professor X's colorful personality has become a campus legend.

Professor X is better at lecturing than at leading discussions.

Professor X's youthful good looks have created awkward problems in class.

If you need more than one relatively uncomplicated sentence, chances are either that the thesis isn't as unified as it ought to be or that it's too ambitious for a short paper.

Limited Subject	Thesis Statement
Professor X	Professor X is an incompetent teacher.
Interracial marriages	Hostility to interracial marriages is the prejudice least likely to die.
People who don't vote	Not voting may sometimes be a responsible decision.
Commercials	Television commercials are great entertainment.
Baseball salaries	Many baseball players are paid far more than their abilities can justify.

Writing with a thesis obviously gives a paper a sense of purpose and eliminates the problem of aimless drift. Your purpose is to back up the thesis. As a result, writing with a thesis also helps significantly in organizing the paper. You use only what enables you to accomplish your purpose. Weight problems and religion have nothing to do with Professor X's abilities as a teacher; so you don't bother with them. Most of all, writing with a thesis gives a paper an intrinsic dramatic interest. You commit yourself. You have something at stake: "This is what I believe, and this is why I'm right." You say, "Professor X is incompetent." Your reader says, "Tell me why you think so." You say, "I'll be glad to." Your reader says, "I'm listening." And you're ready to roll.

So far, then, it's been established that a thesis is the main idea that all elements in the paper should support and that you should be able to express it in a single sentence. It's been established that a thesis has several important practical benefits. That's the bird's-eye view, but the concept is important enough to demand a closer look.

WHAT A THESIS ISN'T

A Thesis Is Not a Title.   A title can often give the reader some notion of what the thesis is going to be, but it is not the thesis itself. The thesis itself, as presented in the thesis statement, does not suggest the main idea—it *is* the main idea. Remember, too, that a thesis statement will always be a complete sentence; there's no other way to make a statement.

Title: Not a Thesis	Thesis Statement
Homes and Schools	Parents ought to participate more in the education of their children.
James Cagney: Hollywood Great	James Cagney was one of the greatest actors ever to appear in movies.
Social Security and Old Age	Continuing changes in the Social Security System make it almost impossible to plan intelligently for one's retirement.
A Shattering Experience	My first visit to the zoo was a shattering experience.
The Fad of Divorce	Too many people get divorced for trivial reasons.

A Thesis Is Not an Announcement of the Subject.   A thesis takes a stand. It expresses an attitude toward the subject. It is not the subject itself.

Announcement: Not a Thesis	**Thesis Statement**
My subject is the incompetence of Professor X.	Professor X is an incompetent teacher.
I want to share some thoughts with you about our space program.	Our space program is a waste of money.
The many unforeseen problems I encountered when I went camping are the topic of this theme.	I encountered many unforeseen problems when I went camping.
This paper will attempt to tell you something about the emotions I felt on viewing the Grand Canyon.	The Grand Canyon was even more magnificent than I had imagined.
The thesis of this paper is the difficulty of solving our environmental problems.	Solving our environmental problems is more difficult than many environmentalists believe.

A Thesis Is Not a Statement of Absolute Fact. A thesis makes a judgment or interpretation. There's no way to spend a whole paper supporting a statement that needs no support.

Fact: Not a Thesis

Jane Austen is the author of *Pride and Prejudice.*

The capitol of California is Sacramento.

Suicide is the deliberate taking of one's own life.

President Lincoln's first name was Abraham.

The planet closest to the sun is Mercury.

A Thesis Is Not the Whole Essay. A thesis is your main idea, often expressed in a single sentence. Be careful not to confuse the term as it is used in this text with the book-length "thesis" or "dissertation" usually required of candidates for advanced degrees in graduate schools.

WHAT A GOOD THESIS IS

It's possible to have a one-sentence statement of an idea and still not have a thesis that can be supported effectively. What characterizes a good thesis?

A Good Thesis Is Restricted.   In certain respects, devising a thesis statement as you plan your paper can sometimes be a way in itself of limiting, or restricting, your subject even further. A paper supporting the thesis that Professor X is incompetent, besides taking a stand on its subject, has far less territory to cover than a paper on Professor X in general. Thesis statements themselves, however, may not always have been sufficiently narrowed down. A good thesis deals with restricted, bite-size issues rather than issues that would require a lifetime to discuss intelligently. The more restricted the thesis, the better the chances are for supporting it fully.

Poor	Better
The world is in a terrible mess.	The United Nations should be given more peace-keeping powers.
People are too selfish.	Human selfishness is seen at its worst during rush hour.
The American steel industry has many problems.	The worst problem of the American steel industry is lack of funds to renovate outdated plants and equipment.
Crime must be stopped.	Our courts should hand out tougher sentences to habitual criminals.

A Good Thesis Is Unified.   The thesis expresses *one major idea* about its subject. The tight structural strength of your paper depends on its working to support that one idea. A good thesis may sometimes include a secondary idea if it is strictly subordinated to the major one, but without that subordination the writer will have too many important ideas to handle, and the structure of the paper will suffer.

Poor	Better
Detective stories are not a high form of literature, but people have always been fascinated by them, and many fine writers have experimented with them.	Detective stories appeal to the basic human desire for thrills.
The new health program is excellent, but it has several drawbacks, and it should be run only on an experimental basis for two or three years.	The new health program should be run only on an experimental basis for two or three years. *or*

Poor	**Better**
(Continued)	Despite its general excellence, the new health program should be run only on an experimental basis for two or three years.
The Columbus Cavaliers have trouble at the defensive end and linebacker positions, and front-office tensions don't help, but the team should be able to make the play-offs.	The Columbus Cavaliers should be able to make the play-offs. *or* Even granting a few troubles, the Columbus Cavaliers should be able to make the play-offs.

A Good Thesis Is Specific.   A satisfactorily restricted and unified thesis may be useless if the idea it commits you to is vague. "The new corporate headquarters is impressive," for example, could mean anything from impressively beautiful to impressively ugly. With a thesis statement like "Hemingway's war stories are very good," you would probably have to spend so many words defining what on earth "good" means that there would be no room for anything else. Even when there's no likelihood of confusion, vague ideas normally come through as so familiar or dull or universally accepted that the reader sees no point in paying attention to them.

Poor	**Better**
Hemingway's war stories are very good.	Hemingway's war stories helped create a new prose style.
Drug addiction is a big problem.	Drug addiction has caused a huge increase in crimes of violence.
Our vacation was a tremendous experience.	Our vacation enabled us to learn the true meaning of sharing.
My parents are wonderful people.	Everything my parents do is based on their loving concern for the welfare of the family.

You may also extend your thesis statement to include the major points you will discuss in the body of the paper. The previously cited thesis statements could be extended as follows:

Specific	**Extended Specific**
Hemingway's war stories helped create a new prose style.	Hemingway's war stories helped create a new prose style by

Specific	Extended Specific
(Continued)	employing extensive dialog, shorter sentences, and strong Anglo-Saxon words.
Drug addiction has caused a huge increase in crimes of violence.	Drug addiction has caused a huge increase in crimes of violence in the home, at school, and on the streets.
Our vacation enabled us to learn the true meaning of sharing.	Our vacation enabled us to learn the true meaning of sharing our time, space, and possessions.
Everything my parents do is based on their loving concern for the welfare of the family.	Everything my parents do is based on their loving concern for the welfare of the family by keeping us in touch with our past, helping us to cope with our present, and inspiring us to build for our future.

These extended thesis statements have certain virtues, but they have their drawbacks, too. They can be considered summaries or mini-outlines, in some respects, and therefore they can be useful because they force you to think through the entire essay beforehand. They may be especially helpful if you are uneasy about your organizing abilities. In short essays, on the other hand, extended thesis statements frequently may not be necessary or desirable. They may, for example, tell readers more than you want them to know and tell it to them too soon. If a summary belongs anywhere, after all, it usually belongs at the end of an essay, not at the beginning. Be sure you know if your instructor has any preference. Remember the main point, though: it is essential that the thesis be specific.

EXERCISES FOR REVIEW

A. Write *T* next to each thesis statement below. Write *NT* if there is no thesis statement.
    1. My sister is a terrible cook because she seldom follows essential recipe instructions, forgets the time variable in meal preparation, and knows absolutely nothing about foods that clash.
    2. I want to tell you about the many defects in the administration's proposals for decreasing the budget deficit.

3. Al Capone, the Chicago gang leader, was nicknamed "Scarface."
4. Justice delayed is justice denied.
5. My thesis asks whether affirmative action programs are just a new form of racism.
6. It's not only poor people who get government handouts.
7. How to Grow Prize-Winning Roses.
8. This paper will examine recent efforts to ease the parking problem on campus by pointing out new regulations, identifying schedule possibilities outside prime-time parking hours, and suggesting alternative transportation.
9. Christmas shopping shows that the law of the jungle is still with us.
10. My husband cooks all the meals for our family, his hunting club, and the patrons at Al's Shrimp O'Rama where he works.

B. Write *G* next to each good thesis statement. Write *NG* next to each statement that is not sufficiently restricted, unified, or specific, and be prepared to suggest revisions.

1. The history of the United States is dominated by lust for money, possessions, and power.
2. Common sense is sometimes the enemy of genius.
3. British and American poets through the centuries have vastly overrated the glories of romantic love.
4. Thirst is harder to endure than hunger.
5. Exercise is a worthwhile activity.
6. Jogging can add years to one's life by improving cardiovascular function, strengthening muscles, and enriching emotional health.
7. Teaching tricks to a dog is easier than most people think.
8. Men's mustaches can reveal something about their characters.
9. Natural beauty must be preserved, but government agencies often make foolish decisions on this matter, and jobs must also be preserved.
10. In *Moby-Dick,* Melville does a very good job.

THE THESIS AT WORK IN THE PAPER

The thesis statement is a tool, not an end in itself. It has two outstanding values. First, it serves as a test of whether your main idea meets the requirements we have just discussed: whether it is a firm concept that can actually be put into words or only a fuzzy notion that is not yet ready for development. Second, the thesis statement is a constant, compact reminder of the point your paper must make, and it is therefore an indispensable means of determining the relevancy or irrelevancy, the logic or lack of logic, of all the material that goes into the paper.

In itself, however, the thesis statement is a deliberately bare-bones presentation of your idea. In your paper you will attempt to deal with the idea in a far more interesting way. The thesis statement, for example, may quite likely never appear word for word in your final paper. There's not even any special rule that in the final paper you must declare the thesis in a single sentence. In some rare cases, the thesis may only be hinted at rather than stated openly. The proper places for the bare-bones thesis statement are in your mind with every word you write, on any piece of scratch paper on which you jot down the possible ingredients of your essay, and at the beginning of a formal outline. (If you are ever required to construct such outlines, all of the student papers in Chapters 2–10 begin with formal topic outlines which you can use as examples. Your instructor will probably give you further guidance.)

In most short papers, the thesis is presented in the first paragraph, the *introduction*. Again, no absolute rule states that this must always be the case— just as no rule demands that an introduction must always be just one paragraph (the last "Sample Introduction" below is three paragraphs)—but in practice most papers do begin that way. It's simply what seems to work for most people most of the time. As a general guideline, then, it's helpful to think of the first paragraph's job as presenting the thesis in an interesting way.

The word *interesting* is important. The introduction should not ordinarily be a one-sentence paragraph consisting solely of the unadorned thesis statement. The introduction certainly should indicate clearly what the thesis is, but it also should arouse curiosity or stress the importance of the subject or establish a particular tone of humor, anger, solemnity, and so forth.

Thesis Statement	**Sample Introduction**
Professor X is an incompetent teacher.	Any school the size of State is probably going to get its share of incompetent teachers. I'm told that last year an elderly history professor came to class to give a final exam and then realized he'd forgotten to make one up. Professor Z tells jokes nobody understands and keeps chuckling to himself about them through the whole class period. Professor Y doesn't return term

Thesis Statement	**Sample Introduction**
(Continued)	papers until the last day of class; so her students never know how they're doing until it's too late. As far as I'm concerned, though, the biggest dud of all is Professor X.
Hostility to interracial marriages is the prejudice least likely to die.	Progress in relations between the races often seems grotesquely slow. Looking at bundles of years instead of days, however, one can see that there has been real progress in jobs, education, and even housing. The most depressing area, the area in which there has been no progress, in which no progress is even likely, in which progress is not even discussed, is the area of interracial marriages.
Not voting may sometimes be a responsible decision.	Public service ads tell us to be good citizens and make sure to vote. On election eves, the candidates tell us to exercise our sacred rights and hustle down to the polling booth, even if we're not going to cast our ballots for them. Network philosophers tell us that the country is going downhill because so few people vote for President. But my neighbor Joe is totally indifferent to politics; he knows little and cares less. My neighbor Jennifer thinks both candidates are equally foul. I believe that Joe, Jennifer, and thousands like them are making intelligent, responsible decisions when they stay home on Election Day, and I admire them for not letting themselves be bullied.
Television commercials are great entertainment.	I like television commercials. It's a terrible confession. I know I'm supposed to sneer and brood and write letters to people who want to

Thesis Statement	**Sample Introduction**
(Continued)	protect me, but I like commercials. They're great entertainment, and it's time somebody said so.

Many baseball players are paid far more than their abilities can justify.	An essay in *Forbes Magazine* by sports commentator Dick Schaap tells a story about the great Baseball Hall of Famer and Detroit Tiger of the 1930s and 40s, Hank Greenberg, the first player to make $100,000 a year. Greenberg's son Steve, now an important baseball official, was once an agent negotiating contracts. He told his father about a player he was representing whose batting average was .238. "What should I ask for?" Steve inquired.
	    "Ask for a uniform," Hank replied.
	    Today, unfortunately, any agent would also ask for a million dollars—and would probably get it. Baseball players' salaries have become ridiculously high and have little or nothing to do with actual athletic abilities.

The function of subsequent paragraphs—paragraphs generally referred to as the *body*—is to support the thesis. All sorts of paragraph arrangements are possible. The important consideration is that the body paragraphs, individually and as a whole, must persuade your reader that your thesis makes sense.

One of the most common paragraph arrangements is worth studying at this time since it's the easiest to follow and since our concern here is with the essential connection between body paragraphs and thesis, not with fine points. This arrangement gives a separate paragraph to each supporting point and the specific evidence necessary to substantiate it. In sketchy outline form, the progression of paragraphs might look something like this:

> ¶ 1—Presentation of thesis: There are at least three good reasons for abolishing capital punishment.

> Start of ¶ 2—First, statistics show that capital punishment is not really a
> deterrent . . .
> Start of ¶ 3—Second, when capital punishment is used it is forever
> impossible to correct a mistaken conviction . . .
> Start of ¶ 4—Third, capital punishment has traditionally been used
> in a discriminatory fashion against poor people and
> blacks . . .

Using the same form of one paragraph for each supporting idea, but abandoning the neatness of numbered points, we might find the following:

> ¶ 1—Presentation of thesis: Dieting can be dangerous.
> Start of ¶ 2—Some diets can raise cholesterol levels alarmingly . . .
> Start of ¶ 3—In other cases, over an extended period, some diets can
> lead to serious vitamin deficiencies . . .
> Start of ¶ 4—One further danger is that already existing medical
> problems such as high blood pressure can be drastically
> aggravated . . .

Most papers also have a distinct *conclusion,* a last paragraph that provides a needed finishing touch. The conclusion can be a quick summary of your thesis and main supporting points. It can emphasize or reemphasize the importance of your thesis. It can relate a seemingly remote thesis to people's everyday lives. It can make a prediction. It can issue a call for action. In one way or another, the conclusion reinforces or develops the thesis; it should never introduce a totally unrelated, brand-new idea. The conclusion should bring your paper to a smooth stop. Just as the introduction steers clear of direct announcements, likewise the conclusion should avoid the blatant "Well, that's about it" ending. There are dozens of possible conclusions, but almost all papers benefit from having one. (For specific examples of different kinds of conclusions, see pages 308–310.)

The group of readings that follows shows the persuasive principle in action by offering contrasting examples of good and not-so-good writing. From short thank-you notes to freshman English compositions, the results of writing with and without a thesis can be explored in detail. Later chapters will comment on and provide examples of the techniques appropriate for particular patterns of writing: classification, description, and so on. Patterns change depending on subjects and approaches. Principles do not change. The basic nature of good writing, as discussed in this chapter, remains constant.

Two Ads on the Community Bulletin Board

A.   Babysitter

Experienced high school student available, weekdays to midnight, week-ends to 2 A.M. Reasonable rates. Call Sandy, 335-0000.

B.   Babysitter

A HIGH SCHOOL STUDENT WHO KNOWS <u>THE THREE R'S</u>
Ready—any weekday to midnight, weekends to 2 A.M.
Reliable—four years' experience, references available.
Reasonable—$2.00 per hour, flat fee for more than five hours.
Call Sandy, 335-0000

DISCUSSION AND QUESTIONS

Even a little "position wanted" ad can use the persuasive principle to its advantage. Two dozen high school students pin two dozen different typed or handwritten index cards to the bulletin board at the local library or supermarket. Most of the cards convey lifeless facts. One or two cards make the same facts come alive by using them to support an idea. Those are the cards that get a second look—and get their writers a phone call.

1. Which ad has a thesis?
2. Does the ad support its thesis?
3. Which ad uses more specific facts?

Two Sets of Directions

A.

How to Get from Town to Camp Wilderness

Take Freeway west to Millersville Road exit. Go north on Millersville Road to Route 256. West on 256 to Laurel Lane. North on Laurel Lane until you see our sign. Turn right, and you're there.

B.

How to Get from Town to Camp Wilderness

You'll have an easy trip if you avoid *three trouble spots.*

1. You have to take the MILLERSVILLE ROAD Exit as you go west on the Freeway, and it's a *left-hand* exit. Start bearing left as soon as you see the "Millersville 5 miles" sign.
2. After turning north (right) on Millersville Road, don't panic when you see Route 526. You want ROUTE 256 and that's 8 more miles.
3. Go west (left) on Route 256 to LAUREL LANE. The street signs are almost impossible to read, but Laurel Lane is the second road on the right after the Mobil station.

Once on Laurel Lane, you're all set. Go 2 miles until you see our sign. Turn right, and you're there.

DISCUSSION AND QUESTIONS

Writing competent directions is a difficult task. When you are explaining something you know well, it's hard to put yourself in the place of a total novice. You may be excessively casual about some step or even forget to mention it. Directions can also be hard to read: for novices they can seem to be a series of one disconnected step after another. Writing with a thesis helps the steps come together in the readers' minds and gives them a comforting sense of security.

1. Which set of directions has a thesis?
2. Which tries to anticipate difficulties?
3. Explain the unconventional capitalization in B.

Two Thank You Notes

A.

July 23, 1993

Dear Aunt Molly,

   "Thanks for everything" is an old, old phrase, but I've never meant it more. Thanks for your generous, great big check. Thanks for coming to the graduation ceremonies. Thanks for years of hugs and funny comments and good advice. Thanks for caring for me, and thanks for being Aunt Molly.

Much love,

Alice

B.

July 23, 1993

Dear Aunt Molly,

   Thank you so much for your generous check. I was really happy that you could come to my graduation, and I hope you had a good time. Thank you so much again.

Much love,

Alice

DISCUSSION AND QUESTIONS _____

Back in the days before long-distance phone calls became routine, people wrote many more personal letters than they do now. For a good number of people today, the thank-you note is probably the only personal letter writing they do, other than a cheerful "Hi, there!" on postcards or Christmas cards. Graduates, newlyweds, new parents, and grieving widows and widowers all need to write thank-you notes. There's not much choice of subject, of course, and even most of the ideas are predetermined. How can the writer make a thank-you note sound like a sincere expression of emotion, not just good manners? The persuasive principle is a valuable aid.

1. Which note has a thesis?
2. How many pieces of "evidence" support the thesis?
3. How does the choice of words in the supporting evidence further reinforce the thesis?
4. Which note communicates more feeling?

Two Letters of Complaint

A.

13 Pier Street
New York, NY 10016
July 23, 1993

Customer Complaints
Maybach Company
123 Fifth Avenue
New York, NY 10001

Subject: Defective Coffee Table

I have tried calling three different times and have not received any satisfaction, so now I am going to try writing.

I have absolutely no intention of paying any $749.60. I returned my coffee table more than a month ago. One of the legs was wobbly and the top had a bad scratch. Two times the pickup men did not come on the day they said they would. I returned the first bill for the table, and now you just sent me another one, and all I get from people when I call the store is "We'll look into it."

Also the price was $174.96, not $749.60. I await your reply.

Yours very truly,

Augusta Briggs
Augusta Briggs

B.

13 Pier Street
New York, NY 10016
July 23, 1993

Customer Complaints
Maybach Company
123 Fifth Avenue
New York, NY 10001

Subject: Defective Coffee Table

When you folks make mistakes, you don't kid around. You make big ones. Phone calls haven't done me much good, so I'm hoping that this letter can clear things up.

Early last month—probably June 9 or 10—I returned a defective coffee table. Since you had no more in stock, I canceled the order.

When the bill came for the table, I returned it with a note of explanation. Exactly one week ago, July 16, I received a second bill. To add to the fun, this second bill was for $749.60 instead of the original $174.96.

When I called the store, I was told I'd be called back by the next day at the latest. I'm still waiting.

I'm sure you agree that these are too many mistakes, and that they are big enough to be extremely annoying. Shall we get this matter settled once and for all?

Thank you for your attention.

Yours very truly,

Augusta Briggs
Augusta Briggs

DISCUSSION AND QUESTIONS ───────────────────────

The letter to a friend may not be as common as it once was, but business writing—and business plays a role in our private lives as well as in our jobs—is as important as ever. An employee makes a good suggestion and is told to "put it in writing." When the clear and methodical statement of ideas and facts is essential, putting it into writing becomes inevitable.

The writer of a letter of complaint has two special difficulties, both of which must be resolved if the letter is to be effective. On the one hand, the writer must communicate the gravity of the complaint, or the complaint may be treated casually, perhaps even ignored. On the other hand, the writer must simultaneously come through as a rational human being calmly presenting a grievance. It's essential that the writer not be dismissed as a crackpot or crank. Letters from crackpots and cranks get shown around the office, everyone has a good laugh, and then the letter goes to the bottom of the fattest pile of unanswered correspondence.

1. Which letter has a thesis?
2. Does the letter support the thesis with specific evidence?
3. Does the letter have a conclusion to reinforce or develop the thesis?
4. Why does the writer of letter B say nothing specific about what was wrong with the coffee table?
5. What is the purpose of the slang ("you folks," "kid around") and humorous touches in letter B?
6. Are there elements in letter A that might allow the reader to dismiss the writer as a crank?
7. Why do business-letter paragraphs tend to be so short?

Two Replies to the Second Letter of Complaint

A.

MAYBACH COMPANY
123 Fifth Avenue
New York, NY 10001
(212) 333-3333

Customer Relations   July 26, 1993

Ms. Augusta Briggs
13 Pier Street
New York, NY 10016

Dear Ms. Briggs:

We apologize. We made a lot of mistakes, and we are truly sorry.

We tried to phone you with our apology as soon as we got your letter of July 23, but you weren't at home. Therefore, we're taking this opportunity to apologize in writing. We also want to tell you that your bill for the coffee table has been canceled once and for all, and you won't be bothered again. If something should go wrong, please call me directly at extension 4550.

Good service makes happy customers, and happy customers are the heart of our business. We appreciate your letting us know when our service isn't so good, and we want to assure you that we've taken steps to see that these mistakes don't recur.

Again, please accept our sincere regrets. Do we dare call your attention to the storewide furniture sale all of next month, including an excellent stock of coffee tables?

Yours very truly,

Rose Alonso

Rose Alonso
Manager

B.

MAYBACH COMPANY
123 Fifth Avenue
New York, NY 10001
(212) 333-3333

Customer Relations   July 26, 1993

Ms. Augusta Briggs
13 Pier Street
New York, NY 10016

Dear Ms. Briggs:

Pursuant to your letter of July 23, please be advised that your bill for the returned coffee table has been canceled.

This department attempted to phone you immediately upon receipt of your letter, but no answer was received.

We apologize for any inconvenience you may have experienced, and we hope that we may continue to deserve your patronage in the future. There is a storewide furniture sale all of next month in which you may have a special interest.

Yours very truly,

Rose Alonso

Rose Alonso
Manager

DISCUSSION AND QUESTIONS

The Maybach Company needs to apologize, correct its error, and keep its customer. Keeping the customer is the hard part, of course. It will require something far more than the traditional cold and dry business letter.

1. Which letter develops a thesis? Which is a collection of separate sentences?
2. Which letter makes the phone call seem an indication of the company's concern? Which makes the call seem as if the company had been inconvenienced?
3. Which letter is superior in convincing the customer that her problems are finally over?
4. Both letters express hope for the customer's continued trade. Why is letter A far better in this respect?

Two "How I Spent My Summer Vacation" Essays

(In-Class Assignment)

A.

I couldn't find a job this summer, and it's hard to write much about my summer vacation.

Every morning I would get up between 8:30 and 9:00. My breakfast would usually be juice, toast, and coffee, though sometimes I would have eggs, too.

For a couple of weeks, after breakfast I would mow some neighbors' lawns, but after a while I got bored with that, and mostly I just hung around. Usually I read the paper and then straightened up my room.

For lunch I had a sandwich and a glass of milk. I remember once my mother and I had a real argument because there wasn't anything for a sandwich.

After lunch, if my mother didn't need the car, I'd usually drive over to the big shopping center with some of my friends. We'd walk around to see what was happening, and sometimes we'd try to pick up some girls. Mostly, we'd just look at the girls. Sometimes, instead of going to the shopping center, we'd go swimming.

After supper, it was usually television or a movie. Television is mostly re-runs in the summer, and it was a bad scene. Some of the movies were okay, but nothing sensational.

In the middle of the summer, my older sister and her family came to visit from out of town. That was fun because I like my two little nephews a lot, and we fooled around in the backyard. My brother-in-law kept asking what I was doing with my time, and my mother said at least I was staying out of trouble.

B.

I couldn't find a job this summer, and most people would probably say that I spend my summer doing nothing. In fact, I spent most of my summer practicing very hard to be a pest.

To start with, I developed hanging around the house into an art. It drove my mother crazy. After breakfast, I'd read the paper, spreading it out over the entire living room, and then take my midmorning nap. Refreshed by my rest, I'd then ask my mother what was available for lunch. Once when there was no Italian salami left and the bread was a little stale, I looked at her sadly and sighed a lot and kept opening and closing the refrigerator. She didn't take my suffering too well. As I recall, the expression she used was "no good bum" or something of that order. In the evenings, I'd sigh a lot over having to watch television reruns. When my mother asked me why I watched if I didn't enjoy myself, I sighed some more.

The other main center for my activities as a pest was at the big shopping center a short drive from home. My friends and I—we figured we needed protection—would stand in people's way on the mall and make them walk around us. We'd try on clothes we had no intention of buying and complain about the price. We'd make eyes, and gestures, and offensive remarks at any pretty girls. We'd practice swaggering and strutting and any other means of looking obnoxious that occurred to us.

Miscellaneous other activities during the summer included splashing people at the beach, laughing in the wrong places at movies, and honking the car horn madly at pedestrians as they started to cross the street. These are small-time adventures, I realize, but difficult to do with real style.

Basically, I had myself a good summer. It's always a pleasure to master a set of skills, and I think I've come close to being an expert pest. I wonder what new thrills lie in wait next summer.

DISCUSSION AND QUESTIONS

Here, in all its mythic tiresomeness, is the worst of all possible subjects: "How I Spent My Summer Vacation." Students boo. The *Peanuts* comic strip makes fun of the subject. Even teachers laugh about it. That's why it's been chosen for this book.

The subject is deadly. To make matters worse, here are two students who spent a remarkably uneventful summer. One blunders along and writes a frightful paper. The other develops a thesis, supports it, and ends with an appealing little paper. It's no candidate for a prize, but it's an appealing little paper. Enough said.

1. In paper A, is "it's hard to write much about my summer vacation" a thesis? Is it a good thesis? Does the writer support it?
2. If both papers have a thesis, are the theses basically the same?
3. What topics mentioned in paper A are not mentioned in paper B? Why?
4. Which paper has a conclusion? Is it effective?
5. Both papers use many specific details. Which uses them better? Why?
6. Which paper has better developed paragraphs?
7. Which paragraphs in paper A do not have topic sentences? Do all the paragraphs in paper B have topic sentences?
8. Which paper handles the argument about lunch better? Why?

TWO FRESHMAN ENGLISH ESSAYS ON A LITERARY SUBJECT

Essay topic: Shirley Jackson's "The Lottery" has a longstanding reputation as a story with a powerful surprise ending. Write a 300–500 word essay evaluating the validity of that reputation.

A.

"The Lottery," written by the author Shirley Jackson, takes place on the morning of June 27th. June 27th is the day the lottery is always held, and everything seems normal. But the reader is in for a surprise.

The children assemble first. With school just out, they don't know what to do with themselves and start gathering stones. Then the men come telling quiet jokes. We are told that "they smiled rather than laughed." Then the women come, gossiping and summoning the children.

Finally, it is time for the head of the lottery, Mr. Summers, and we are told about the long history of the lottery: the old black box, the slips of paper, the old rituals, and the complicated procedures for drawing. Tessie Hutchinson's late arrival adds a touch of humor.

All the family names are called in alphabetical order, and there seems to be a little nervous tension in the air. Old Man Warner gets angry when told that other towns are thinking of giving up the lottery.

When the Hutchinson family is chosen, Tessie gets very upset and complains that the drawing was not fair because Bill, her husband, was not given enough time to draw. Bill had as much time as anyone else. Mrs. Delacroix tells Tessie to "be a good sport," and even Bill is embarrassed and says, "Shut up, Tessie."

Then there is a second drawing where each member of the Hutchinson family draws individually. Tessie turns out to have the paper with the spot on it. She has won the lottery.

The surprise comes when we find out that Tessie has been chosen to be executed. She is going to be stoned to death, and we remember the stones from the beginning of the story. "The Lottery" by Shirley Jackson shows how people follow traditions, sometimes bad ones, without ever thinking about what they are doing.

B.

Shirley Jackson's "The Lottery" is a wonderful story, but the only thing that surprised me at the end was the stones. I admit that I had pretty much forgotten about the stones, but I knew long before the ending that something terrible was going to happen. "The Lottery" is a powerful story, certainly, but its reputation for having a "powerful surprise ending" is undeserved.

It takes no more than two pages before we realize that the annual village lottery is more mysterious and sinister than any drawing for a trip to Hawaii or a new Buick. To begin with, there's an air of mystery about the shabby black box: shabby as it is, we are told directly that it represents tradition of some kind, and no one wants to replace it. People nervously hesitate to hold it still while Mr. Summers mixes the paper inside it.

As if the mystery and tradition of the black box were not enough, we learn that the whole institution of the lottery goes back to the "first people" who settled the village and that it involved all sorts of mysterious ceremonies and rituals. There had been some sort of "chant," some sort of "ritual salute." We're not just at a lottery—we're practically going to church.

The sense of church-like solemnity continues when Mrs. Dunbar, whose husband has a broken leg, is asked, "Don't you have a grown boy to do it for you, Janey?" When young Jack Watson, now old enough to draw for his family, walks up to the box, he is told, "Glad to see your mother's got a man to do it." What's going on here? What is so awesome that picking up a slip of paper is considered a job appropriate only for menfolk?

As the drawing proceeds, the story stresses the tension. People wet their lips. If they grin, they do so "humorlessly and nervously."

Any surviving thoughts about the lottery being a pleasant social occasion have to disappear with Old Man Warner's hysterical reaction to the news that some villages are thinking about abandoning the lottery. He calls them a "pack of crazy fools" and virtually predicts the end of the world—"they'll be wanting to go back to living in caves." He quotes an old saying: "Lottery in June, corn be heavy soon." We're dealing with ancient rites and rituals here—famines, and gods of the harvest, and keeping the gods happy.

We're still a long way from the end, but the author keeps pouring it on. The Hutchinson family wins the drawing, and Tessie Hutchinson, instead of packing her bags for Hawaii, complains that "It wasn't fair!" She wants someone else to win because it's obvious that something bad happens to the winner. As the individual members of the Hutchinson family participate in the second drawing, a girl's voice from the crowd says, "I hope it's not Nancy," because the girl knows what happens, too.

Any reader by this time knows from the seriousness of the reactions that we are dealing with matters of life and death. The stones are a surprise, and an important one. They fit into the story well because stoning as a means of execution is ancient, connected to religion, and involves the whole community. The stones are a surprise, but nothing else is.

DISCUSSION AND QUESTIONS

Students sometimes say that it's easy to bluff when writing an essay examination or at-home essay on a literary subject. Maybe so, but most teachers are as aware of the hazards as anyone else and make a special effort to spot bluffing.

A good, non-bluffing essay on a literary subject, especially on a "What's-your-opinion?" question, can go in many different directions, but it always displays the following characteristics:

A. It discusses the subject assigned, not the one the student wishes had been assigned. Inexperienced or nervous students might see the title "The Lottery" and haphazardly start writing everything they have ever heard or thought about the story. *Stick to the subject.*

B. It uses specific details to support its thesis. The instructor wants an essay from someone who has read and remembered and understood the story, not from someone who, from all the essay shows, has merely turned up in class and gotten the general drift of what the story must be about.

C. It does not get sidetracked into a plot summary unless the assignment specifically calls for one. Any references to the plot should support a thesis, not tell the story all over again.

1. Which essay has a thesis?
2. Is the thesis supported with specific details?
3. Which essay is mostly a plot summary?
4. Compare first sentences. Which is more directly related to the assignment?
5. Does the writer of the essay that has a thesis keep the thesis in mind throughout, or are there some digressions?
6. Can the relative merits of both essays be determined even by a reader unfamiliar with "The Lottery?"

2

NARRATION

T ell me a story," children say again and again. They're bored or restless, and they know the wonders a good story can perform.

In the New Testament we can see that Jesus, like other great religious leaders, knew of those wonders, too. Time after time he used parables—short tales directly embodying moral or spiritual lessons—to link general, abstract truths to the immediate experiences of his audience, and so help make the truths clear, memorable, and fresh. The Parable of the Good Samaritan is one among many that have helped to shape our culture.

Narration, then, is the telling of a story, and the shared experience of the human race suggests that a well-told story has few rivals in lasting fascination.

This chapter, of course, is concerned with telling a story as one of the patterns by which a thesis can be supported. That's by no means the only purpose of narration. Although Jesus's parables and Aesop's fables (a fable is a parable in which animals often replace human beings and the moral is almost always specifically stated) tell stories to support a point, many modern writers of stories are far more interested in conveying a sense of life than in conveying ideas. "Yes," says the reader of these stories, "that's what a family argument"—or a first kiss or being a soldier or having the air conditioner break down—"is really like." A thesis, as such, either does not exist or is so subordinate to other concerns that it may as well not exist. This approach to narration has produced plenty of great fiction, but it's not what your narration theme is about.

Chances are that your narration theme, in fact, isn't going to be fiction at all. Nothing is wrong with trying your hand at making up a parable, fable, or other piece of fiction, but most narration themes proceed in far different ways. You'll probably be telling the story of what once really happened to you or to people you know. (Like any good storyteller, naturally, you'll emphasize some elements and de-emphasize or ignore others, depending on the point of the story.) All the reading selections in this chapter deal with authentic events in the lives of real people.

Imagine a scene in which some friends are uttering what strikes you as sentimental foolishness about the glories of jogging. You say, "I think jogging is horrible. Let me tell you what happened to me." And you tell your story. That's the essence of the narration paper: a point, and a story to back it up.

There are millions of stories and thousands of ways to tell them. *Tell your own story in your own way* is as good a piece of advice as any. As you do so, it's reasonable to remember the various bores you may have listened to or read and try to avoid their mistakes: the bores who worried about what day of the week it was when they were bitten by a snake, who constantly repeated the same phrases *(you know, and then I, you see),* who went on long after the interesting part of their story had been told. Profit from their examples, but tell your own story in your own way.

That advice has a fine ring to it, but it's certainly on the abstract side. "Your own way," for example, will undoubtedly change from one story to another. To get less abstract, in *most* narration papers *most* of the time, you should keep the following suggestions in mind:

Stress the Story.   The story must have a thesis, but the story itself is what gives life to the paper. *Write a story, not a sermon.* Your thesis is usually a sentence or two at the beginning or end of the paper. Sometimes the thesis can be so clearly part of the story itself that it may not even need to be expressed directly. In any event, most of your words are devoted to the telling of your story, not to lecturing and moralizing.

Remember That a Good Story Has Conflict.   Some critics would be prepared to argue that without conflict it's impossible to have a story at all. In any event, conflict is usually the starting point for readers' interest. Three patterns of conflict are the most common. First, *conflict between people:* you went jogging in the park with a group of friends, and while you were gasping for breath, one friend was driving you mad with lofty philosophical comments about appreciating the outdoors and feeling good about our bodies.

Second, *conflict between people and their environment* (a social custom or prejudice, a religious tradition, a force of nature such as a hurricane, and so on): at the end of the jogging trail, after you had managed to survive the intolerably hot weather and a killer pebble that had worked its way into one of your sneakers, your friends happily began to discuss a time and place for jogging the next day; you wanted to say "Never again," but the social pressure was too great to resist, and you went along with the crowd. Third, *conflict within a person:* all through your jogging miseries, one side of you was calling the other side a soft, overcivilized snob, incapable of appreciating the simple pleasures of life. Clearly, you do not need to confine your story to only one kind of conflict.

Use Lots of Convincing Realistic Details.   The good story will give a sense of having actually happened, and convincing realistic details are your best device for transmitting that sense, as well as for preventing the sermon from taking over the story. Don't just mention the insect pests that kept bothering you as you jogged through the park—mention mosquitoes. Don't just mention mosquitoes—mention the huge one with blood lust that got onto your neck and summoned up dim memories of a malaria victim in an old Tarzan movie.

Play Fair.   Stories of pure innocence versus pure evil, of totally good guys versus totally bad guys, tend to be unconvincing because they are gross distortions of what everyone knows about the complexities of life. Support your thesis energetically, by all means, but don't neglect to show some awareness of the complexities. The paper on jogging, for example, will be more powerful and persuasive if it grudgingly concedes somewhere that the park was beautiful, after all, and that while hating every minute of your journey through it, you were able occasionally to notice the beauty.

WRITING SUGGESTIONS FOR NARRATION THEMES

Choose one of the famous quotations or proverbs below and write a narration that supports it. You will probably draw on personal experience for your basic material, but you should also feel free to decorate or invent whenever convenient. Some of the suggestions might be appropriate for a fable or parable.

1. What a tangled web we weave / When first we practice
   to deceive.

   Walter Scott

2. Haste makes waste.
3. You cannot have harmony without noise.

   Albanian proverb

4. Nobody ever went broke underestimating the
   intelligence of the American public.

   H.L. Mencken

5. Faith is believing what you know ain't so.

   Mark Twain

6. Absence makes the heart grow fonder.
7. The bridge between laughing and crying is
   not long.

   Jamaican proverb

8. The way to a man's heart is through his stomach.
9. Few things are harder to put up with than the
   annoyance of a good example.

   Mark Twain

10. Patriotism is the last refuge of a scoundrel.

    Samuel Johnson

11. Genius is one percent inspiration and ninety-nine
    percent perspiration.

    Thomas A. Edison

12. Winning isn't the most important thing. It's the
    only thing.

    Vince Lombardi

13. When the fox starts preaching look to your hens.

    Basque proverb

14. Those who do not know history are condemned
    to repeat it.

    George Santayana

15. Wickedness is a myth invented by good people to
    account for the curious attractiveness of others.

    Oscar Wilde

16. There is an exception to every rule.
17. The mass of men lead lives of quiet desperation.

    Henry David Thoreau

18. Whoever rides on a tiger can never dismount.

    Chinese proverb

19. Fools and their money are soon parted.
20. A man who hates dogs and children can't be all bad.

W. C. Fields

21. A thing of beauty is a joy forever.

John Keats

22. Everything I like is either illegal, immoral,
or fattening.

Alexander Woollcott

23. In America, nothing fails like success.

F. Scott Fitzgerald

24. Luck is the residue of design.

Branch Rickey

25. Advice to those about to marry: Don't.

Punch Magazine

READINGS

Readings in this chapter and in all remaining chapters are intended to provide you with practical models for your own writing. The readings begin with a student-written essay (two essays in Chapter 6 on Comparison and Contrast) together with an outline to stress the importance of careful organization. The student work is followed by a group of professional models with notes and detailed comments and questions on organization, content, and style.

When to Keep Quiet

Steve Robinson (student)

Thesis: The adage "It is better to keep your mouth shut and appear stupid than to open it and remove all doubt" is true.

    I.   Before the Blunders
        A. Magazines
        B. Car enthusiasts

   II. Car Conversation
        A. Fords
        B. Two-doors

 III. The Blunders
        A. Kind of engine
        B. Size of engine

The inner workings of an automobile have always been somewhat of a mystery to me. I've often found myself envious of "shade tree" mechanics as they engaged in shop talk pertaining to their high performance cars. Usually I would simply sit, listen, and inwardly ponder these conversations. However, I once broke my standard policy of adhering to the principle that states "It is better to keep your mouth shut and appear stupid than to open it and remove all doubt," and actually decided to contribute to the conversation. It was then that the truth of this adage struck me.

It all started one day as I was taking my lunch break at the grocery store where I work. I was sitting in the brightly lit room at a table with car magazines strewn all over the top, mulling over the latest issue of *Hot Rod* when into the room strode the day-stocking crew preparing to take their collective lunch. I must digress at this point so that the reader may note that each person who had just entered the room owns the equivalent of a Grand Prix race car that he built from spare parts found on the side of the road and in old junk yards. Anyway, this group sat down and started comparing notes as I adopted my usual attentive, but mute attitude.

The point at which my mistake came was about 15 minutes into the discussion. I must say to my credit that I only acted as I did under extreme provocation. Hank, a short burly young man with hair growing from his nose and grease under his fingernails, began to expound on the virtues of Ford motorcars. At the end of his proud little speech, he looked around the room for approval and his gaze soon fell on me. "You have a Ford, don't you, Steve?" he asked. This seemed a simple enough question to answer since I had noticed the letters F-O-R-D sprinkled in several spots on my car. I responded with a vigorous, "Yes, yes!" He then asked, "Is it a two-door?" The moment was going great, or so I thought. I was actually engaging in car talk and knew the answers. To Hank's two-door question, I smugly replied, "You bet it is!" Unfortunately, my new-found euphoria was short-lived.

I realized my error with the next question Hank posed. He inquired, "What kind of engine do you have?" Feeling like a freshman at registration, I frantically searched my brain for an answer. Finally I squeaked out three little words that signalled my downfall, one to me almost as catastrophic as Napoleon's must have felt. "A car engine . . . ," I asked, more than stated. The immediate laughter sounded like a pack of hyenas, high-pitched and uproariously loud. Hank choked out, "Seriously, Steve, what size is your engine?" I quickly pounced on the keyword "size." I knew a little bit about engine size I told myself. Many car conversations are centered around some person's engine, and as I usually tried to be present at such times, I had seen many different sizes of engines. Since I had seen my engine only last week when the service station attendant had shown me how to open my hood, all I had to do was compare my engine to all the others I had seen. "I've got them now," I thought. I leaned back in my chair, slowly looked at every face in the room, then drawled, "Oh, about a medium, I'd say."

Although that incident did cause me some embarrassment and I'm no longer allowed to sit in on "car talk" sessions, I feel I learned a fine-tuned lesson from it all. I think the best thing to do in such situations is to sit obscurely in a corner, nod wisely at the appropriate times, and, above all else, keep quiet.

COPING WITH SANTA CLAUS

DELIA EPHRON

Delia Ephron has written humorous books and stories for young people, though many appeal to adults as well. Her books include *How to Eat Like a Child and Other Lessons in Not Being a Grown-up* (1978), *Teenage Romance or How to Die of Embarrassment* (1981), *Alex and Santa* (1983), and *Do I Have to Say Hello?* (1989). Readers of "Coping with Santa Claus" will agree that dying of embarrassment is by no means limited to teenagers.

Words to check:

ecstatic (paragraph 9)   reproachfully (32)
modicum (10)

1   Julie had turned 8 in October and as Christmas approached, Santa Claus was more and more on her mind. During the week before Christmas, every night she announced to her father, "I know who really brings the presents. You do!" Then, waiting a moment, she added, "Right?"

2   Jerry didn't answer. Neither he nor I, her stepmother, was sure she really wanted the truth. We suspected she did, but couldn't bring ourselves to admit it to her. And we both felt uncomfortable saying something hedgy. Something pretentious. Something like, "But Santa does exist, dear. He exists in spirit—in the spirit of giving in all of us." That sounded like some other parents in some other house with some other child.

3   I actually resented Julie for putting us on the spot. Wasn't the truth about Santa something one learned from a classmate? The same classmate who knows a screwed-up version of the facts of life. Or else from a know-it-all older sister—as I did. Mine sneaked into my room on Christmas Eve, woke me and said, "Go into the hall and look. You'll see who really puts out the presents."

4   There was another problem. Jerry and I were reluctant to give up Santa Claus ourselves. We got to tell Julie and her younger brother, Adam, to put out the cookies in case Santa was hungry. We made a fuss about the fire being out in the fireplace so he wouldn't get burned. We issued a few threats about his list of good children and bad. It was all part of the tension and thrill of Christmas Eve—the night the fantasy comes true. And that fantasy of a fat jolly man who flies through the sky in a sleigh drawn by reindeer and arrives via chimney with presents—that single belief says everything about the innocence of children. How unbearable to lose it. For them and for us. So Jerry and I said nothing. And the next night Julie announced it again.

5   Christmas Eve Julie appeared with a sheet of yellow, lined paper. At the top she had written, "If you are real, sign here." It was, she said, a letter to Santa. She insisted that on this letter each of us—her father, Adam and I—write the words "Santa Claus," so if Santa were to sign it, she could compare our handwriting with his. Then she would know she had not been tricked.

6   Jerry signed. I signed. Adam, who was 5 and couldn't write, gave up after the letter "S." Julie folded the paper into quarters, wrote "Santa Claus" on the outside and stuck it on a ledge inside the chimney along with two Christmas cookies.

7   After much fuss, Julie and Adam were tucked into bed. Jerry and I put out the presents. We were not sure what to do about the letter.

8   After a short discussion, and mostly because we couldn't resist, we opted for deceit. Jerry took the note and, in the squiggliest printing imaginable, wrote "Merry Christmas, Santa Claus." He put the note back in the fireplace and ate the cookies.

9   The next morning, very early, about 6, we heard Julie and Adam tear down the hall. Jerry and I, in bed, listened for the first ecstatic reactions to the presents. Suddenly, we heard a shriek. "He's real! He's real! He's really real!!!!" The door to our room flew open. "He's REAL!!!" she shouted. Julie showed us the paper with the squiggly writing.

10   Somehow, this was not what we had bargained for. I had expected some modicum of disbelief—at least a "Dad, is this for real?"

11   Julie clasped the note to her chest. Then she dashed back to the presents.

12   That afternoon, our friend Deena came over to exchange gifts. "Santa Claus is real," said Julie.

13   "Oh," said Deena.

14   "I know for sure, for really, really sure. Look!" And Julie produced the proof.

15   Just then the phone rang. Knowing it was a relative calling with Christmas greetings, Julie rushed to answer it. "Santa Claus is real," I heard her say to my sister Nora, the same sister who had broken the bad news about Santa Claus to me 30 years ago. Julie handed me the phone.

16   "What is this about?" asked Nora.

17   I told her the story, trying to make it as funny as possible, hoping she wouldn't notice how badly Jerry and I had handled what I was beginning to think of as "the Santa issue." It didn't work.

18   "We may have made a mistake here," said Nora, diplomatically including herself in the mess.

19   "You're telling me!" I said. "Do you think there's any chance Julie will forget all this?" That was what I really wanted, of course—for the whole thing to go away.

20   "I doubt it," said Nora.

21   We had a wonderful day—good food, good presents, lots of visitors. Then it was bedtime.

22   "Dad?" said Julie, as he tucked her in.

23   "What?"

24   "If Santa's real, then Rudolph must be real, too."

25   "What!"

26   "If Santa's real—"

27   "I heard," said Jerry. He sat down on her bed and took a deep breath. "You know, Julie," and then he stopped. I could see he was trying to think of a way, any way, to explain our behavior so it wouldn't sound quite as deceptive, wrong and stupid as it was. But he was stumped.

28   "Yeah," said Julie.

29   "I wrote the note," said Jerry.

30   She burst into tears.

31   Jerry apologized. He apologized over and over while Julie sobbed into her pillow. He said he was wrong, that he shouldn't have tricked her, that he should have answered her questions about Santa Claus the week before.

32   Julie sat up in bed. "I thought he was real," she said reproachfully. Then suddenly she leaned over the bed, pulled out a comic from underneath and sat up again. "Can I read for five minutes?" she said.

33   "Sure," said Jerry.

34   And that was it. One minute of grief at Santa's death, and life went on.

35   Jerry and I left Julie's room terribly relieved. I immediately got a craving for leftover turkey and headed for the kitchen. I was putting the bird back in the refrigerator when I heard Adam crying. I went down the hall. The door to his room was open and I heard Julie, very disgusted, say: "Oh, Adam, you don't have to cry! Only babies believe in Santa Claus."

WHAT DID THE WRITER SAY AND WHAT DID YOU THINK? _____

1. What were the reasons for not telling Julie the truth about Santa Claus? Were the reasons valid?
2. Julie is not totally naive. What test does she devise to establish Santa's existence? What does she do to prevent fraud?
3. What is Julie's reaction to the apparent proof that Santa does exist?
4. What makes Jerry finally decide to tell the truth?
5. Express the thesis in your own words.
6. What are the conflicts in this narration? (see pp. 30-31)
7. Does your own experience confirm this story? Do you remember when you stopped believing in Santa Claus?

HOW DID THE WRITER SAY IT?

1. Is the thesis ever stated specifically? If so, where?
2. Paragraphs 2, 3, and 4 use a number of sentence fragments. Are they justified?

WHAT ABOUT *YOUR* WRITING?

Punctuation isn't always a matter of rules. Sometimes it can be a matter of taste.

"He's real! He's real! He's really real!!!! . . . He's REAL!!!"

Delia Ephron can afford to indulge here in comic-book punctuation because she's quoting a hysterical child—and hysterical children tend to sound childish. Writers anxious to avoid sounding childish themselves, however, will always avoid comic-book punctuation, the pouring on of artificial aids like exclamation points, question marks, italics, and capital letters to create emphasis. Writers guilty of these practices usually cheapen their effects and betray a lack of confidence in their command of words or their readers' intelligence.

When the words themselves haven't done the job adequately, the words need to be changed. The only way to fix a lame sentence is to fix the language; tossing in a pushy exclamation point doesn't make the sentence more powerful but only lets the reader know you wish it were more powerful. And two exclamation points are twice as bad, not twice as good. If your intended sarcasm in a sentence hasn't come through effectively with your words, a pushy little question mark isn't going to help, either.

Comic-book Punctuation	Improved
I had never seen anyone with such an ego! Never!!	Never had I seen anyone with such an ego.
Art?? The movie was filth!	The movie was not art. It was filth.
Professor Jones was a teacher (?) in Art History.	Professor Jones was a poor Art History teacher.

Don't assume that punctuation has suddenly been banned. All the resources of the language, including punctuation, are at your disposal. When a character in a novel is choking to death, nobody will object to the exclamation point when he says "Aaargh!" In a textbook nobody will object to the italics in a sentence like "The first principle of good writing is the *persuasive principle.*" The more spectacular forms of punctuation, however, require extreme caution. It's a matter of taste.

ANGELS ON A PIN

ALEXANDER CALANDRA

An amusing narrative by a university professor, "Angels on a Pin" leads to some
serious speculation about student-teacher relationships and the nature of
education. Scholasticism, referred to in Calandra's last paragraph, was a medieval
school of philosophy and theology broadly devoted to creating harmony between
reason and faith. The significant achievements of Scholastic philosophers often
tend to be forgotten today, and scholasticism is now associated by many with
hairsplitting logical disputation on trivial subjects such as the semilegendary
debate about how many angels can stand on the head of a pin. Calandra is a
physics professor at Washington University in St. Louis, Missouri.

Words to check:

arbiter (paragraph 1)   pendulum (11)
pedantic (13)

1   Some time ago, I received a call from a colleague who asked if I would be the
referee on the grading of an examination question. He was about to give
a student a zero for his answer to a physics question, while the student
claimed he should receive a perfect score and would if the system were not
set up against the student. The instructor and the student agreed to submit
this to an impartial arbiter, and I was selected.

2   I went to my colleague's office and read the examination question: "Show
how it is possible to determine the height of a tall building with the aid of a
barometer."

3   The student had answered: "Take the barometer to the top of the building,
attach a long rope to it, lower the barometer to the street, and then bring it
up, measuring the length of the rope. The length of the rope is the height of
the building."

4   I pointed out that the student really had a strong case for full credit, since
he had answered the question completely and correctly. On the other hand,
if full credit were given, it could well contribute to a high grade for the student in his physics course. A high grade is supposed to certify competence
in physics, but the answer did not confirm this. I suggested that the student
have another try at answering the question. I was not surprised that my colleague agreed, but I was surprised that the student did.

5   I gave the student six minutes to answer the question, with the warning
that his answer should show some knowledge of physics. At the end of five
minutes, he had not written anything. I asked if he wished to give up, but he
said no. He had many answers to this problem; he was just thinking of the

best one. I excused myself for interrupting him, and asked him to please go on. In the next minute, he dashed off his answer, which read:

6 "Take the barometer to the top of the building and lean over the edge of the roof. Drop the barometer, timing its fall with a stopwatch. Then, using the formula $S = 12at^2$, calculate the height of the building."

7 At this point, I asked my colleague if *he* would give up. He conceded, and I gave the student almost full credit.

8 In leaving my colleague's office, I recalled that the student had said he had other answers to the problem, so I asked him what they were. "Oh, yes," said the student. "There are many ways of getting the height of a tall building with the aid of a barometer. For example, you could take the barometer out on a sunny day and measure the height of the barometer, the length of its shadow, and the length of the shadow of the building, and by the use of simple proportion, determine the height of the building."

9 "Fine," I said. "And the others?"

10 "Yes," said the student. "There is a very basic measurement method that you will like. In this method, you take the barometer and begin to walk up the stairs. As you climb the stairs, you mark off the length of the barometer along the wall. You then count the number of marks, and this will give you the height of the building in barometer units. A very direct method.

11 "Of course, if you want a more sophisticated method, you can tie the barometer to the end of a string, swing it as a pendulum, and determine the value of 'g' at the street level and at the top of the building. From the difference between the two values of 'g,' the height of the building can, in principle, be calculated."

12 Finally, he concluded, there are many other ways of solving the problem. "Probably the best," he said, "is to take the barometer to the basement and knock on the superintendent's door. When the superintendent answers, you speak to him as follows: 'Mr. Superintendent, here I have a fine barometer. If you will tell me the height of this building, I will give you this barometer.'"

13 At this point, I asked the student if he really did not know the conventional answer to this question. He admitted that he did, but said that he was fed up with high school and college instructors trying to teach him how to think, to use the "scientific method," and to explore the deep inner logic of the subject in a pedantic way, as is often done in the new mathematics, rather than teaching him the structure of the subject. With this in mind, he decided to revive scholasticism as an academic lark to challenge the Sputnik-panicked classrooms of America.*

* The first man-made satellite, Sputnik I, was launched by the Soviet Union on October 4, 1957. The Soviet success helped stimulate a renewed emphasis on science in American education.

WHAT DID THE WRITER SAY AND WHAT DID YOU THINK?

1. What is Calandra's thesis?
2. What is the conventional answer to the examination question?
3. Express in your own words what irritated the student and what he was trying to prove.
4. Is the author's opinion the same as the student's?
5. Was the student treated fairly?

HOW DID THE WRITER SAY IT?

1. Except for intelligence, the student is individualized very little. Why? Can you find *any* instances where he is given some individuality?
2. Which seemingly trivial details increase the drama and believability of the narration?
3. Most writing patterns present the thesis early. Why is the thesis here not presented until the last paragraph?
4. What are some of the specific examples used in this selection?

=WHAT ABOUT *YOUR* WRITING?=

Watch out for *very*. Of all the trouble-making words in the language, *very* has possibly contributed most to sloppy writing. *Very* is an intensifier. You can smack it in front of nearly any adjective and strengthen—intensify—the meaning: *very pretty, very silly,* and so forth. The trouble is that the strengthening tends to be so generalized and imprecise that usually little of any substance is actually added to meaning. Sometimes meaning is even diminished or confused.

"There is a very basic measurement method that you will like," says the student in Calandra's article (paragraph 10). What did the student intend to say? If something is basic in itself, can it be any more basic? To be basic is to be the foundation, the core, the nucleus, the *base*. Did the student, in fact, intend to suggest ultrafine distinctions between measurement methods that are very basic and those that are only a little bit basic, quite basic, and very very basic? It's more likely that he was merely using *very* as most people do—carelessly. When he refers to "a very direct method" later in the paragraph, is he truly comparing it to other methods that are direct, but not *very* direct, just somewhat direct? And if the other methods are only somewhat direct, why bother thinking of them as direct at all? There are better words.

In fairness to the student, he is supposed to be talking, and conversation can never be as precise as writing. No speaker can take a break of a few minutes to ponder a choice of words, as a writer can. This is a book about writing, however, and in writing, the vague intensifier *very* is far more irritating than in speech. Nobody suggests that the word be outlawed, but in your own writing you'd do well to avoid it whenever you can. Start by looking for one-word synonyms: Instead of *very pretty*, try *beautiful;* instead of *very silly*. try *ridiculous.*

Really is another overused intensifier, particularly when used as the equivalent of *very. Very* may not mean much, but at least it means itself. *Really* doesn't even have that much going for it in the following sentences:

They ate a really fine dinner.

The stairs are really steep.

The new furniture was really expensive.

So watch out for *really,* too. Its only legitimate use occurs when the writer has in mind a distinction between what is factual or *real* in opposition to what is false or imaginary. Calandra uses the word correctly when he writes

I pointed out that the student really had a strong case for full credit.

I asked the student if he really did not know the conventional answer to this question.

SALVATION

LANGSTON HUGHES

Poet, playwright, short story writer, and essayist, Langston Hughes (1902–1967) is referred to by the *Encyclopedia Britannica* as "one of the foremost interpreters to the world of the black experience in the U. S." Hughes achieved great popularity with readers of all races, and when he died an astonishing twenty-seven of his books were still in print. "Salvation," from the 1940 autobiographical volume *The Big Sea,* shows Hughes's great gift for treating essentially serious subjects with a mixture of sensitivity and humor.

Words to check:

revival (paragraph 1)	knickerbockered (11)
dire (3)	punctuated (14)
gnarled (4)	

1   I was saved from sin when I was going on thirteen. But not really saved. It happened like this. There was a big revival at my Auntie Reed's church. Every night for weeks there had been much preaching, singing, praying, and shouting, and some very hardened sinners had been brought to Christ, and the membership of the church had grown by leaps and bounds. Then just before the revival ended, they held a special meeting for children, "to bring the young lambs to the fold." My aunt spoke of it for days ahead. That night I was escorted to the front row and placed on the mourners' bench with all the other young sinners, who had not yet been brought to Jesus.

2   My aunt told me that when you were saved you saw a light, and something happened to you inside! And Jesus came into your life! And God was with you from then on! She said you could see and hear and feel Jesus in your soul. I believed her. I have heard a great many old people say the same thing and it seemed to me they ought to know. So I sat there calmly in the hot, crowded church, waiting for Jesus to come to me.

3   The preacher preached a wonderful rhythmical sermon, all moans and shouts and lonely cries and dire pictures of hell, and then he sang a song about the ninety and nine safe in the fold, but one little lamb was left out in the cold. Then he said: "Won't you come? Won't you come to Jesus? Young lambs, won't you come?" And he held out his arms to all us young sinners there on the mourners' bench. And the little girls cried. And some of them jumped up and went to Jesus right away. But most of us just sat there.

4   A great many old people came and knelt around us and prayed, old women with jet-black faces and braided hair, old men with work-gnarled hands. And the church sang a song about the lower lights are burning, some poor sinners to be saved. And the whole building rocked with prayer and song.

5   Still I kept waiting to *see* Jesus.

6   Finally all the young people had gone to the altar and were saved, but one boy and me. He was a rounder's son named Westley. Westley and I were surrounded by sisters and deacons praying. It was very hot in the church, and getting late now. Finally Westley said to me in a whisper: "God damn! I'm tired o' sitting here. Let's get up and be saved." So he got up and was saved.

7   Then I was left all alone on the mourners' bench. My aunt came and knelt at my knees and cried, while prayers and songs swirled all around me in the little church. The whole congregation prayed for me alone, in a mighty wail of moans and voices. And I kept waiting serenely for Jesus, waiting, waiting— but he didn't come. I wanted to see him, but nothing happened to me. Nothing! I wanted something to happen to me, but nothing happened.

8   I heard the songs and the minister saying: "Why don't you come? My dear child, why don't you come to Jesus? Jesus is waiting for you. He wants you. Why don't you come? Sister Reed, what is this child's name?"

9   "Langston," my aunt sobbed.

10   "Langston, why don't you come? Why don't you come and be saved? Oh, Lamb of God! Why don't you come?"

11   Now it was really getting late. I began to be ashamed of myself, holding everything up so long. I began to wonder what God thought about Westley, who certainly hadn't seen Jesus either, but who was now sitting proudly on the platform, swinging his knickerbockered legs and grinning down at me, surrounded by deacons and old women on their knees praying. God had not struck Westley dead for taking his name in vain or for lying in the temple. So I decided that maybe to save further trouble, I'd better lie, too, and say that Jesus had come, and get up and be saved.

12   So I got up.

13   Suddenly the whole room broke into a sea of shouting, as they saw me rise. Waves of rejoicing swept the place. Women leaped in the air. My aunt threw her arms around me. The minister took me by the hand and led me to the platform.

14   When things quieted down, in a hushed silence, punctuated by a few ecstatic "Amens," all the new young lambs were blessed in the name of God. Then joyous singing filled the room.

15   That night, for the last time in my life but one—for I was a big boy twelve years old—I cried. I cried, in bed alone, and couldn't stop. I buried my head

under the quilts, but my aunt heard me. She woke up and told my uncle I was crying because the Holy Ghost had come into my life, and because I had seen Jesus. But I was really crying because I couldn't bear to tell her that I had lied, that I had deceived everybody in the church, that I hadn't seen Jesus, and that now I didn't believe there was a Jesus any more, since he didn't come to help me.

WHAT DID THE WRITER SAY AND WHAT DID YOU THINK?

1. What is the narrative point or thesis in "Salvation"?
2. Do you think that the adults were unfair in their pressures on the children? Why or why not?
3. How does the young Langston define "see"? Why, then, is he disappointed?
4. How is Westley's reaction different from Langston's?
5. Do you think that Hughes wants his essay to be read as a comment about adults' failure to remember the fears of childhood? Explain.

HOW DID THE WRITER SAY IT?

1. Why is Hughes's thesis implied rather than expressed directly?
2. In what order does Hughes present his narrative? Does this order create suspense for the reader? How?
3. Do you think the audience should be acquainted with the concept of religious revivals in order to comprehend Hughes's narrative? If you think so, what details could support your answer?
4. How do the hymn lyrics contribute to the pressures the young Langston feels?
5. In paragraph 13, Hughes compares the church to an ocean. How is this metaphor significant to the pressures that consume the young "sinner"?

WHAT ABOUT *YOUR* WRITING?

Part of the appeal of "Salvation" is its awakening of memories. Reading about the author's childhood, readers return to their own childhoods and remember the relatives, the boredom, the illusions, the ideals. Everything starts coming back.

It's hard to beat nostalgia as subject matter for papers. The friendly trivia contests at parties and the popularity of games like "Trivial Pursuit," the "Whatever Happened to . . ." and "Remember When?" features in newspapers and magazines, are only superficial signs of that appeal. In the midst of a world seemingly devoted to impermanence and the celebration of "future shock," many people find themselves drawn to keep in touch with, to keep faith with, their pasts.

The writer's age doesn't matter much with nostalgia. Our pasts may be different, but each of us has one. One person will remember Jackie Robinson and Joe DiMaggio, rationing during World War II, and "The Shadow" suspense program on radio. Another will remember the first day of being bused to a desegregated school, the seeing of *Jaws* four times in one week, and the killing of John Lennon. There are recent and less recent memories, funny ones and tragic ones, memories to treasure and memories to fear—but no normal person ever lived without memories.

Nostalgia can work in almost any paper, but bear one warning in mind: Avoid oozing sentimentality. Don't make the mistake of assuming automatically that everything about the past was glorious and everything about the present terrible. With that warning, though, a nostalgic trip into your own past can often result in a surprisingly easy solution to the problem of being stuck for a subject.

WHEN FATHER DOESN'T KNOW BEST

ANDREW MERTON

Andrew Merton is on the faculty of the University of New Hampshire in Durham, about an hour and a half by car from Boston's Fenway Park where much of this narrative essay takes place. Merton has a great deal to tell us about the right and wrong way to bring up children—but as you read, notice how much of the author's time, energy, and words go to telling a good story and how little direct philosophizing the essay contains.

Words to check:

insidious (paragraph 3)   tentative (15)
catacombs (6)

1   On Nov. 25, 1983, the prizefighter Marvis Frazier, 23 and inexperienced, was knocked out by the heavyweight champion of the world, Larry Holmes, after 2 minutes and 57 seconds of the first round. Frazier was sucker-punched. Holmes faked a left jab and Frazier went for it, leaving himself open for the decisive punch, a right. Frazier managed to stay on his feet while Holmes pummeled him with 19 consecutive punches. Finally, with three seconds left in the round, the referee stopped the fight. At that moment, Marvis Frazier's father and manager, the former heavyweight champion Joe Frazier, embraced his son and repeated over and over: "It's all right. It's all right. I love you."

2   Later, responding to criticism that he had overestimated his son's abilities, Joe Frazier said, "I knew what I was doing." In the face of indisputable evidence to the contrary, Joe Frazier was unable to give up the notion that Marvis would succeed him as champion, that he would continue to reign through his son.

3   It is an insidious business, this drive for immortality, usually much more subtle than thrusting one's son naked into the ring. Often it is simply a matter of expecting the boy to repeat one's own boyhood, step for step.

4   In July 1983, my son Gabriel was 4 and extremely conscious of it. In fact, he defined and justified much of his behavior by his age: "Four-year-olds can buckle their own sandals." Or "I can run faster than Mike. That's because I'm 4 and he's only 3." A 4-year-old, I thought, was ready for a major-league baseball game. So on Saturday, July 16, I drove him to Boston to see the Red Sox play the Oakland A's.

5   It was a clear, hot day—very hot, in fact, setting a record for Boston on that date at 97 degrees—but, rare for Boston, it was dry. A good day for hitters. Jim Rice, Tony Armas, Carl Yastrzemski and Wade Boggs had been on a tear. I expected a slugfest. I had packed a bag with fruit and vegetables. Gabe slept through the entire 90-minute drive to Boston, a good sign; he'd be fresh for the game. Another good sign: I found a free, legal parking space. And as we entered the ball park, Gabe seemed excited. Gravely he heeded my advice to go to the bathroom now, so we would not have to move from our seat during the action.

6   As we walked through the catacombs beneath the stadium, I remembered my own first game, in Yankee Stadium in 1952. My only previous view of major-league baseball had come via the flickering images of black-and-white television. As my father and I emerged into the sun, I was overwhelmed by the vast, green expanse of the outfield. A stubble-faced pitcher named Vic Raschi fired strike after strike, a Yankee first baseman named Joe Collins hit

a home run and the Yankees won, 3-2. The opponent had been the old Philadelphia Athletics, direct ancestors of the Oakland team. I felt joy and anticipation as Gabe and I now emerged into the sun for his first look at the left-field wall at Fenway, the Green Monster. Gabe said nothing, but he must have felt the excitement.

7   We found our seats, on the right-field side of the park halfway between first base and the foul pole. Good seats, from which we could see every part of the playing field. We were about a half-hour early, and we settled down to watch the end of batting practice. Then, as the ground crew manicured the infield, Gabe said he was hungry. I gave him a carrot stick, which he munched happily. When he finished that, he asked what else I had in the bag. I gave him some grapes, then an apple. Within 15 minutes he had polished off most of the contents of the bag. And then he said: "I think I've had enough baseball. I want to go home now."

8   "But the game hasn't started yet," I said. "You haven't seen any baseball."

9   "Yes, I have. And I want to go home."

10   "That was only batting practice. Don't you want to see the real game?"

11   "No."

12   I considered staying anyway. It was *my* day with my son that was being ruined here, wasn't it?

13   But I knew better. I knew now that if I insisted on staying, it would be *his* day that would be ruined so Dad could watch a ball game. Submitting to the logic of this, I gritted my teeth. In a foul mood, I carried him out of the park on my shoulders just as the Red Sox took the field. I was muttering to myself, almost audibly, "It's *his* day, dammit."

14   "Daddy? Can I have an ice-cream cone?"

15   Without much grace, I bought him an ice-cream cone. Then we got in the car, and I drove away from my precious parking space, still fuming. He was well aware that I was upset; I could see the tentative look on his face, a combination of fear and pain. I hated that look. But I could not shake my mood. I was not looking forward to the drive back to New Hampshire.

16   Then on Storrow Drive, I spotted the Boston Museum of Science, just across the Charles River. Gabe had been there before, and he had loved it, although he still referred to it, quite seriously, as the "Museum of Silence." Still angry, I managed to say, "Gabe, would you like to go to the museum?"

17   "Yeah," he said.

18   We had the museum nearly to ourselves. As we walked through the wonderfully cool exhibition halls, I acknowledged to myself how much I wanted Gabe to be like me. He was supposed to like the baseball game, not for his

sake, but for mine, and I had gotten angry at him when he didn't measure up to my expectations. It was those expectations, and not Gabe's actions, that were out of line. And it was those expectations that had to change.

19   I also thought about the competition between us: what had happened at the ball park was, after all, a battle of wills. He had won. He had prevailed because he was persistent and stubborn and stood up for what he thought was right.

20   We spent three quick hours at the museum, viewing the life-sized tyrannosaurus rex from different angles, trying out the space capsule, making waves and viewing exhibits on everything from centrifugal force to probability. Each time Gabe made a discovery, he called me over to share his excitement. And I *was* excited.

21   Son and father, together, had saved the day—he by holding out for something he enjoyed and I by having the sense, finally, to realize that he was right, and to let go of my dream of how things should be.

22   This time, anyway.

23   And then I remembered something else. When my own father took me to Yankee Stadium, I was 6 years old, not 4.

24   Maybe in a couple of years. . . .

**WHAT DID THE WRITER SAY
AND WHAT DID YOU THINK?** ⎯⎯⎯⎯⎯⎯⎯⎯⎯⎯⎯⎯⎯⎯⎯

1. What is the thesis? Where and how is it stated?
2. Why does the author begin his essay with the story of the Frazier-Holmes prizefight?
3. What "signs" make Merton think that the baseball game is a good idea?
4. Why does the author get so angry with his son? How do the two of them deal with his anger?
5. How does Gabe express his boredom?
6. Why is the Boston Museum of Science a better choice for Gabe than a baseball game?

HOW DID THE WRITER SAY IT? ⎯⎯⎯⎯⎯⎯⎯⎯⎯⎯⎯⎯⎯⎯⎯⎯⎯

1. Does the author attack his own thesis in the last three sentences of this essay? How seriously are we meant to take these sentences?
2. What details does Merton use to establish his own love of baseball?

3. How do Joe Frazier's parental attitudes compare and contrast with the author's?

═══════════════════**WHAT ABOUT *YOUR* WRITING?**═══════════════════

Merton's title "When Father Doesn't Know Best" arouses our curiosity. It reminds us of a famous saying—and television show—and simultaneously surprises us by changing the expected wording. We sense that a fresh point is going to be made, perhaps with a touch of humor, and we read on.

A good title is worth fussing about. It usually helps identify your subject, as well as your attitude toward the subject. It enables the reader to become properly oriented even before looking at your opening sentence. A good title also stimulates curiosity: it makes the reader willing to bother with your opening sentence in the first place. A good title won't save a bad piece of writing, and a bad title won't destroy good writing, but good titles help, and writers shouldn't be shy about accepting all the help they can get.

Boring Title	Better Title
The Making of the Constitution	A More Perfect Union
Three Kinds of Teachers	Teach, Teacher, and Sir
Great Vampire Movies	Fangs for the Memory
The New Father	Have a Baby, My Wife Just Had a Cigar
Problems of Medical Expenses	Your Money or Your Life

A CULTURAL DIVORCE

ELIZABETH WONG

Elizabeth Wong's essay about her school days spectacularly avoids the danger of becoming sweetly sentimental about the past: classrooms, the innocence of children, the joys of family life (see pp. 46–47). After you finish this essay, consider whether it can be thought of as a story with an abrupt surprise ending or whether the surprise is anticipated anywhere earlier.

Words to check:

stoically (paragraph 1)	kowtow (6)
dissuade (2)	ideographs (7)
flanked (5)	pidgin (10)

1   It's still there, the Chinese school on Yale Street where my brother and I used to go. Despite the new coat of paint and the high wire fence, the school I knew 10 years ago remains remarkably, stoically the same.

2   Every day at 5 P.M., instead of playing with our fourth- and fifth-grade friends or sneaking out to the empty lot to hunt ghosts and animal bones, my brother and I had to go to Chinese school. No amount of kicking, screaming, or pleading could dissuade my mother, who was solidly determined to have us learn the language of our heritage.

3   Forcibly, she walked us the seven long, hilly blocks from our home to school, depositing our defiant tearful faces before the stern principal. My only memory of him is that he swayed on his heels like a palm tree, and he always clasped his impatient twitching hands behind his back. I recognized him as a repressed maniacal child killer, and knew that if we ever saw his hands we'd be in big trouble.

4   We all sat in little chairs in an empty auditorium. The room smelled like Chinese medicine, an imported faraway mustiness. Like ancient mothballs or dirty closets. I hated that smell. I favored crisp new scents. Like the soft French perfume that my American teacher wore in public school.

5   There was a stage far to the right, flanked by an American flag and the flag of the Nationalist Republic of China, which was also red, white and blue but not as pretty.

6   Although the emphasis at the school was mainly language—speaking, reading, writing—the lessons always began with an exercise in politeness. With the entrance of the teacher, the best student would tap a bell and everyone would get up, kowtow, and chant, "Sing san ho," the phonetic for "How are you, teacher?"

7   Being ten years old, I had better things to learn than ideographs copied painstakingly in lines that ran right to left from the tip of a *moc but,* a real ink pen that had to be held in an awkward way if blotches were to be avoided. After all, I could do the multiplication tables, name the satellites of Mars, and write reports on "Little Women" and "Black Beauty." Nancy Drew, my favorite book heroine, never spoke Chinese.

8   The language was a source of embarrassment. More times than not, I had tried to disassociate myself from the nagging loud voice that followed me wherever I wandered in the nearby American supermarket outside Chinatown. The voice belonged to my grandmother, a fragile woman in her seventies who could outshout the best of the street vendors. Her humor was raunchy, her Chinese rhythmless, patternless. It was quick, it was loud, it was unbeautiful. It was not like the quiet, lilting romance of French or the gentle refinement of the American South. Chinese sounded pedestrian. Public.

9   In Chinatown, the comings and goings of hundreds of Chinese on their daily tasks sounded chaotic and frenzied. I did not want to be thought of as mad, as talking gibberish. When I spoke English, people nodded at me, smiled sweetly, said encouraging words. Even the people in my culture would cluck and say that I'd do well in life. "My, doesn't she move her lips fast," they would say, meaning that I'd be able to keep up with the world outside Chinatown.

10   My brother was even more fanatical than I about speaking English. He was especially hard on my mother, criticizing her, often cruelly, for her pidgin speech—smatterings of Chinese scattered like chop suey in her conversation. "It's not 'What it is,' Mom," he'd say in exasperation. "It's 'What *is* it, what *is* it, what *is* it!'" Sometimes Mom might leave out an occasional "the" or "a," or perhaps a verb of being. He would stop her in midsentence: "Say it again, Mom. Say it right." When he tripped over his own tongue, he'd blame it on her: "See, Mom, it's all your fault. You set a bad example."

11   What infuriated my mother most was when my brother cornered her on her consonants, especially "r." My father had played a cruel joke on Mom by assigning her an American name that her tongue wouldn't allow her to say. No matter how hard she tried, "Ruth" always ended up "Luth" or "Roof."

12   After two years of writing with a *moc but* and reciting words with multiples of meanings, I finally was granted a cultural divorce. I was permitted to stop Chinese school.

13   I thought of myself as multicultural. I preferred tacos to egg rolls; I enjoyed Cinco de Mayo* more than Chinese New Year.

14   At last, I was one of you; I wasn't one of them.

15   Sadly, I still am.

WHAT DID THE WRITER SAY AND WHAT DID YOU THINK?

1. What is Wong's thesis? Does she state it directly? Does she need to?
2. What are the implications of the last sentence of this reading?
3. When the author was a child she hated speaking Chinese. Why?
4. What are Wong's current feelings about being forced to attend Chinese school?
5. What is the "cruel joke" of the author's mother's name?

* May 5, a holiday celebrating the defeat of French troops in Mexico at the Battle of Puebla, 1862.

HOW DID THE WRITER SAY IT? ————————————————

1. What specific details does the author use to emphasize her childhood distaste for all that was Chinese and love for all that was American?
2. What does the phrase "a cultural divorce" mean?
3. How and where does Wong indicate that her childhood attitudes have changed?

════════════WHAT ABOUT *YOUR* WRITING?════════════

Once writers are ready to go beyond the obvious ingredients of grammar, mechanics, and organization, they frequently find themselves working hardest on specific details. That's what they should be doing. Writing that lacks effective specific details is almost always dull and sometimes unclear. Writing that uses effective specific details has energy, character, and conviction. Yes, of course, writers must generalize; a thesis statement is a generalization, after all. To a great extent, however, it's by specific details that the writing lives or dies. Without them, no matter how sensible or important or even brilliant the ideas, a paper is likely to perish from malnutrition.

In "A Cultural Divorce," Elizabeth Wong uses specific details to bring her subject to life. She does not settle for writing accurately but ploddingly, "I was proud of my American schooling and contemptuous of my Chinese schooling." Instead, she makes the same general point with specific details— and the writing becomes twice as interesting, twice as forceful, and twice as convincing: "After all, I could do the multiplication tables, name the satellites of Mars, and write reports on 'Little Women' and 'Black Beauty.' Nancy Drew, my favorite book heroine, never spoke Chinese." Wong does not *tell* us in general terms that her mother had trouble speaking English. Instead, we see Wong's mother unable to pronounce her own name, and we share some of the pain and embarrassment. We start to care, and we care intensely. And that's why specific details are so important.

3

DESCRIPTION

*D*escription is nothing new. You undoubtedly noted the descriptions you encountered in the previous narration chapter. Narrative writing draws much of its life from sensory description. In "Coping with Santa Claus" when Delia Ephron wrote " . . . Julie appeared with a sheet of yellow, lined paper," and in "Salvation" when Langston Hughes wrote " . . . swinging his knickerbockered legs and grinning down at me, surrounded by deacons and old women on their knees praying," these authors were using descriptive details to help the reader sense the scene. If you have already written a narrative essay, you, too, probably relied on description to advance your ideas. In your essays to come, you will also find that description is essential. Description is not new, but devoting an entire paper to it is new and demands separate consideration.

Some descriptions can be completely *objective:* they can describe the size and color of measles spots, the size and speed of a missile. Objective descriptions make no judgments about the ugliness of the spots or the morality of the missile. Ordinarily intended to meet special needs, objective descriptions are not within the province of this chapter.

The *impressionistic* or *interpretive* description paper is our basic concern. The writer of this paper uses description to convey an attitude. Any objective description of measles spots, for instance, is subordinate here to convincing the reader of the ugliness or triviality or seriousness of the spots.

Rules, guidelines, and handy hints are of less practical value than usual in writing the comparatively freewheeling description paper. Only three major points need to be stressed, and none of them is especially restrictive.

EMOTIONAL APPEAL

First, *description papers tend to rely more than others on a direct appeal to the reader's emotions.* A description of a room will more probably have a thesis like *The room was frightening* than *The room was big.* To make their emotional appeal, description papers also tend to concentrate more than others on using colorful language. Moreover, such hard-to-pin-down elements as mood and tone tend to be major concerns. These are pretty spectacular generalizations, of course; they don't apply to all description papers, and they certainly shouldn't be interpreted as implying that other patterns of writing can't or shouldn't appeal to emotions, use colorful language, and so on. As a whole, though, good description papers do receive praise more for their insight and sensitivity than for their masterful logic.

Nobody can teach you how to make your writing tingle with deep perceptions. Insight and sensitivity come from within. It might help, however, to suggest a few approaches that can give your writing a push in the right direction toward attaining the lively emotional appeal of good description.

1. Try a Deliberately Unconventional Thesis. If a room would strike ninety-nine people out of a hundred as ugly, try pointing out its hidden beauties. If everyone agrees that a young woman is painfully shy, try showing that she really has a superiority complex. Don't lie, and don't attempt to support a thesis you believe is idiotic; do see if you can make a case for an unconventional idea.

2. Show Your Powers of Observation by Stressing Specific Details. Virtually all good writing uses specifics, lots of them. A description paper absolutely depends on them. Try to take a seemingly trivial detail and show its surprising relevancy. Demonstrate that you had the ability to notice the detail in the first place and then to have its significance register on your mind. If you write a paper attempting to show that a certain man pays no attention to his appearance, don't just say that he looks messy; bring up the bread crumbs in his moustache and the toe protruding through the hole in his tennis sneakers. Too trivial? Not at all. As long as the details support the thesis, they add life to the paper.

3. Use Specific Language. Another principle of most good writing is of particular importance in description. The effect of a specific detail can be weakened if the language used to present the detail is not itself specific. *There were bread crumbs in his mustache* shows observation of specific details. *Forgotten bread crumbs, slowly hardening in his mustache, had the same revolting inappropriateness as paint stains on a fur coat* shows observation of specific details dramatized by specific language.

4. Stress the Psychological Impact of What You Describe. A good description will be accurate, but it will be exciting, too. Your description of a dusty old room won't convey a sense of immediacy by itemizing the locations of all the clumps of dust; your reader should have not only a picture of what the room looks like but also a strong sense of how depressed or indignant or philosophical the room made you feel.

So much for emotional appeal.

ORGANIZATION

Second, *choose an appropriate organizing principle, and stick to it.* Some authorities suggest that in describing the appearance of a person, the writer might start with the head and go down to the toes (or vice versa, of course). In describing a landscape, the writer might start with objects farthest away and progress to those closest. Many writers should be able to do better. The authorities want to achieve order but sometimes seem to invite rigidity.

Still, they have a case, and cautious agreement with them is the only reasonable course. Nobody wants rigidity, but chaos is even worse. Certainly, a writer needs enough of a predetermined organizing principle to decide which descriptive details come first and which come last. It's easy to understand hesitation about the cut-and-dried mathematics of top-to-bottom or far-to-near, but not all the formulas need to be that definite. Some description papers may be organized on a looser principle like attractive features/ unattractive features, first impressions/second impressions, impact on senses like sight, touch, and hearing. Structure of some kind is necessary. In addition, even the top-to-bottom and far-to-near principles seldom turn out to be as dreary as they sound. A good writer, after all, doesn't ordinarily make formal announcements like "moving down from the forehead, I shall now discuss the nose" or "The next closest object is . . ." Don't adopt an organizing principle, then, that makes a prisoner of you and your reader, but do adopt a principle. There's freedom of choice, but you have to make a choice.

PERSUASIVE PRINCIPLE

Third, *the description paper must commit itself to the discipline of the persuasive principle.* With all this material on freedom and emotional appeal, this last point is particularly important. It's precisely because of the relatively free-form nature of much descriptive writing that the persuasive principle has to be insisted on so strongly. Freedom and sloppiness are not the same. Thesis and support of thesis in many respects are the main ingredients for holding the description paper together. Without a thesis, a process paper (see Chapter 5) can still trace a process. Without a thesis, a description paper goes off in all directions and disintegrates into a shapeless mass. It doesn't describe; it simply takes inventory. Without a thesis, a description paper has no backbone—and, like a body without a backbone, has no freedom to do, or be, anything.

There's not much this book can say about the general nature of the persuasive principle that it hasn't already said. Throughout much of Chapter 1, the book showed how a paper on education was narrowed down to a description of Professor X with the thesis "Professor X is an incompetent teacher." On page 11 a sample first paragraph showed how such a paper might begin. A description paper doesn't merely benefit from a thesis. It needs one in order to exist.

WRITING SUGGESTIONS FOR DESCRIPTION THEMES ⎯⎯⎯⎯⎯⎯

Some of the suggested topics here are more specific than usual. Don't feel hemmed in. Use them only as starting points for your own ideas. Notice that many topics can be treated in two different ways. You can write a description of a general or composite type of airline flight attendant or lifeguard or hospital waiting room, having no one specific person, place, or thing in mind; you can also write a description of an *individual* person, place, or thing: flight attendant Susan Early, lifeguard John Braun, the waiting room at St. Luke's.

1. Beggars
2. Know-it-all car mechanics
3. Traffic jams
4. Lifeguards
5. Spoiled children
6. Haunted houses
7. People eating lobster or corn on the cob
8. Thunderstorms
9. Dentists
10. Animals in the zoo
11. Bus drivers

12. Airline flight attendants
13. Pinball or video game fanatics
14. Normally busy places, now deserted
15. Stutterers
16. Retarded children
17. Drunks
18. Hospital waiting rooms
19. The contents of a pocketbook
20. Overcommercialized tourist attractions
21. Housing developments
22. Amusement parks
23. Vans or campers
24. Sports stadiums

The Glorious Fourth

Allen Robertson (student)

Thesis: When I was a kid, the Fourth of July was the best holiday there was.

    I.   Daytime
        A. Playing games
        B. Lying in the hammock

   II. Evening
        A. Barbecuing
        B. Playing with sparklers
        C. Eating dinner

  III. Night
        A. Waiting for the fireworks
        B. Watching fireworks

Conclusion: I still try to hold on to the beauty and excitement that was the Fourth of July.

    When I was a kid the Fourth of July was the best holiday there was. It was better than Easter or Christmas because I didn't have to waste any of the day in church. It was better than Thanksgiving because there was more to do. And it was better than a birthday because absolutely everybody was celebrating with me.

    We always spent the sunlit half of the day doing very little indeed. Maybe we would run through the sprinkler, or have a water fight, or play catch in the street, or maybe we'd just lie in the hammock and watch the green leaves and the gold sunshine and the blue shadows changing shape above our heads.

Around five o'clock, Dad would light the barbecue, and the tingly smoke would creep out to wherever my brothers and I were playing. We'd start feeling hungry and wander on home. To keep us out of his way while he cooked the spicy, smoky barbecued chicken, Dad would give us sparklers. He'd light the ends of these mysterious gray metal sticks with his cigarette lighter. We watched impatiently, waiting for them to burst into a waterfall of golden sparks that always seemed to last just five seconds short of long enough.

One or more of us always tried to sneak a sparkler into the kitchen to share with Mom, but she always chased us out, sending us off to clean up for dinner. We moved pretty fast when we heard the word dinner, because there was never anything better than a plate filled with Dad's barbecued chicken and Mom's once-a-year-and-I-only-do-it-because-I-love-you potato salad.

After dinner, when the dishes were cleaned up and put away, and the sky was getting dark and the bugs were coming out, and just when we kids were starting to worry that we might miss the main event, Mom and Dad would pile us into the car. Like all the other families from our neighborhood, we drove out to the top of the hill overlooking the town. We kids climbed up on the roof of the car for the best possible view, and Mom and Dad handed up cookies and lemonade when they weren't talking with old friends. Then, as the night got darker and quieter, we'd wait for the fireworks.

When the fireworks started and everyone else oohed and aahed, I would lie on my back on the top of the car, on the top of the world, and try to hang on to all the beauty and excitement. I knew they couldn't last, not any more than the sparks that made the fireworks could, but I still tried to hang on.

LEVI'S

MARILYN SCHIEL

As you might guess, this essay gives a memorable description of Levi's. Marilyn Schiel doesn't think Levi's are just long-lasting work pants, however. What else does she describe?

Words to check:

shirtwaist (paragraph 4)	chamois (12)
anachronism (4)	trestle (14)
acumen (9)	worldliness (15)

1   They weren't boot cut, or spiked leg, or 501. They weren't stone washed, or acid bleached, or ice black. They weren't Guess, or Zena, or Jordache. They were just blue jeans—old, worn Levi's.

2   My ten-year-old brother wore blue jeans. I wore slacks. In summer, cotton pastel pants with embroidered bunnies or ducks. In winter, grey-corduroys with girl-pink flannel lining. I wanted to wear blue jeans.

3   As a five-year-old I didn't understand the difference between cause and co-incidence. My brother's jeans meant he could wander his two-wheel bike blocks from home after school; he could, with a crew of blue-jeaned boys, build a tree house in the oak in the vacant lot next door; he could carry a BB gun all the way to the cemetery to shoot at squirrels. I had to be content trik-ing my embroidered bunnies up and down the driveway; I had to settle for building domino houses on the living room floor; I could shoot only caps at imaginary black-hatted cowboys in the basement. I wanted to wear blue jeans.

4   But little girls in my 1950 world didn't wear blue jeans. Big girls didn't wear them either. Big girls didn't even wear pastel cotton slacks or winter corduroys. At least my mother, the big girl I knew best, didn't. When the family gathered for breakfast, seven days a week sharp at 7:30, Mom was already in uniform, a shirtwaist dress garnished with a colored, beaded necklace that matched clip-on earrings. By the 1960s June Cleaver* may have been an anachronism, but in the early 1950s she lived at my house.

5   Mothers stayed home. Unlike dads, mothers didn't work. Mothers made the beds, cooked the meals, cleaned the house, baked the cookies, tended the garden, canned the vegetables, squeezed the clothes through the wringer-washer, hung washed clothes to dry on lines strung through the basement, ironed everything—including sheets and towels—scrubbed the floors while kneeling on pink rubber pads, walked seven blocks pulling an empty Red-flyer wagon to buy groceries, struggled seven blocks home with a week's worth of carefully budgeted supplies, and picked out the clothes their children would wear. My brother got blue jeans. I got embroidered bunnies.

6   Then, in 1953, my world changed. Elvis took us all to Heartbreak Hotel; Eisenhower brought us home from Korea; and my mother went to work. The hardware store Dad bought pulled Mom from the home to the business.

---

* The perfect mother of the perfect family on the television program *Leave It to Beaver*.

Her transition from the breadbaker to a breadwinner taught my mother that women, big or little, didn't have to wear embroidered bunnies anymore.

7   The change was more evolutionary than revolutionary. She still wore the housewife uniform—but now she wore it to work. She still did the laundry, but now with an automatic washing machine and electric dryer. We still ate breakfast together at 7:30, but now cereal and milk replaced eggs and bacon. The ironing went out every Tuesday night to a house on the hill behind the railroad tracks and came back folded every Wednesday evening. And as a businesswoman, my mother discovered that sometimes function was more important than fashion, at least for little girls.

8   Those old, worn Levi's of my brother's met the expectations of the advertisements. They survived an entire season of his hard wear and, unlike most of his clothes, were outgrown before worn out. And as mother used to say about anything that might be salvaged for use, "These old pants still have a little life left in them."

9   Not only did they have some life left in them, but they were going to give that life to me. A year earlier they would have been boxed with other we-don't-want-them-anymore clothes for the "naked children" of some foreign country I'd never heard of or, if the postage wasn't too expensive, shipped off to my poor cousins in South Dakota. With her newfound economic acumen and with her slowly evolving awareness of a woman's place, my mother looked at those blue jeans differently than she would have the year before. Maybe she looked at me a little differently, too.

10   "Marilyn, come here," she called from my brother's room. That in itself tripped anticipation. Now that Bob was approaching adolescence, his room held the mystery earned of secrecy. The door to his room was open; my mother leaned over the bed folding and sorting boy-clothes. Shirts in one stack, pants in another, worn to see-through-thin garments in still a third pile. But smoothed out full length along the edge of Bob's bed were a pair of old, worn Levi's.

11   "Here, try these on." She held them up against my seven-year-old middle. "I think these will fit you if you roll up the legs."

12   And fit they did, more like a gunnysack than a glove, but they were blue jeans and they were my brother's—and they were now mine. Cinched tightly with an Indian-beaded belt scrounged from my brother's dresser, the chamois-soft denim bunched in unplanned pleats at my waist. No more sissy elastic for me. Triple-roll cuffs still scuffed the ground by my shoe heels when I walked—my excuse for the swaggering steps those Levi's induced. After a time sidewalk burns frayed the bottom edge, finally denoting my singular ownership.

Metal rivets marked the pockets and seam overlaps. Gone were the telltale girl-white overstitching outlines. And those pockets. Real pockets. Not that patch pocket pretend stuff of girl-pants, but deep inside pockets of white, soft, gather-in-my-fist material that could be pulled inside out in search of the disappeared dime.

13   But those Levi's marked more than my move from little-girl clothes to big-brother clothes. Indeed, they were the only hand-me-downs ever handed down. Instead, those old ratty pants marked my move to freedom, freedom from the conventional girl-stuff my mother had so carefully fostered only one year earlier. Maybe my mother—who was learning the difference between roofing nails and wood screws, who was learning to mix paint in the vise-gripping shake-machine bolted to the floor in the back room of the hardware store, who would later teach me to cut glass, make keys, and clean Surge milk pumpers—wanted me to know what she was learning about women's work and men's work. I don't know. I just know that those Levi's—old, worn, with a difficult-to-manage button fly—meant the world to me, at least the limited world offered by my neighborhood.

14   The next summer I got my first two-wheeled bike, a full-size, blue, fat-tire Schwinn off the store's showroom floor. It was Mother who convinced Dad that I didn't need training wheels. "If you want her to learn to ride, put her on it and let her ride." Oh, I dented the fenders some that summer and suffered some scars from the inescapable tip-overs, but I learned to ride as well as the boys. And by the end of the summer, Mom was packing peanut butter sandwiches for me to take on fishing expeditions down at the Chippewa River below the railroad trestle.

15   Along with the traditional dolls and play cookware, Christmas Eve brought chemistry kits and carpenter tools. Even my brother acknowledged my new-found worldliness. Better than any gift were the after-school hours spent helping him rebuild an old auto engine in the basement. I didn't do much, but watching him work and occasionally fetching wrenches taught me where pistons went and what they did, and that my big brother didn't mind having me around.

16   By junior high, I had my own .22. Our family Sundays in the fall found three of us in the woods searching for squirrel. My brother elected to hunt a more dangerous game, senior high school girls. Dad wore that goofy brown billed hat with cold-weather earflaps; I wore wool side-zipping slacks from the juniors department at Daytons, topped by a crew-neck matching sweater—style in a seventh-grade girl mattered even in the woods; Mom wore a turtleneck under one of Dad's wool shirt-jacs pulled out to hang over her blue jeans—old, worn Levi's.

WHAT DID THE WRITER SAY AND WHAT DID YOU THINK?

1. What is the thesis?
2. How does the author contrast herself with her brother?
3. How did Schiel make her brother's jeans uniquely hers?
4. Does the author really believe that "mothers didn't work?" How do you know?
5. What was the author's mother learning about "women's work and men's work?"
6. How are Schiel and her mother alike?
7. Does the author believe that "clothes make the man (or woman)?"

HOW DID THE WRITER SAY IT?

1. The first three sentences are almost exactly alike and the fourth is only slightly different. Why is such a simple paragraph so effective?
2. What details emphasize the mother's growing independence?
3. Why does Schiel bother telling her audience about her first bike, her experiences watching her brother fix a car, and her squirrel hunts? Do these things relate to her first blue jeans at all?

WHAT ABOUT *YOUR* WRITING?

To avoid monotony, the good writer varies sentence length. Long and short sentences are neither good nor bad in themselves: variety is the key.

In the Schiel selection, notice how paragraph 3, ending with a sentence of merely six words, is preceded by two much longer sentences of 52 and 39 words respectively. Notice how two short sentences begin and end paragraph 5, but between those sentences is an unusually long sentence of 83 words.

Mathematical formulas are inapplicable, of course. There's no magic number of words at which a sentence ceases to be short and suddenly becomes long. There's no special point, for that matter, at which readers suddenly cease to be interested and become bored. Monotonous sentence length, however, contributes to boredom, and variety can often contribute to interest. So try to vary sentence length.

BE SCARED FOR YOUR KIDS

AL SICHERMAN

Al Sicherman writes a humor column for the *Minneapolis Star Tribune*, so his readers must have been astonished one day in 1989 to see this extraordinary and moving description of his son and his son's funeral. Note that in addition to being a personal tribute and farewell to a beloved son, the essay is intended to present a powerful public message to all parents.

Words to check:

chronicle (paragraph 3)	acerbic (27)
parries (5)	raucous (32)
pinnacle (17)	dulcimers (44)
cantor (23)	heady (48)

1　Dear, dear friends: This isn't going to be easy.

2　Nor is it going to be funny.

3　My older son, Joe, of whom I was very, very proud, and whose growing-up I've been privileged to chronicle occasionally in the newspaper, died last month in a fall from the window of his seventh-floor dorm room in Madison, Wisconsin. He had taken LSD. He was eighteen years old.

4　To say he had his whole life ahead of him is unforgivably trite—and unbearably sad.

5　I saw him a week before he died. It was my birthday, and he spent the weekend with his stepmother and me. He was upbeat, funny, and full of his new activities, including fencing. He did a whole bunch of very impressive lunges and parries for us.

6　The next time I was with him, he was in a coffin.

7　He must not have known how treacherous LSD can be. I never warned him, because, like most adults, I had no idea it was popular again. I thought it had stopped killing kids twenty years ago. Besides, Joe was bright and responsible; he wouldn't "do" drugs. It didn't occur to me that he might dabble in them.

8　His mother had warned him about LSD, though; she knew it was back because Joe had told her about a friend who had taken it. Obviously he didn't listen to her advice. At eighteen, kids think they're invulnerable. They're wrong.

9　*Joey was a very sweet, very funny kid. And even before he had anything particularly funny to say, he had great timing. When he was about six, I asked him what he wanted to be when he grew up. He paused, just long enough, and said, "A stand-up physicist."*

10   I went to the mortuary in Milwaukee several hours before the funeral to have a chance to be with him. I spent most of the time crying and saying dumb things like "I would have caught you" and "I would have traded with you." I wish I could say that I sang him a lullaby, but I didn't think of it until several days later. I went ahead and did it then, but it was too late. It would have been too late in any case.

11   Joe was not a reckless kid: Last summer he turned down my wife's suggestion that the family go on a rafting trip through the Grand Canyon; although he loved amusement-park rides, he thought that sounded too risky. So we went sailing and miniature golfing instead. But he took LSD. Apparently he figured that wasn't as dangerous.

12   *When he was about seven or eight, Joey attended a camp for asthma sufferers. When asked "What do you do at asthma camp?" he responded, cheerfully, "Wheeze!"*

13   The coffin is always closed in traditional Jewish funerals, and as I sat with him that morning before the funeral, I minded that. I felt so far from him. I finally decided that I had the right to open if briefly, even if it was against some rule. In fact, I rationalized, Joe probably would like my breaking the rule. So I raised the lid.

14   He was in a body bag.

15   I'm not surprised that kids don't listen to their parents about drugs. Adults' standards of risk are different from theirs, and they know it; and they discount what we tell them. But we must tell them anyway.

16   Joe's aunt, a teacher, says that when you warn kids about something dangerous—something that kills people—they always say "Name one." OK, I will. Joe Sicherman. You may name him, too. Please.

17   *Joe's first job was in Manchester, New Hampshire, where his mother had moved with him and his younger brother nine years ago. He was a carry-out boy in a supermarket. One day he came to the rescue of a clerk faced with a customer who spoke only French and who wanted to use Canadian money. Armed with his two years of high-school French, Joe stepped forward and explained "Madame, non!" She seemed not to understand. That, he said, was when he rose the very pinnacle of linguistic and supermarket expertise: "Madame," he said, with a Gallic shrug of his shoulders, "augghhhh!" The woman nodded and left.*

18   Because the coffin is always closed, nobody expected anyone to look inside. There were blood splatters on the body bag.

19   It's entirely possible that warning your kids won't scare them away from LSD. But maybe it will. I wish I could tell you how to warn them so it would work, but I can't.

20   This is the generation gap reduced to its most basic: It is parents' worst fear that something terrible will happen to their kids; it is kids' constant struggle to be free of the protection of their parents.

21   *Joe's next job was in Shorewood, Wisconsin, a Milwaukee suburb, where his family moved just before his junior year in high school. It was a summer job as a soda jerk. He confided to me that he worked alongside a "soda idiot" and that his boss was "a soda &#%@." Actually, I think he enjoyed it. He told me one day that he was "acquiring meaningful insights into the Sundae Industry." Like: If you say "yes" to "Do you want a lid on that?" you're going to get less whipped topping.*

22   Traditional Jewish funerals leave no room for the stage of grief that psychologists call "denial." When you leave the cemetery, you have no doubt that the person is dead. In fact, you might say that these funerals are brutal. I could avoid telling you about it, and spare us both some pain, but I think I owe it to Joe—and to every parent—to let this be as forceful as possible.

23   When the graveside prayers were over, workmen lowered Joe's coffin into the ground and then eased a concrete cover down into the hole until it covered the metal burial vault. The cover had Joe's name on it. They pulled the green fake-grass cloth off the pile of dirt next to the grave, and the rabbi and the cantor each threw a shovelful of earth onto the vault lid.

24   Then they handed the shovel to Joe's fifteen-year-old brother, David.

25   It occurs to me now that what I might have done is ask Joe what kind of drugs were around. Maybe my genuine alarm at the reemergence of LSD would have registered with him. I'm certainly going to be less self-assured about how I deal with this subject with David. He's a wonderful kid, too, and while I don't want to smother him, I don't want to assume anything, either.

26   I didn't take Joe for granted; I think I encouraged him and delighted in him and celebrated with him. But I certainly took his *life* for granted. Parents must not do that. We must be scared for them. They don't know when to be scared for themselves.

27   *Although his humor had become somewhat acerbic recently, Joe remained a sweet, thoughtful kid. When, as I often did, I wound up apologizing to him because a weekend or a vacation hadn't worked out the way I'd hoped, he always patted my hand—literally or figuratively—and let me know he loved me anyway.*

28 *He took good care of others, too. He spent most of his grandfather's nine-tieth birthday party making sure that his stepmother had somebody to talk to besides my ex-wife's family.*

29 *And on that last birthday visit with me in early October, he talked a little about his concerns and hopes for his brother. One of those concerns was drugs.*

30 Then they handed the shovel to me.

31 Later I overheard my wife say that the expression on my face when I turned away, having shoveled dirt onto my son's coffin, was the most awful thing she'd ever seen.

32 Whenever I thought about Joe recently, it was about college and indepen-dence and adulthood, and his latest involvements: His attempt to produce an English paper that was more interesting than what the instructor had asked for, the raucous rock band he and his friend put together over the summer, his plans to rent a cabin with a bunch of kids at winter break.

33 Now, suddenly, I'm no longer looking at the moment, but instead at the whole life. And in some automatic averaging-out, in my mind I'm sometimes calling him "Joey," his little-boy name.

34 *He told his mother a year ago that he wanted his senior year in high school to be the best year he'd ever had, and on the drive to Madison to start college this fall, he told her that, despite lots of typical teenage domes-tic tension, it had been. He said he'd accomplished everything he'd set out to do—except to have a mad, passionate affair with a woman he didn't even know.*

35 *She refrained from asking the obvious question.*

36 Then they handed the shovel to his mother.

37 Even though it is only three weeks since his death, I find that the reality of Joey is beginning to turn sepia. He will be forever eighteen. And his life will forever stop in 1989. That saddens me so much. It's not just that he won't have a career, maybe get married, have kids, all those things we hope might happen for a promising young person. He won't go out for pizza anymore either, or come into a warm house on a cold night, or imitate Martin Short imitating Katharine Hepburn, or scuff through piles of leaves.

38 And I won't ever see him again.

39 *Joe had been very involved in high-school journalism. He won a statewide award for feature writing in New Hampshire, and he was news editor of the school paper in Shorewood. He contributed a great deal of that paper's humor edition in May, including a large advertisement that read, in part:*

40   *"Attention! All available slightly twisted females: Marry Me! I am a nice guy, a National Merit semifinalist, devastatingly handsome, relatively inexpensive, housebroken, handy with tools, easily entertained, a gentleman in the truest sense of the word, and I think I am extremely funny. In fact, I think I am the funniest guy on earth! . . . Please call immediately. Operators are standing by. (I am in great demand.) . . . Kids—Please get permission from your parents before calling."*

41   Then they handed the shovel to his stepmother.

42   In his sermon at David's bar mitzvah last year, the rabbi used a phrase I'd never heard before. It caused me to weep at the time; I wasn't sure why. It's come back to me again and again recently. It isn't consoling, nor even helpful. But it is pretty, and in an odd way it puts events into a much larger perspective.

43   "All things pass into mystery."

44   *At one point during that last visit, we went to a craft fair where Joe noticed someone selling hammered dulcimers. He had never played one, but he'd played the guitar for quite a few years, which must have helped. He picked up the hammers and began to fool around, and soon he drew a small crowd with something that sounded like sitar music. He asked about the price; they were expensive. I keep finding myself thinking that it would be neat to get him one. I should have done it then.*

45   Then they handed the shovel to his only living grandmother; it took her two tries to get enough dirt on the shovel. Neither of his grandfathers could bring himself to do it. But many of Joe's friends, weeping, took a turn.

46   I hope someday to be able to write about Joe again; I probably won't be writing a humor column for a while. In the meantime, I want folks to know how I think he would have turned out. He would have been a *mensch*—a decent, sincere man, the kind you're proud to know. He already was. Damn drugs.

47   *A year or so ago, the four of us played charades, a vacation tradition. Joe drew "The Sun Also Rises," which he did in one clue. He stretched an imaginary horizon line between his hands then slowly brought his head above it at one end and traversed an arc, grinning from ear to ear. It took us about five seconds to get it. Body bag or no, that's how I want to remember him.*

48   The last thing I wrote about him appeared in the newspaper the morning he died. He told me that he and a friend decided one Saturday afternoon to hitchhike to a rock concert near Milwaukee. He realized, he said, that now that he was away from home, he didn't have to ask anybody if he could go or

tell anybody that he was going. He just decided to do it, and he did it. I wrote about what a heady experience that was, to be independent at last.

49   There's a fair measure of irony in that column. We're told that the rock concert is where he got the LSD, and where he took his first trip.

50   That trip, I understand, went OK. This one killed him.

51   Although Joe apparently was with friends most of the evening, the police said he was alone when he went out the window. We'll probably never know exactly what happened in those last minutes, but judging by our own reading of him and by what lots of others have told us, we're sure he wasn't despondent. Many of his friends, including one who spoke at his funeral, said that he was very happy and enjoying his life in Madison.

52   The likeliest explanation we've heard is that he had the LSD hallucination that makes a person think he can fly. In any case, a little after one o'clock Sunday morning, October 15, somebody studying across the courtyard saw a curtain open and then a body fall. Joe didn't cry out.

53   I have since, many times.

WHAT DID THE WRITER SAY AND WHAT DID YOU THINK?

1. How does the author help his audience to get to know and care about Joe?
2. What is Sicherman's thesis, and why does he wait so long to state it?
3. Is the author's telling of Joe's story an effective anti-drug warning?
4. The author concentrates mostly on Joe's life, rather than on his death. Why? Is it true that Joe's funeral left no room for denial?
5. This essay is from the author's regular, and usually humorous, column. With this in mind, is his opening appropriate?

HOW DID THE WRITER SAY IT?

1. The author addresses his readers directly in the first sentence. Where else would the readers of his column feel they were being communicated with directly?
2. What is the subject matter of the italicized portions of this essay? How are they organized?
3. Comment on the various possible interpretations that can be given to the last sentence.

=====================**WHAT ABOUT *YOUR* WRITING?**=====================

The normal body paragraph in an essay has a topic sentence and a varying number of additional sentences that develop or support the topic sentence. Specialized one-sentence transitional paragraphs are traditionally acceptable for their own special purpose—"Now that we have finished the mixing, we are ready to bake," for example.

"Be Scared for Your Kids" has a great many short one-sentence paragraphs, including the first and last ones—not transitional paragraphs by any stretch of the imagination. Notice the second paragraph, too. Notice "Then they handed the shovel to me (30)," "Then they handed the shovel to his mother (36)," and "Then they handed the shovel to his stepmother (41)." There are many other examples, as well. How is it that this exceptionally powerful piece of writing can break, or seem to break, so many basic rules?

One answer is that Al Sicherman writes for a newspaper, and newspaper paragraphs have to be kept short no matter what textbooks say. The words in a newspaper appear in thin columns, not on 8½- by 11-inch sheets of typing paper. A normal-sized paragraph in that thin column would present readers with an excessively long solid block of print with no convenient place for the eyes to rest. Physical reality has to take precedence over rules: Readers with eyestrain don't stay readers for long.

A second, more important reason for the one-sentence paragraphs is that they stand out, and the author wants them to stand out. Precisely because most paragraphs most of the time are much longer—and for good reason—readers will tend to pay special attention to unexpected, dramatic exceptions to the usual. Sicherman does not want the tragic impact of those shovels at the grave site to be lost in the middle of a paragraph. He wants them to stand out.

Like this.

Rules let us know what works for almost all writers almost all the time. Rules can save us painful years of effort, because without them we are forced to discover all the basic truths for ourselves. Rules are not meant to enslave us, however.

Don't let them enslave you.

OBJECTS

JULIUS LESTER

Julius Lester, who now teaches at the University of Massachusetts, was active in the Student Nonviolent Coordinating Committee (SNCC) during the civil rights campaigns of the mid-1960s. He gained national attention with his memorably titled first book, *Look Out, Whitey! Black Power's Gon' Get Your Mama!* (1968) and has since written extensively on black folktales. "Objects" comes from Lester's recent book *Falling Pieces of the Broken Sky* (1990).

Words to check:

minutiae (paragraph 1)   permeated (5)
samovar (3)

1   When my father died, one of the tasks that fell to me was to sort through the minutiae of his life and decide which objects to save and which to throw away. Now I look at the objects of my life as if I were dead, wondering, what will my children do with the human skull that sits on the bookcase next to my desk? I couldn't blame them if they threw it out. They've been wanting to do that for some years, but will they know how much can be learned from living with a skull? And what about my books? Surely they can find someplace in their apartments for ten thousand books. However, I know they will look at the white, plastic head of a horse on my desk and throw it into a Glad trash bag without a thought, never knowing that it is the only piece remaining from the first chess set I owned. It is me at age twelve.

2   But that is the order of things. The final decisions about who we were are left to those who knew us least—our children. I was the closest to my father and knew him well, and yet, only when I was going through his study did I learn he had collected picture postcards of hotels. Had he ever shown the huge scrapbook to anyone? And what was I to do with it now? What was I to do with all the objects that had been him? The grieving part of me wanted to put everything in my car and take it home. The rational prevailed, however, and I filled trash bag after trash bag with old newspapers, magazines, paper clips, pamphlets of all kinds, apologizing to his spirit as I did. I could not throw out the thousands of slides he had taken on his travels. He was not an artistic photographer; he was not a good one even, but he was a loving one. I brought the slides home, though I will

never look at them. And I brought home the postcards, too. I brought twelve boxes of my father home.

3   How many boxes of me will my children keep? Or will they look in the yellow pages under Trash Hauling and tell some unshaven man with a cigar in his jaw to take me to the landfill? Can I trust my children with my life? How would they know that the tiny replica of a samovar sitting on a windowsill of my study is a miniature of the one Tolstoy* used? Every object of our lives is a memory, and emotion swirls around it like fog, hiding and protecting a tiny truth of the heart.

4   I look at the objects that are my life and the only way my children can satisfy me is by not touching a thing. But they must if they are to go on with their lives. They must if I am to go on with my death.

5   I look at these objects that are me and know, too, that they are symbols of how alone I am, how alone each of us is, for no one knows what any object means except he or she who owns it. Only I have the memories of when and how each one was acquired; only I have the memory of taking it home like one of my newly born children from the hospital; only I have the memory of what it looked like when I lived in that apartment and where it sat in that house. I look at the objects that are me, and the memories are warm and permeated with love. I look at the objects that are me and know that I'm going to miss me very much.

WHAT DID THE WRITER SAY
AND WHAT DID YOU THINK? _____

1. What is Lester's thesis?
2. The author spends a great deal of time writing about death and dying. Is he depressing?
3. Why did Lester keep twelve boxes of his father's slides and postcards?
4. What specific items does the author value even though he knows that others find them useless?
5. Is the author wrong to define himself by what he owns rather than by what he is?
6. Does Lester really expect his children to find room for ten thousand books? How do you know?

* Leo Tolstoy (1828–1910), Russian writer and philosopher.

HOW DID THE WRITER SAY IT? _____

1. The author asks a great number of questions in a very short essay. What is the effect of this tactic?
2. What specific details does the author use to accent the joys of daily life?
3. How do you know that the author loved his father very much?

═══════════WHAT ABOUT *YOUR* WRITING?═══════

Effective repetition of words and phrases—sometimes exact repetition, sometimes repetition with a slight variation—is one of a writer's most direct means of driving home a point and achieving a touch of stylistic power. In paragraph 4, to emphasize the painful necessity of cleaning up and cleaning out after a death, Lester writes, "They must if they are to go on with their lives. They must if I am to go on with my death." Lester uses repetition for emotional emphasis again in paragraph 5 with "they are symbols of how alone I am, how alone each of us is."

Repetition can be abused, of course. If not handled well, it can become monotonous and irritating. Thus Lester would not start listing the specific names of all the individuals he actually knows who are "alone." Used properly, however, repetition has produced some of the most memorable phrases in the language:

Gentlemen may cry peace, peace—but there is no peace.

We have nothing to fear but fear itself.

It was the best of times, it was the worst of times.

Good bread, good meat, good God, let's eat!

THE BARRIO

ROBERT RAMIREZ

A former employee in the Latin American division of Chicago's Northern Trust Bank, Robert Ramirez has also been a news producer for KGBT-TV in Edinburg,

Texas. He has also worked as a news anchor, reporter, and cameraman. In "The Barrio," Ramirez gives lavish descriptive attention to this unique district.

Words to check:

paradoxical (paragraph 2)
eludes (2)
perpetuate (2)
leprous (4)
pariahs (4)
complacently (9)
familial (12)

pervades (12)
countenances (12)
mutely (14)
impenetrable (15)
fissures (17)
adverse (19)
elusive (19)

1   The train, its metal wheels squealing as they spin along the silvery tracks, rolls slower now. Through the gaps between the cars blinks a streetlamp, and this pulsing light on a barrio streetcorner beats slower, like a weary heartbeat, until the train shudders to a halt, the light goes out, and the barrio is deep asleep.

2   Throughout Aztlán (the Nahuatl term meaning "land to the north"), trains grumble along the edges of a sleeping people. From Lower California, through the blistering Southwest, down the Rio Grande to the muddy Gulf, the darkness and mystery of dreams engulf communities fenced off by railroads, canals, and expressways. Paradoxical communities, isolated from the rest of the town by concrete columned monuments of progress, and yet stranded in the past. They are surrounded by change. It eludes their reach, in their own backyards, and the people, unable and unwilling to see the future, or even touch the present, perpetuate the past.

3   Leaning from the expressway or jolting across the tracks, one enters a different physical world permeated by a different attitude. The physical dimensions are impressive. It is a large section of town which extends for fifteen blocks north and south along the tracks, and then advances eastward, thinning into nothingness beyond the city limits. Within the invisible (yet sensible) walls of the barrio, are many, many people living in too few houses. The homes, however, are much more numerous than on the outside.

4   Members of the barrio describe the entire area as their home. It is a home, but it is more than this. The barrio is a refuge from the harshness and the coldness of the Anglo world. It is a forced refuge. The leprous people are isolated from the rest of the community and contained in their section of town. The stoical pariahs of the barrio accept their fate, and from the angry seeds of rejection grow the flowers of closeness between outcasts, not the thorns

of bitterness and the mad desire to flee. There is no want to escape, for the feeling of the barrio is known only to its inhabitants, and the material needs of life can also be found here.

5   The *tortilleria* [tortilla factory] fires up its machinery three times a day, producing steaming, round, flat slices of barrio bread. In the winter, the warmth of the tortilla factory is a wool *sarape* [blanket] in the chilly morning hours, but in the summer, it unbearably toasts every noontime customer.

6   The *panaderia* [bakery] sends its sweet messenger aroma down the dimly lit street, announcing the arrival of fresh, hot sugary *pan dulce* [sweet rolls].

7   The small corner grocery serves the meal-to-meal needs of customers, and the owner, a part of the neighborhood, willingly gives credit to people unable to pay cash for foodstuffs.

8   The barbershop is a living room with hydraulic chairs, radio, and television, where old friends meet and speak of life as their salted hair falls aimlessly about them.

9   The pool hall is a junior level country club where *'chucos* [young men], strangers in their own land, get together to shoot pool and rap, while veterans, unaware of the cracking, popping balls on the green felt, complacently play dominoes beneath rudely hung *Playboy* foldouts.

10   The *cantina* [canteen or snackbar] is the night spot of the barrio. It is the country club and the den where the rites of puberty are enacted. Here the young become men. It is in the taverns that a young dude shows his *machismo* through the quantity of beer he can hold, the stories of *rucas* [women] he has had, and his willingness and ability to defend his image against hardened and scarred old lions.

11   No, there is no frantic wish to flee. It would be absurd to leave the familiar and nervously step into the strange and cold Anglo community when the needs of the Chicano can be met in the barrio.

12   The barrio is closeness. From the family living unit, familial relationships stretch out to immediate neighbors, down the block, around the corner, and to all parts of the barrio. The feeling of family, a rare and treasurable sentiment, pervades and accounts for the inability of the people to leave. The barrio is this attitude manifested on the countenances of the people, on the faces of their homes, and in the gaiety of their gardens.

13   The color-splashed homes arrest your eyes, arouse your curiosity, and make you wonder what life scenes are being played out in them. The flimsy, brightly colored, wood-frame houses ignore no neon-brilliant color. Houses trimmed in orange, chartreuse, lime-green, yellow, and mixtures of these and other hues beckon the beholder to reflect on the peculiarity of each home.

Passing through this land is refreshing like Brubeck,* not narcoticizing like revolting rows of similar houses, which neither offend nor please.

14   In the evenings, the porches and front yards are occupied with men calmly talking over the noise of children playing baseball in the unpaved extension of the living room, while the women cook supper or gossip with female neighbors as they water the *jardines* [gardens]. The gardens mutely echo the expressive verses of the colorful houses. The denseness of multicolored plants and trees gives the house the appearance of an oasis or a tropical island hideaway, sheltered from the rest of the world.

15   Fences are common in the barrio, but they are fences and not the walls of the Anglo community. On the western side of town, the high wooden fences between houses are thick, impenetrable walls, built to keep the neighbors at bay. In the barrio, the fences may be rusty, wire contraptions or thick green shrubs. In either case you can see through them and feel no sense of intrusion when you cross them.

16   Many lower-income families of the barrio manage to maintain a comfortable standard of living through the communal action of family members who contribute their wages to the head of the family. Economic need creates interdependence and closeness. Small barefooted boys sell papers on cool, dark Sunday mornings, deny themselves pleasantries, and give their earnings to *mamá*. The older the child, the greater the responsibility to help the head of the household provide for the rest of the family.

17   There are those, too, who for a number of reasons have not achieved a relative sense of financial security. Perhaps it results from too many children too soon, but it is the homes of these people and their situation that numbs rather than charms. Their houses, aged and bent, oozing children, are fissures in the horn of plenty. Their wooden homes may have brick-pattern asbestos tile on the outer walls, but the tile is not convincing.

18   Unable to pay city taxes or incapable of influencing the city to live up to its duty to serve all the citizens, the poorer barrio families remain trapped in the nineteenth century and survive as best they can. The backyards have well-worn paths to the outhouses, which sit near the alley. Running water is considered a luxury in some parts of the barrio. Decent drainage is usually unknown, and when it rains, the water stands for days, an incubator of health hazards and an avoidable nuisance. Streets, costly to pave, remain rough, rocky trails. Tires do not last long, and the constant rattling and shaking grind away a car's life and spread dust through screen windows.

---

* Jazz composer, conductor, and pianist, Dave Brubeck is known for his many innovations in contemporary music.

19   The houses and their *jardines,* the jollity of the people in an adverse
world, the brightly feathered alarm clock pecking away at supper and cautiously eyeing the children playing nearby, produce a mystifying sensation at
finding the noble savage alive in the twentieth century. It is easy to look at
the positive qualities of life in the barrio, and look at them with a distantly
envious feeling. One wishes to experience the feelings of the barrio and not
the hardships. Remembering the illness, the hunger, the feeling of time running out on you, the walls, both real and imagined, reflecting on living
in the past, one finds his envy becoming more elusive, until it has vanished
altogether.

20   Back now beyond the tracks, the train creaks and groans, the cars jostle
each other down the track, and as the light begins its pulsing, the barrio, with
all its meanings, greets a new dawn with yawns and restless stretchings.

WHAT DID THE WRITER SAY
AND WHAT DID YOU THINK? _____

1. What is Ramirez's thesis?
2. What are some of the words Ramirez uses to define a barrio?
3. Why do people wish to remain in the barrio rather than moving into a
   more modern setting?
4. Can you think of other cultural groups who stay within a limited
   environment so that they may cling to the past?
5. How can the barrio meet all the physical needs of its inhabitants?
6. What are some similarities between the barrio and mainstream
   neighborhoods?
7. How does Ramirez use fences as a point of contrast between the
   barrio and the Anglo community?
8. Although the barrio offers refuge, it is not always a pleasant
   environment. Why does Ramirez end his essay with the harsh
   realities of the barrio?

HOW DID THE WRITER SAY IT? _____

1. For what audience is Ramirez writing? How can you tell?
2. Ramirez uses numerous figures of speech, especially similes and
   metaphors. Identify one of each and explain why they are effective.
   (See What About *Your* Writing?, pp. 107–108.)

3. Ramirez uses words such as "home," "family," "shelter," and "closeness" to describe the barrio. What connotations do these words share? Do they make his description clearer?

4. The author also uses the words "fences" and "walls" several times throughout the essay. Why are these words significant to his overall description?

5. Reread Ramirez's first and last paragraphs. At what time of day does he begin the essay? At what time does he close the essay? How is this relationship between the first and last paragraphs significant? Are these two paragraphs essential to the description of the barrio?

=========================WHAT ABOUT *YOUR* WRITING?=========================

One of the fundamental ingredients of English style is *parallelism:* using the same (parallel) grammatical forms to express elements of approximately the same (parallel) importance. This definition may seem more formidable than it really is. Parallelism is so fundamental that we use it all the time.

Three parallel adjectives:
    The man was *tall, dark,* and *handsome.*

Four parallel nouns:
    We have to buy a *rug,* a *sofa,* two *chairs,* and a *lamp.*

Three parallel prepositional phrases:
    . . . *of the people, by the people, for the people.*

Three parallel independent clauses:
    I want you. I need you. I love you.

Two parallel imperatives:
    Sit down and *relax.*

Four parallel infinitives:
    "*To strive, to seek, to find,* and not *to yield.*"

The parallel grammatical forms point to and reinforce the parallels in thought and importance. Moreover, parallelism is what readers normally expect; it's the normal way that words are put together. Notice how a breakdown in expected parallelism adversely affects these sentences:

The man was tall, dark, and an athlete.

. . . of the people, by the people, and serving the people.

To strive, to seek, to find, and we must not yield.

In "The Barrio," Robert Ramirez uses parallelism effectively. For instance, in paragraph 12 he casts parallel prepositional phrases when he writes, ". . . familial relationships stretch out *to immediate neighbors, down the block, around the corner,* and *to all parts of the barrio,*" and again in, ". . . this *on the countenances of the people, on the faces of their homes,* and *in the gaiety of their gardens.*" Then in paragraph 16, he uses both parallel adjectives and verbs within the following: ". . . boys *sell* papers on *cool, dark* Sunday mornings, *deny* themselves pleasantries, and *give* their earnings . . . ." Had Ramirez written, ". . . boys *sell* papers on cool, dark Sunday mornings, *deny* themselves pleasantries, and *giving* their earnings . . ." the structure would break down.

Bear three points in mind for your own writing:

1. Parallelism isn't just a matter of sterile correctness. It can contribute to genuine stylistic distinction. Some of the most memorable phrases in the language draw much of their strength from parallelism:

   Friends, Romans, countrymen . . .

   I have nothing to offer but blood, sweat, toil, and tears.

   . . . life, liberty, and the pursuit of happiness.

   I came, I saw, I conquered.

   . . . with malice toward none, with charity for all.

2. Occasional modifying words do not break the basic parallelism and can sometimes help avoid the danger of monotony. These sentences still show parallelism:

   He was tall, dark, and astonishingly handsome.

   We have to buy a rug, a sofa, two chairs, and most of all a fancy new lamp.

3. Parallelism works only when each member of the parallel series is roughly equivalent in importance. It leads to absurdity in the following cases:

   My teacher has knowledge, enthusiasm, concern, and sinus trouble.

   We must protect society from murderers, perverts, kidnappers, and litterbugs.

HUSH, TIMMY—THIS IS LIKE A CHURCH

KURT ANDERSON

This *Time* magazine essay pays homage to the Vietnam Veterans Memorial. The thesis is clear and strong, but *Time* is a news magazine, after all, and its people are trained reporters. Notice how much of this descriptive essay depends on the fact-gathering skills of the writer.

Words to check:

roster (paragraph 1)	wary (6)
redemptive (3)	erstwhile (6)
apolitical (4)	liturgical (7)
elitist (5)	touchstone (7)
stigmatized (5)	catharsis (7)
sublime (6)	residual (7)
figurative (6)	pathologies (7)
mandarins (6)	amphitheatrical (7)
spectral (6)	totem (8)

1   The veteran and his wife had already stared hard at four particular names. Now the couple walked slowly down the incline in front of the wall, looking at rows of hundreds, thousands more, amazed at the roster of the dead. "All the names," she said quietly, sniffling in the early-spring chill. "It's unreal, how many names." He said nothing. "You have to see it to believe it," she said.

2   Just so. In person, close up, the Viet Nam Veterans Memorial—two skinny black granite triangles wedged onto a mound of Washington sod—is some kind of sanctum, beautiful and terrible. "We didn't plan that," says John Wheeler, chairman of the veterans' group that raised the money and built it. "I had a picture of seven-year-olds throwing a Frisbee around on the grass in front. But it's treated as a spiritual place." When Wheeler's colleague Jan Scruggs decided there ought to be a monument, he had only vague notions of what it might be like. "You don't set out and *build* a national shrine," Scruggs says. "It *becomes* one."

3   Washington is thick with monuments, several of them quite affecting. But as the Viet Nam War was singular and strange, the dark, dreamy, redemptive memorial to its American veterans is like no other. "It's more solemn," says National Park Service Ranger Sarah Page, who has also

worked at the memorials honoring Lincoln, Washington and Jefferson. "People give it more respect." Lately it has been the most visited monument in the capital: 2.3 million saw it in 1984, about 45,000 a week, but it is currently drawing 100,000 a week. Where does it get its power—to console, and also to make people sob?

4   The men who set up the Viet Nam Veterans Memorial Fund wanted something that would include the name of every American killed in Viet Nam, and would be contemplative and apolitical. They conducted an open design competition that drew 1,421 entries, all submitted anonymously. The winner, Maya Ying Lin, was a Chinese-American undergraduate at Yale: to memorialize men killed in a war in Asia, an Asian female studying at an old antiwar hotbed.

5   Opposition to Lin's design was intense. The opponents wanted something gleaming and grand. To them, the low-slung black wall would send the same old defeatist, elitist messages that had lost the war in the '60s and then stigmatized the veterans in the '70s. "Creating the memorial triggered a lot of old angers and rage among vets about the war," recalls Wheeler, a captain in Viet Nam and now a Yale-trained government lawyer. "It got white hot."

6   In the end, Lin's sublime and stirring wall was built, 58,022 names inscribed. As a compromise with opponents, however, a more conventional figurative sculpture was added to the site last fall (at a cost of $400,000). It does not spoil the memorial, as the art mandarins had warned. The three U.S. soldiers, cast in bronze, stand a bit larger than life, carry automatic weapons and wear fatigues, but the pose is not John Wayne-heroic: these American boys are spectral and wary, even slightly bewildered as they gaze southeast toward the wall. While he was planning the figures, sculptor Frederick Hart spent time watching vets at the memorial. Hart now grants that "no modernist monument of its kind has been as successful as that wall. The sculpture and the wall interact beautifully. Everybody won." Nor does Lin, his erstwhile artistic antagonist, still feel that Hart's statue is so awfully trite. "It captures the mood," says Lin. "Their faces have a lost look." Out at the memorial last week, one veteran looked at the new addition and nodded: "That's us."

7   But it is the wall that vets approach as if it were a force field. It is at the wall that families of the dead cry and leave flowers and mementos and messages, much as Jews leave notes for God in the cracks of Jerusalem's Western Wall. Around the statue, people talk louder and breathe easier, snap vacation photos unselfconsciously, eat Eskimo Pies and Fritos. But near the wall, a young Boston father tells his rambunctious son, "Hush, Timmy—this is like a

church." The visitors' processionals do seem to have a ritual, even liturgical quality. Going slowly down toward the vertex, looking at the names, they chat less and less, then fall silent where the names of the first men killed (July 1959) and the last (May 1975) appear. The talk begins again, softly, as they follow the path up out of the little valley of the shadow of death.

8   For veterans, the memorial was a touchstone from the beginning, and the 1982 dedication ceremony a delayed national embrace. "The actual act of being at the memorial is healing for the guy or woman who went to Viet Nam," says Wheeler, who visits at least monthly. "It has to do with the felt presence of comrades." He pauses. "I always look at Tommy Hayes' name. Tommy's up on panel 50 east, line 29." Hayes, Wheeler's West Point pal, was killed 17 years ago this month. "I know guys," Wheeler says, "who are still waiting to go, whose wives have told me, 'He hasn't been able to do it yet.'" For those who go, catharsis is common. As Lin says of the names, chronologically ordered, "Veterans can look at the wall, find a name, and in a sense put themselves back in that time." The war has left some residual pathologies that the memorial cannot leach away. One veteran killed himself on the amphitheatrical green near the wall. A second, ex-Marine Randolph Taylor, tried and failed in January. "I regret what I did," he said. "I feel like I desecrated a holy place."

9   The memorial has become a totem, so much so that its tiniest imperfections make news. Last fall somebody noticed a few minute cracks at the seams between several of the granite panels. The cause of the hairlines is still unknown, and the builders are a little worried.

10   Probably no one is more determined than Wheeler to see the memorial's face made perfect, for he savors the startlingly faithful reflections the walls give off: he loves seeing the crowds of visitors looking simultaneously at the names and themselves. "Look!" he said the other day, gesturing at panel 4 east. "You see that plane taking off? You see the blue sky? No one expected that."

WHAT DID THE WRITER SAY AND WHAT DID YOU THINK?

1. What is Anderson's thesis? Does he have one?
2. Does the author find the choice of Maya Ying Lin as the memorial's designer ironic? How do you know?
3. Why does Anderson feel that the Vietnam memorial is so special?
4. Why does the author include stories of suicide and attempted suicide at the memorial?

HOW DID THE WRITER SAY IT? _____

1. What effect does the author's frequent use of quotations have?
2. Is the title appropriate? Why or why not?
3. The author pays a good deal of attention to numbers and statistics. Does this help support his thesis, or is it a detraction?
4. Andersen writes of "the little valley of the shadow of death." To what work is this an allusion? Why is it fitting?
5. What specific details are used to emphasize the difference between the Vietnam memorial and other memorials?

=================**WHAT ABOUT *YOUR* WRITING?**=================

"'We didn't plan that,' says John Wheeler, chairman of the veteran's group that raised the money and built it."

"'It's more solemn,' says National Park Service Ranger Sarah Page, who has also worked at the memorials honoring Lincoln, Washington, and Jefferson. 'People give it more respect.'"

One way of backing up a thesis is by *citation of authority.* A writer reinforces a point by quoting or referring to sources whose view the reader must take seriously. A writer on religion quotes the Bible. A writer on psychoanalysis quotes Freud. A writer on art quotes Picasso. A writer on the Vietnam Memorial quotes the head of the group that built it and a guard who studies visitors every day and has studied visitors at other memorials. "The people who should know agree with me," says the writer, no longer an isolated voice, but a voice with authority. In addition, the writer conveys the valuable impression of having done a certain amount of serious research before arriving at an opinion.

The citation of authority must be combined with taste and judgment. An authority in one special field, removed from that field, is no longer an authority. Freud's endorsement of an aftershave lotion would be of limited worth. A former star quarterback's comments about a football coach merit attention, but his feelings about instant tea or shampoos are another matter. Comments of authorities must also be kept in context. Quoting a Supreme Court decision that the Supreme Court itself reversed ten years later is flatly irresponsible. Finally, assuming that even within the proper field and context the authority must always be right is another danger. Most people agree that Thomas Jefferson was a great president, but his decision to make the

Louisiana Purchase without consulting Congress was not necessarily correct. Citations of authority can strengthen a point; they can't prove it.

With all these necessary warnings, your own writing can profit from an occasional citation of authority. In Emerson's words, "Next to the originator of a good sentence is the first quoter of it."

4

EXAMPLES

An example is a single item drawn from a larger group to which it belongs. An example is also often viewed as one of a number of specific cases in which a generalization turns out to be true. Smog is one of many possible examples of pollution. Chicken pox is an example of a childhood disease. The egg yolk on Bill's necktie is an example of his sloppy eating habits. The bald eagle is an example that backs up the generalization that endangered species can sometimes be preserved. The French Reign of Terror is an example that supports the idea that violent revolutions often bring about further violence. (The preceding five sentences are examples of examples.)

It's hard to write a good paper of any kind without using at least some examples. Examples *clarify* a writer's thought by bringing remote abstractions down to earth.

> The American Civil War was not all the romantic valor we read about in storybooks. It was the horrors of trench warfare, the medical nightmare of wholesale amputations, and for the South, at least, the agony of slow starvation.

Examples also *add interest:* the most humdrum generalization can take on new life if supported by effective examples. Specific details described in specific language are at the heart of almost all good writing, and examples by their very nature are specific.

Professor Smathers' course in Shakespeare was the worst I have ever taken. Once we spent a whole week listening to students recite—or mumble—sonnets they had been forced to memorize. Another time Professor Smathers devoted an entire period to attacking one of the footnotes in our edition of *Hamlet*. And I never understood the true meaning of boredom until the great day that I heard him discourse on Shakespeare's preference for daisies over roses.

Examples help *persuade*. Without the help of examples, many perfectly valid statements can be perceived as dismal echoes of ideas the author has heard somewhere but has never thought about seriously. If the writer of the following paragraph had omitted the examples, there would be no way to evaluate the merits of the complaint.

Routine city services are in a terrible state. The freeway from West 50th Street to the Downtown exit has been filled with gaping chuckholes since early spring. Rat-infested, condemned, and abandoned buildings still line Water Street despite three-year-old promises to tear them down. Last week the papers reported the story of a man who called the police about a burglar entering his home—and got a busy signal.

An example essay is one that relies entirely on examples to support its thesis. The ordinary pattern for an example essay is elementary, though bear in mind that no pattern should be followed blindly. A first paragraph presents the thesis. A varying number of paragraphs—depending on the subject, complexity of thesis, and material available to the writer—then establishes through examples the validity of the thesis. A concluding paragraph reinforces or advances the thesis. The pattern seems simple, and it is.

What isn't quite so simple is seeing to it that all the examples are relevant and persuasive.

Are There Enough Examples to Support Your Thesis?   Three examples may sometimes be enough. A hundred may often be too few (and in that case you've made a poor choice of thesis for an example essay). Common sense is your best guide. Three in-depth examples of overly sentimental deathbed scenes from Dickens's novels may be enough to establish that Dickens had trouble with deathbed scenes. A hundred examples of middle-aged men with protruding stomachs will not even begin to establish that most middle-aged men have potbellies. As a general rule for a paper of five hundred words or so, choose a thesis that can be supported adequately with no more than fifteen examples, unless your instructor tells you otherwise. Don't use fewer than three examples unless you're extremely confident about the virtues of your paper. Remember, too, that the fewer the examples, the more fully each needs to be developed.

Are the Examples Fairly Chosen?   Your reader must be convinced that the examples represent a reasonable cross-section of the group you're dealing with. Choose typical examples. Anyone can load the dice. You may have an imposing number of dramatic examples showing that the downtown business area of a city is deserted and dying, but if you drew all the examples from only one street or from visiting the area on a Sunday afternoon, you would not have played fair. Plan your paper with the notion of a cross-section constantly in mind. If you're generalizing about teachers in your school, try to pick examples from different departments, age groups, sexes, and so on. If you're attacking television commercials, make sure your examples include significantly different products; otherwise, you might wind up convincing your reader that only ads for soaps and detergents are bad.

Have You Stuck to Your Thesis?   One way of losing sight of your thesis has just been described. Poorly selected examples, besides creating an impression of unfairness, may support only part of the thesis; one writer demonstrates that only a single block is deserted and dying, not the whole downtown area; another shows that commercials about washday products are offensive, not commercials in general.

A second, but equally common, way of drifting off is to forget about writing an example paper. A writer starts out well by providing examples establishing the idea that "routine city services are in a terrible state." Halfway through the paper, the writer gets sidetracked into a discussion of the causes for this condition and the steps the average citizen can take to remedy it. The writer thus manages to produce a paper that is 50 percent irrelevant to the declared thesis.

Have You Arranged Your Examples to Produce the Greatest Impact?
In planning your paper, you've limited your subject, developed a thesis, and jotted down lots of examples. You've eliminated irrelevant and illogical examples. Now how do you handle those that are left? Which comes first? Which comes last?

Unless you're superhuman, some of the examples you're going to use will be clearly superior to others. As a general principle, try to start off with a bang. Grab the attention of your reader as soon as possible with your most dramatic or shocking or amusing or disturbing example. If you have two unusually effective examples, so much the better. Save one for last: Try to end with a bang, too.

A large number of exceptionally strong examples can also lead to a common variation on the orthodox pattern of devoting the first paragraph to a presentation of the thesis. Use the first paragraph instead to present one of the strongest examples. (Humorous anecdotes often work particularly well.) Stimulate curiosity. Arouse interest. Then present the thesis in the second paragraph before going on to the other examples.

Paragraphing itself is important throughout the essay to help the reader understand the nature of your material and the logic of your argument. With a few well-developed examples, there's no problem. Each should get a paragraph to itself. With a great number of examples, however, there's some potential for difficulties. Each example will probably be short—one or two sentences, let's say—because you're writing an essay of only a few hundred words, not a term paper. If each of these short examples gets a separate paragraph, the paper is likely to be extremely awkward and choppy to read. But even without that burden, the physical appearance alone of the page can bother most readers: before getting to the actual reading, they will have thought of the paper as a collection of separate sentences and thoughts rather than as a unified composition.

The solution to this paragraphing problem is to gather the many examples together into a few logical groups and write a paragraph for each group, not for each example. Suppose you have fifteen good examples of declining city services. Instead of writing fifteen one-sentence paragraphs, you observe that four examples involve transportation; five, safety; three, housing; and the rest, pollution and sanitation. Your paragraphing problems are over.

¶ 1   Thesis: *Routine city services are in a terrible state.*

¶ 2   *Transportation*
    Example 1—higher fares for same or worse service
    Example 2—no parking facilities
    Example 3—poor snow removal
    Example 4—refusal to synchronize traffic lights downtown

¶ 3   *Safety*
    Example 1—unrepaired chuckholes
    Example 2—unrepaired traffic lights
    Example 3—busy signals at police station
    Example 4—slow response when police do come

Example 5—releasing of dangerous criminals because of overcrowding at city jail

¶ 4 *Housing*

Example 1—decaying public projects

Example 2—abandoned buildings not torn down

Example 3—housing codes not enforced in some neighborhoods

¶ 5 *Pollution and Sanitation*

Example 1—flooded basements

Example 2—litter in public parks

Example 3—increase in rats

¶ 6 *Conclusion*

WRITING SUGGESTIONS FOR EXAMPLE ESSAYS

Write an example essay supporting one of the following statements or a related statement of your own.

1. Life in _____ [your town] is not as bad as it's cracked up to be.
2. Some teachers try too hard to identify with their students.
3. Junk food has many virtues.
4. Corruption is part of the American way of life.
5. Teenage marriages are likely to end unhappily.
6. People express their personalities through the clothes they wear.
7. The generation gap is a myth.
8. Children's television programs display too much violence.
9. A student's life is not a happy one.
10. Nuns and/or priests are complex human beings, not plaster saints.
11. You can tell a lot about people from their table manners.
12. Student government is a farce.
13. Apparent nonconformists are sometimes the worst conformists.
14. Everyone loves to gossip.
15. Many people never learn from their mistakes.
16. The effort to succeed is more satisfying than success itself.
17. Even at their best, most people are basically selfish.
18. Weddings are a bore.
19. Taking care of a pet can be a great educational experience for children.
20. Newspapers rarely bother to report good news.

Easy Cruelty

David Grey (student)

Thesis: Emotional pain is easier to cause and is far more damaging than physical pain.

    I.   Prejudice
        A. Racist and sexist jokes
        B. Cruel and discriminatory attitudes

    II. Children's cruelty
        A. Exclusion
        B. Long-lasting effects

    III. Adult cruelty
        A. Trampling on love and joy
        B. Making others feel worthless

Conclusion: Although cruelty is easier than kindness, we must learn to work to be kind.

It's easy to hurt people physically. Hit them. Throw something. Kick. Punch. Make them bleed or bruise or burn. Easy though all that is, it's even easier and more damaging to hurt people mentally, to reach inside to their emotions and their minds and cause a wound that can't be fixed by any iodine, band-aid, or sling.

The easiest type of this easy cruelty is prejudice. Jokes about dumb blondes, idiotic Poles, beer-swilling Irishmen, and lazy, incompetent Blacks and Mexicans are very easy to tell. Sometimes they are even funny. The after-effects of these jokes, however, are not funny at all. Sexist, racist, and ethnic jokes strip their subjects and their tellers of their dignity and their pride. The jokes and bigotry also grow from seemingly harmless punchlines into widespread attitudes. The assumption is that all these jokes must be based on fact. All those funny stories about the stupidity of almost any ethnic group have to be true, right? Then, it becomes frighteningly easy to make cruel personal comments, to begin treating others as less than human. Prejudice is simple, but it is also simply evil.

Children, not quite the sweet innocents we may like to think, are experts at this sort of subtle mental torture. They unthinkingly choose the same kids last for every sports team, forget to send unpopular kids party invitations, and exclude others from their cliques without even knowing why. The hideous thing about this type of cruelty is that the effects seem to last forever. I know some adults who are still shy about introducing themselves because their name was judged stupid in grade school, and I know others who are still hurt by their exclusion from the popular crowd in fourth grade.

We adults, neither sadistic bigots nor unthinking children, are just as ruthless with our cruelty. We trample on love and joy without a second's thought saying, "You can't really be serious about her, can you?" and, "You do realize, he's probably her last chance for a husband." We convince people to feel useless and to stop trying by calling them incompetent, stupid, and worthless. We open our mouths and ruin a life without even trying, without even noticing.

Cruelty is so simple. Just stop thinking about what you say, stop worrying about what you do, and stop caring about other people. Each one of us is so fragile that it takes almost nothing to wound us forever. We mustn't let cruelty happen because it is so easy. Work to be kind.

IT'S HOW YOU ASK IT

SIDNEY J. HARRIS

Best known for his syndicated newspaper column "Strictly Personal," Sidney J. Harris has also written the book *Pieces of Eight,* from which "It's How You Ask It" is excerpted. Note how Harris's examples perform all three vital functions of good examples: to clarify, to add interest, and to persuade.

Words to check:

elicit (paragraph 1)	sedate (9)
subdued (7)	rakish (9)
ostentatious (8)	gaudy (9)
shrewder (8)	

1   What a lot of people fail to learn, even as they grow older, is that the way you ask a question can determine the kind of answer you get. The professional pollsters are keenly aware of this and can elicit seemingly contradictory answers by asking the same question in somewhat different ways.

2   As an example, I recall the story of the two priests arguing about whether it was proper to smoke and pray at the same time. One said it was, and the other said it wasn't. To settle the matter, they agreed that both should write to the Pope for his opinion.

3   A few weeks later they met and compared notes. Each claimed that the Pope had supported his view and suspected the other of falsifying the reply he got from the Holy Office.

4   Finally, one asked, "How did you phrase your question?" The other replied, "I asked whether it was proper to smoke while one is praying, and the Pope answered, 'Certainly not, praying is a serious business and permits of no distractions.' And how did you phrase your question?"

5   "Well," said the other, "I asked if it was proper to pray while smoking, and the Pope said, 'Certainly, prayer is always in order.'"

6   Some years ago, two large auto companies made expensive public surveys at much the same time to try to find out what kind of car the American motorist might buy in the future.

7   One company's pollster asked the direct question, "What kind of car would you like to have?" The majority of auto owners replied that they wanted a car that was compact, economical, functional, and subdued in looks.

8   The other company's pollster was far shrewder and more sensitive to the self-deception most of us unconsciously practice. He asked: "What kind of car do you think your neighbor would like to have?" And there the majority replied that their neighbors coveted large, ostentatious, gimmicky models that looked more like boats or airplanes.

9   The first auto maker nearly went broke putting out sedate little cars long before the public was ready for them, while the second enjoyed a banner year with its rakish, gaudy, rear-finned models. In fact, the first company was forced to retool to meet the competition.

10   It is far harder to devise fair and "unweighted" questions than it is to find the answers. Indeed, the most significant advances in science have come not from finding answers, but from beginning to ask the right questions in the right way. Like that simplest one of all, which no one asked until Newton, "Why do apples fall down instead of up?"

WHAT DID THE WRITER SAY AND WHAT DID YOU THINK?

1. What is the thesis? Is it stated directly?
2. Why are professional pollsters so interested in the art of questioning? Does Harris indicate that they sometimes have a better understanding of our tendencies toward self-deception than we do? Use an example to support your answer.
3. What is more important to the advancement of science, the right answer or the right question? Explain your answer.

HOW DID THE WRITER SAY IT?

1. What makes up the body of Harris's essay?
2. Where does Harris state his thesis?
3. Are the two examples that Harris uses sufficient to support his thesis? Why or why not?
4. Why do you suppose the author brings "science" into the conclusion of the essay?

WHAT ABOUT *YOUR* WRITING?

"It's How You Ask It" is a good example of why-didn't-I-think-of-saying-that writing. Who doesn't know the importance of phrasing questions? Who doesn't know there's a difference between asking, "Why don't you do some work for a change?" and "Are you interested in getting better grades?" Who doesn't understand the difference between "Do you support the church?" and "Will you double the amount of your financial pledge?" Many readers probably see in the Harris article a main idea that has occurred to them and that they believe is true, read insights they themselves have probably had, and mutter, "Why didn't I think of saying that?" Maybe they didn't think of it because they were too busy lamenting that they didn't have anything to write about. More likely, they had drifted into the habit of not taking their own ideas seriously.

In "Self-Reliance" Ralph Waldo Emerson presents this moral more memorably when he complains of the person who "dismisses without notice his thought, because it is his. In every work of genius we recognize our own rejected thoughts: they come back to us with a certain alienated majesty." You don't have to believe that Harris's article is a work of genius to agree with Emerson's conclusion: We "should learn to detect and watch that gleam of light which flashes across the mind. . . . Else, tomorrow a stranger will say with masterly good sense precisely what we have thought and felt all the time, and we shall be forced to take with shame our own opinion from another."

WHAT IS INTELLIGENCE, ANYWAY?

ISAAC ASIMOV

Isaac Asimov (1920–1992), author of over 450 books, was one of the best-known and most widely read writers in history. Although his reputation will probably be secured by his trailblazing work in science fiction, he also wrote histories, mysteries, a guide to the Bible, textbooks, humorous works, and nonfiction volumes on scientific subjects.

Words to check:

vitals (paragraph 3)	foist (4)
oracles (3)	arbiter (4)
academician (4)	raucously (6)

1   What is intelligence, anyway? When I was in the Army, I received a kind of aptitude test that all soldiers took and, against a normal of 100, scored 160. No one at the base had ever seen a figure like that, and for two hours they made a big fuss over me. (It didn't mean anything. The next day I was still a buck private with KP as my highest duty.)

2   All my life I've been registering scores like that, so that I have the complacent feeling that I'm highly intelligent, and I expect other people to think so, too. Actually, though, don't such scores simply mean that I am very good at answering the type of academic questions that are considered worthy of answers by the people who make up the intelligence tests—people with intellectual bents similar to mine?

3   For instance, I had an auto repairman once, who, on these intelligence tests, could not possibly have scored more than 80, by my estimate. I always took it for granted that I was far more intelligent than he was. Yet, when

anything went wrong with my car, I hastened to him with it, watched him anxiously as he explored its vitals, and listened to his pronouncements as though they were divine oracles—and he always fixed my car.

4   Well then, suppose my auto repairman devised questions for an intelligence test. Or suppose a carpenter did, or a farmer, or, indeed, almost anyone but an academician. By every one of those tests, I'd prove myself a moron. And I'd *be* a moron, too. In a world where I could not use my academic training and my verbal talents but had to do something intricate or hard, working with my hands, I would do poorly. My intelligence, then, is not absolute but is a function of the society I live in and of the fact that a small subsection of that society has managed to foist itself on the rest as an arbiter of such matters.

5   Consider my auto repairman, again. He had a habit of telling me jokes whenever he saw me. One time he raised his head from under the automobile hood to say, "Doc, a deaf-and-dumb guy went into a hardware store to ask for some nails. He put two fingers together on the counter and made hammering motions with the other hand. The clerk brought him a hammer. He shook his head and pointed to the two fingers he was hammering. The clerk brought him nails. He picked out the sizes he wanted, and left. Well, doc, the next guy who came in was a blind man. He wanted scissors. How do you suppose he asked for them?"

6   Indulgently, I lifted my right hand and made scissoring motions with my first two fingers. Whereupon my auto repairman laughed raucously and said, "Why, you dumb jerk, he used his *voice* and asked for them." Then he said, smugly, "I've been trying that on all my customers today." "Did you catch many?" I asked. "Quite a few," he said, "but I knew for sure I'd catch *you.*" "Why is that?" I asked. "Because you're so goddamned educated, doc, I *knew* you couldn't be very smart."

7   And I have an uneasy feeling he had something there.

WHAT DID THE WRITER SAY AND WHAT DID YOU THINK? _____

1. Is this essay primarily a funny anecdote, or does it have a serious point to make? What is the point, if any?
2. How does the author feel about intelligence tests?
3. What distinction does the mechanic make between "educated" and "smart"?
4. In what ways is Asimov's intelligence "tested" in this essay?

HOW DID THE WRITER SAY IT? ———————————————

1. What would be the effect, if any, of removing the first sentence of this essay?
2. How and where does Asimov's exceptional intelligence show in this essay?
3. Where does the author's word choice reveal his own interest in and knowledge of science?

═══════════════**WHAT ABOUT *YOUR* WRITING?**═══════════

Some students think that developing a thesis makes demands on intellectual powers they do not possess. Isaac Asimov's "What Is Intelligence, Anyway?" demonstrates that if you have adequately interesting material, you can view your thesis primarily as an organizational device for tying things together, not as a blazing new insight or a bold stand on an issue of current controversy. Asimov's thesis, after all, comes to little more than "Intelligence has different meanings for different people," or "People's intelligence depends on what activity they are performing." Don't ignore great controversial ideas when they happen to pop up, but first-rate essays have been built around theses no more profound than "There are two sharply conflicting ways of approaching such and such a subject," "Thomas Hardy's reputation as a poet is still being debated," "Solving the problems of pollution is more complicated than it looks," and so on.

DARKNESS AT NOON

HAROLD KRENTS

Harold Krents was active for many years in working for fair employment practices for handicapped people. A graduate of Harvard College and Harvard Law School, he worked as a lawyer from 1971 until his death in 1986. Harold Krents was the model for the blind protagonist in the play and movie *Butterflies Are Free*.

Words to check:

narcissistic (paragraph 1)	graphically (5)
enunciating (2)	intoned (12)
conversely (2)	cum laude (15)
retina (3)	mandate (17)

1   Blind from birth, I have never had the opportunity to see myself and have been completely dependent on the image I create in the eye of the observer. To date it has not been narcissistic.

2   There are those who assume that since I can't see, I obviously also cannot hear. Very often people will converse with me at the top of their lungs, enunciating each word very carefully. Conversely, people will also often whisper, assuming that since my eyes don't work, my ears don't either.

3   For example, when I go to the airport and ask the ticket agent for assistance to the plane, he or she will invariably pick up the phone, call a ground hostess and whisper: "Hi, Jane, we've got a 76 here." I have concluded that the word "blind" is not used for one of two reasons: Either they fear that if the dread word is spoken, the ticket agent's retina will immediately detach, or they are reluctant to inform me of my condition of which I may not have been previously aware.

4   On the other hand, others know that of course I can hear, but believe that I can't talk. Often, therefore, when my wife and I go out to dinner, a waiter or waitress will ask Kit if "*he* would like to drink" to which I respond that "indeed *he* would."

5   This point was graphically driven home to me while we were in England. I had been given a year's leave of absence from my Washington law firm to study for a diploma in law degree at Oxford University. During the year I became ill and was hospitalized. Immediately after admission, I was wheeled down to the X-ray room. Just at the door sat an elderly woman—elderly I would judge from the sound of her voice. "What is his name?" the woman asked the orderly who had been wheeling me.

6   "What's your name?" the orderly repeated to me.

7   "Harold Krents," I replied.

8   "Harold Krents," he repeated.

9   "When was he born?"

10 "When were you born?"

11 "November 5, 1944," I responded.

12 "November 5, 1944," the orderly intoned.

13 This procedure continued for approximately five minutes at which point even my saint-like disposition deserted me. "Look," I finally blurted out, "this is absolutely ridiculous. Okay, granted I can't see, but it's got to have become pretty clear to both of you that I don't need an interpreter."

14 "He says he doesn't need an interpreter," the orderly reported to the woman.

15 The toughest misconception of all is the view that because I can't see, I can't work. I was turned down by over forty law firms because of my

blindness, even though my qualifications included a cum laude degree from Harvard College and a good ranking in my Harvard Law School class.

16   The attempt to find employment, the continuous frustration of being told that it was impossible for a blind person to practice law, the rejection letters, not based on my lack of ability but rather on my disability, will always remain one of the most disillusioning experiences of my life.

17   Fortunately, this view of limitation and exclusion is beginning to change. On April 16, [1978] the Department of Labor issued regulations that mandate equal-employment opportunities for the handicapped. By and large, the business community's response to offering employment to the disabled has been enthusiastic.

18   I therefore look forward to the day, with the expectation that it is certain to come, when employers will view their handicapped workers as a little child did me years ago when my family still lived in Scarsdale.

19   I was playing basketball with my father in our backyard according to procedures we had developed. My father would stand beneath the hoop, shout, and I would shoot over his head at the basket attached to our garage. Our next-door neighbor, aged five, wandered over into our yard with a playmate. "He's blind," our neighbor whispered to her friend in a voice that could be heard distinctly by Dad and me. Dad shot and missed; I did the same. Dad hit the rim: I missed entirely: Dad shot and missed the garage entirely. "Which one is blind?" whispered back the little friend.

20   I would hope that in the near future when a plant manager is touring the factory with the foreman and comes upon a handicapped and nonhandicapped person working together, his comment after watching them work will be, "Which one is disabled?"

WHAT DID THE WRITER SAY AND WHAT DID YOU THINK? _____

1. What is the thesis? Is it ever stated directly?
2. Into what categories does the author divide the sighted people he meets?
3. What is a "76"?
4. Why does Krents feel that discrimination against the handicapped in the workplace will change?
5. What is important about the way the neighbor's friend reacts to Krents and his father?
6. Do you think that the author is overly sensitive?

HOW DID THE WRITER SAY IT? ⎯⎯⎯⎯⎯⎯⎯⎯⎯⎯⎯⎯⎯⎯⎯

1. Most of the essay is written in a very casual tone. One section, however, is much more formal. Where is it, and why is it so different?
2. Why is the tone of cheerfulness and good humor so important to the success of this essay?
3. How does Krents relate his basketball experience to his main point?

══════════WHAT ABOUT *YOUR* WRITING?══════════

"Look . . . this is absolutely ridiculous. Okay, granted I can't see, but it's got to have become pretty clear to both of you that I don't need an interpreter."

"He says he doesn't need an interpreter," the orderly reported to the woman.

Good dialogue, a few lines or a lengthy conversation, can add life to almost any writing, nonfiction as well as fiction. The sense of immediacy can be remarkable. These are the words the people spoke, and readers are on their own. The author may mention a tone of voice or a gesture or may drop in an occasional *he said* or *she said* so that readers can keep track of the speaker, but essentially the author butts out. Good dialogue is direct, dramatic, persuasive. Apart from anything else, it gives the reader a pleasurable sense of recognition: "This is the way people talk," the reader says. "This is authentic."

Among the less obvious uses of dialogue could be its occasional use in original and lively introductions.

"Did you have a good time on your date, dear?"
"Aw, Mom."
"Was she a nice girl?"
"Aw, Mom."
"What does her father do?"
"Aw, Mom."
The generation gap—in my house, at least—is more than a myth.

"So what should we do about protecting the environment?" my teacher asks. If I had the nerve, I'd like to answer, "First of all, let's stop talking about it every single minute. Enough is enough."

Many creative writing teachers are inclined to feel that writing good dialogue is a gift. You have it or you don't. You were born with an ear for dialogue or you weren't. Still, some elementary pointers might be helpful.

Keep Your Comments Simple. Confine yourself to *he said, she said, he asked, she answered,* and similar phrases. Avoid fancy variations like *he asserted, he expostulated, she queried, she gasped, he hissed.*

Don't Worry about Standard English. If the person who's talking would swear, say *ain't,* confuse *who* and *whom,* make the person talk that way. Don't, whatever you do, use swear words to show off how tough and courageous and unflinchingly honest you are. Just be accurate.

Change Paragraphs with Each Speaker. You'll find violations of this advice among some of the best writers, but it seems ordinary common sense. Changing paragraphs makes the dialogue easier to follow by giving the reader a direct visual indication that there's been a change of speaker.

CLUTTER

WILLIAM ZINSSER

William Zinsser is a well-known writer, editor, and critic. His work has appeared in such newspapers and magazines as the *New York Herald Tribune, New York Times, Life,* and *The New Yorker.* Zinsser is the author of a wide range of books, including several editions of the delightful *On Writing Well.* "Clutter" is Chapter 3 of that book.

Words to check:

debasing (paragraph 3)	layman (11)
pompous (5)	pretentious (11)
euphemism (6)	jargon (11)
ponderous (6)	insidious (13)
vaporous (9)	festooned (16)
arsenal (11)	

1   Fighting clutter is like fighting weeds—the writer is always slightly behind. New varieties sprout overnight, and by noon they are part of American speech. Consider what Nixon's aide John Dean accomplished in just one day of testimony on TV during the Watergate hearings. The next day everyone in America was saying "at this point in time" instead of "now."

2   Consider all the prepositions that are draped onto verbs that don't need any help. We no longer head committees. We head them up. We don't face

problems anymore. We face up to them when we can free up a few minutes. A small detail, you may say—not worth bothering about. It *is* worth bothering about. The game is won or lost on hundreds of small details. Writing improves in direct ratio to the number of things we can keep out of it that shouldn't be there. "Up" in "free up" shouldn't be there. Can we picture anything being freed *up?* To write clean English you must examine every word you put on paper. You'll find a surprising number of words that don't serve any purpose.

3   Take the adjective "personal," as in "a personal friend of mine," "his personal feeling" or "her personal physician." It's typical of the words that can be eliminated nine times out of ten. The personal friend has come into the language to distinguish him from the business friend, thereby debasing both language and friendship. Someone's feeling *is* his personal feeling—that's what "his" means. As for the personal physician, he is that man summoned to the dressing room of a stricken actress so that she won't have to be treated by the impersonal physician assigned to the theater. Someday I'd like to see him identified as "her doctor." Physicians are physicians, friends are friends. The rest is clutter.

4   Clutter is the laborious phrase that has pushed out the short word that means the same thing. Even before John Dean, people had stopped saying "now." They were saying "at the present time," or "currently," or "presently" (which means "soon"). Yet the idea can always be expressed by "now" to mean the immediate moment ("Now I can see him"), or by "today" to mean the historical present ("Today prices are high"), or simply by a form of the verb "to be" ("It is raining"). There's no need to say, "At the present time we are experiencing precipitation."

5   Speaking of which, we are experiencing considerable difficulty getting *that* word out of the language. Even your dentist will ask if you are experiencing any pain. If he had one of his own children in the chair he would say, "Does it hurt?" He would, in short, be himself. By using a more pompous phrase in his professional role he not only sounds more important, he blunts the painful edge of truth. It's the language of the airline stewardess demonstrating the oxygen mask that will drop down if the plane should somehow run out of air. "In the unlikely possibility that the aircraft should experience such an eventuality," she begins—a phrase so oxygen-depriving in itself that we are prepared for any disaster, and even gasping death shall lose its sting. As for her request to "kindly extinguish all smoking materials," I often wonder what materials are smoking. It's a terrifying sentence.

6   Clutter is the ponderous euphemism that turns a slum into a depressed socioeconomic area, a salesman into a marketing representative, garbage

collectors into waste-disposal personnel and the town dump into the volume reduction unit. I think of Bill Mauldin's cartoon showing two hoboes riding a freight train. One of them says, "I started as a simple bum, but now I'm hard-core unemployed."

7   Clutter is the official language used by the American corporation—in its news releases and its annual report—to hide its mistakes. When one big company recently announced that it was "decentralizing its organizational structure into major profit-centered businesses" and that "corporate staff services will be realigned under two senior vice-presidents," it meant that it had had a lousy year.

8   Clutter is the language of the interoffice memo ("The trend to mosaic communication is reducing the meaningfulness of concern about whether or not demographic segments differ in their tolerance of periodicity") and the language of computers ("Congruent command paradigms explicitly represent the semantic oppositions in the definitions of the commands to which they refer").

9   Clutter is the language of the Pentagon throwing dust in the eyes of the populace by calling an invasion a "reinforced protective reaction strike" and by justifying its vast budgets on the need for "credible second-strike capability" and "counterforce deterrence." How can we grasp such vaporous double-talk? As George Orwell pointed out in "Politics and the English Language," an essay written in 1946 but cited frequently during the Vietnam and Cambodia years of Johnson and Nixon, "In our time, political speech and writing are largely the defense of the indefensible. . . . Thus political language has to consist largely of euphemism, question-begging and sheer cloudy vagueness." Orwell's warning that clutter is not just a nuisance but a deadly tool has come true in the recent decades of American military adventurism in Southeast Asia, Central America and other parts of the world.

10   Verbal camouflage reached new heights of invention during General Alexander Haig's tenure as secretary of state in the Reagan administration. Before Haig, nobody had ever thought of saying "at this juncture of maturization" to mean "now." He told the American people that he saw "improved pluralization" in El Salvador, that terrorism could be fought with "meaningful sanctionary teeth" and that intermediate nuclear missiles were "at the vortex of cruciality." As for any worries that the public might harbor about such matters, his message—reduced to one-syllable words—was "leave it to Al." What he actually said was, "We must push this to a lower decibel of public fixation. I don't think there's much of a learning curve to be achieved in this area of content."

11   I could go on quoting examples from various fields—every profession has its growing arsenal of jargon to fire at the layman and hurl him back from its walls. But the list would be depressing and the lesson tedious. The point of raising it now is to serve notice that clutter is the enemy, whatever form it takes. It slows the reader and makes the writer seem pretentious.

12   Beware, then, of the long word that is no better than the short word: "numerous" (many), "facilitate" (ease), "individual" (man or woman), "remainder" (rest), "initial" (first), "implement" (do), "sufficient" (enough), "attempt" (try), "referred to as" (called), and hundreds more. Beware, too, of all the slippery new fad words for which the language already has equivalents: overview and quantify, paradigm and parameter, optimize and maximize, prioritize and potentialize. They are all weeds that will smother what you write. Don't dialogue with someone you can talk to. Don't interface with anybody.

13   Nor are all the weeds so obvious. Just as insidious are the little growths of ordinary words with which we explain how we propose to go about our explaining, or which inflate a simple preposition or conjunction into a whole windy phrase.

14   "I might add," "It should be pointed out," "It is interesting to note that"— how many sentences begin with these dreary clauses announcing what the writer is going to do next? If you might add, add it. If it should be pointed out, point it out. If it is interesting to note, *make* it interesting. Being told that something is interesting is the surest way of tempting the reader to find it dull; are we not all stupefied by what follows when someone says, "This will interest you"? As for the inflated prepositions and conjunctions, they are the countless phrases like "with the possible exception of" (except), "due to the fact that" (because), "he totally lacked the ability to" (he couldn't), "until such time as" (until), "for the purpose of" (for).

15   Is there any way to recognize clutter at a glance? Here's a device that my students at Yale found helpful. I would put brackets around any component in a piece of writing that wasn't doing useful work. Often it was just one word that got bracketed: the unnecessary preposition that is appended to a verb ("order up"), or the adverb that carries the same meaning as the verb ("smile happily"), or the adjective that states a known fact ("tall skyscraper"). Often my brackets surrounded the little qualifiers that weaken any sentence they inhabit ("a bit," "sort of"), or the announcements like "I'm tempted to say," or the phrases like "in a sense" that don't mean anything at all. Sometimes my brackets surrounded an entire sentence—the one that essentially repeats what the previous sentence said, or that says something that readers don't need to know or can figure out for themselves. Most first

drafts can be cut by 50 percent—they're swollen with words and phrases that do no new work.

16   My reason for bracketing the extra words instead of crossing them out was to avoid violating the student's sacred prose. I wanted to leave the sentence intact for the student to analyze. I was saying, "I may be wrong, but I think this can be deleted and the meaning won't be affected at all. But *you* decide: read the sentence without the bracketed material and see if it works." In the early weeks of the term I gave back papers that were festooned with brackets. Entire paragraphs were bracketed. But soon the students learned to put mental brackets around their own clutter, and by the end of the term their papers were almost clean. Today many of those students are professional writers, and they tell me, "I still see your brackets—they're following me through life."

17   You can develop the same eye. Look for the clutter in your writing and prune it ruthlessly. Be grateful for everything you can throw away. Reexamine each sentence that you put on paper. Is every word doing new work? Can any thought be expressed with more economy? Is anything pompous or pretentious or faddish? Are you hanging on to something useless just because you think it's beautiful?

18   Simplify, simplify.

WHAT DID THE WRITER SAY AND WHAT DID YOU THINK? ─────────────

1. What is Zinsser's thesis?
2. Define *clutter* in your own words.
3. What does the author do to give variety to his examples?
4. Why does the author particularly dislike the word *experiencing?*
5. Why does the author hate all clutter so much?
6. What are Zinsser's complaints about airline language?

HOW DID THE WRITER SAY IT? ─────────────

1. Is there any clutter in the author's own writing?
2. What is the purpose of the last paragraph?
3. How does the frequent use of humor help to strengthen the impact of this essay?

WHAT ABOUT *YOUR* WRITING?

"Fighting clutter is like fighting weeds," Zinsser writes. The comparison works in a number of ways. It successfully communicates the ideas of being obnoxious, common, and hard to eliminate. For the general reader, it connects the relatively remote academic issue of writing style to the more immediate concerns of backyards and gardens. Moreover, the comparison to weeds is echoed throughout the essay, reinforcing the thought and adding color to the style: "New varieties sprout overnight" (paragraph 1), "They are all weeds that will smother what you write" (12), "little growths of perfectly ordinary words" (13), "Prune it ruthlessly" (17).

Comparisons can sometimes add a spark to your own writing. Instead of settling for "I was embarrassed," for example, you might try to finish off the thought with a comparison:

I was as embarrassed as a poolroom hustler hitting the cue ball off the table.

I hadn't been so embarrassed since I was six and my mother caught me playing doctor with Jimmy Fisher next door.

I was so embarrassed it was like having a simultaneous attack of dandruff, noisy stomach, and underarm perspiration.

The two most common kinds of comparisons are similes and metaphors. *Similes* make the comparison explicit by using *like* or *as.*

> The friction of the great beast's foot had stripped the skin from his back as neatly as one skins a rabbit.

Metaphors are sometimes defined as similes without the *like* or *as.* The simile, "The moon was like a silver dollar," becomes a metaphor when expressed, "The moon was a silver dollar." A metaphor can be more sophisticated than that, however, and the term is best defined as a word or phrase ordinarily associated with one context that is transferred to another. Some metaphors have become part of the language—so much so that they are either hopelessly trite or barely recognizable as metaphors.

Life is a rat race.

He ought to come down from his ivory tower.

Keep your paws off me.

She has a good nose for news.

. . . branches of knowledge

. . . key to the problem

. . . legs of a table

. . . hit below the belt

Other metaphors are waiting to be created to add impact, originality, and excitement to your writing.

Cautiously, the psychiatrist started to enter the haunted castle of his patient's mind.

It was the same thing all over again. My whole life had turned into a summer rerun.

His childhood daydreams had gone forever. Facing the fact that success took hard work, he realized that he could not expect to shazam his way to greatness.

Two cautions are necessary. First, use comparisons in moderation; otherwise, your style, instead of becoming enlivened, will bog down through carrying excess baggage. Second, don't be tempted into using the ready-made trite comparisons that fill the language: "as easy as pie," "so hungry I could eat a horse," "like taking candy from a baby," "like a bolt out of the blue," and so on. Trite phrases, by definition, are dead, and good comparisons are intended to be life-giving.

AMERICA: THE MULTINATIONAL SOCIETY

ISHMAEL REED

Twice nominated for National Book Awards, Ishmael Reed has written numerous novels, plays, essays, and songs and has taught at Harvard, Yale, Dartmouth, and the University of California at Berkeley. Among his novels are *The Free Lance Pall Bearers* (1967), *Mumbo Jumbo* (1978), and *Reckless Eyeballing* (1986). Volumes of essays include *Shrovetide in New Orleans* (1979) and *Writin' Is Fightin'* (1988). As you read "America: The Multinational Society," observe how careful Reed is to distribute his examples over as wide an area as possible (see p. 89), not merely to pour on a great number of examples.

Words to check:

mosques (paragraph 2)   archetypal (9)
ostracism (4)   incarceration (9)
monocultural (4)   patriarchs (10)
bouillabaisse (6)   lecterns (10)
entity (6)   calypso (11)
monolithic (6)   meticulous (12)
cubists (6)   repository (15)
surrealists (6)   bereft (15)
dissidents (7)

1   At the annual Lower East Side Jewish Festival yesterday, a Chinese woman ate a pizza slice in front of Ty Thuan Duc's Vietnamese grocery store. Beside her a Spanish-speaking family patronized a cart with two signs: "Italian Ices" and "Kosher by Rabbi Alper." And after the pastrami ran out, everybody ate knishes.

(New York Times, 23 June 1983)

2   On the day before Memorial Day, 1983, a poet called me to describe a city he had just visited. He said that one section included mosques, built by the Islamic people who dwelled there. Attending his reading, he said, were large numbers of Hispanic people, forty thousand of whom lived in the same city. He was not talking about a fabled city located in some mysterious region of the world. The city he'd visited was Detroit.

3   A few months before, as I was leaving Houston, Texas, I heard it announced on the radio that Texas's largest minority was Mexican American, and though a foundation recently issued a report critical of bilingual education, the taped voice used to guide the passengers on the air trams connecting terminals in Dallas Airport is in both Spanish and English. If the trend continues, a day will come when it will be difficult to travel through some sections of the country without hearing commands in both English and Spanish; after all, for some western states, Spanish was the first written language and the Spanish style lives on in the western way of life.

4   Shortly after my Texas trip, I sat in an auditorium located on the campus of the University of Wisconsin at Milwaukee as a Yale professor—whose original work on the influence of African cultures upon those of the Americas has led to his ostracism from some monocultural intellectual circles—walked up and down the aisle, like an old-time southern evangelist, dancing and drumming the top of the lectern, illustrating his points before some serious Afro-American intellectuals and artists who cheered and applauded his performance and his mastery of information. The professor was "white."

After his lecture, he joined a group of Milwaukeeans in a conversation. All of the participants spoke Yoruban,* though only the professor had ever traveled to Africa.

5   One of the artists told me that his paintings, which included African and Afro-American mythological symbols and imagery, were hanging in the local McDonald's restaurant. The next day I went to McDonald's and snapped pictures of smiling youngsters eating hamburgers below paintings that could grace the walls of any of the country's leading museums. The manager of the local McDonald's said, "I don't know what you boys are doing, but I like it," as he commissioned the local painters to exhibit in his restaurant.

6   Such blurring of cultural styles occurs in everyday life in the United States to a greater extent than anyone can imagine and is probably more prevalent than the sensational conflict between people of different backgrounds that is played up and often encouraged by the media. The result is what the Yale professor, Robert Thompson, referred to as a cultural bouillabaisse, yet members of the nation's present educational and cultural Elect still cling to the notion that the United States belongs to some vaguely defined entity they refer to as "Western civilization," by which they mean, presumably, a civilization created by the people of Europe, as if Europe can be viewed in monolithic terms. Is Beethoven's Ninth Symphony, which includes Turkish marches, a part of Western civilization, or the late nineteenth- and twentieth-century French paintings, whose creators were influenced by Japanese art? And what of the cubists, through whom the influence of African art changed modern painting, or the surrealists, who were so impressed with the art of the Pacific Northwest Indians that, in their map of North America, Alaska dwarfs the lower forty-eight in size?

7   Are the Russians, who are often criticized for their adoption of "Western" ways by Tsarist dissidents in exile, members of Western civilization? And what of the millions of Europeans who have black African and Asian ancestry, black Africans having occupied several countries for hundreds of years? Are these "Europeans" members of Western civilization, or the Hungarians, who originated across the Urals in a place called Greater Hungary, or the Irish, who came from the Iberian Peninsula?

8   Even the notion that North America is part of Western civilization because our "system of government" is derived from Europe is being challenged by Native American historians who say that the founding fathers, Benjamin Franklin especially, were actually influenced by the system of government

---

* Language of the Yoruba people, who live mainly in southwest Nigeria.

that had been adopted by the Iroquois hundreds of years prior to the arrival of large numbers of Europeans.

9   Western civilization, then, becomes another confusing category like Third World, or Judeo-Christian culture, as man attempts to impose his small-screen view of political and cultural reality upon a complex world. Our most publicized novelist recently said that Western civilization was the greatest achievement of mankind, an attitude that flourishes on the street level as scribbles in public restrooms: "White Power," "Niggers and Spics Suck," or "Hitler was a prophet," the latter being the most telling, for wasn't Adolph Hitler the archetypal monoculturalist who, in his pig-headed arrogance, believed that one way and one blood was so pure that it had to be protected from alien strains at all costs? Where did such an attitude, which has caused so much misery and depression in our national life, which has tainted even our noblest achievements, begin? An attitude that caused the incarceration of Japanese-American citizens during World War II, the persecution of Chicanos and Chinese Americans, the near-extermination of the Indians, and the murder and lynchings of thousands of Afro-Americans.

10   Virtuous, hardworking, pious, even though they occasionally would wander off after some fancy clothes, or rendezvous in the woods with the town prostitute, the Puritans are idealized in our schoolbooks as "a hardy band" of no-nonsense patriarchs whose discipline razed the forest and brought order to the New World (a term that annoys Native American historians). Industrious, responsible, it was their "Yankee ingenuity" and practicality that created the work ethic. They were simple folk who produced a number of good poets, and they set the tone for the American writing style, of lean and spare lines, long before Hemingway. They worshiped in churches whose colors blended in with the New England snow, churches with simple structures and ornate lecterns.

11   The Puritans were a daring lot, but they had a mean streak. They hated the theater and banned Christmas. They punished people in a cruel and inhuman manner. They killed children who disobeyed their parents. When they came in contact with those whom they considered heathens or aliens, they behaved in such a bizarre and irrational manner that this chapter in the American history comes down to us as a late-movie horror film. They exterminated the Indians, who taught them how to survive in a world unknown to them, and their encounter with the calypso culture of Barbados resulted in what the tourist guide in Salem's Witches' House refers to as the Witchcraft Hysteria.

12   The Puritan legacy of hard work and meticulous accounting led to the establishment of a great industrial society; it is no wonder that the American

industrial revolution began in Lowell, Massachusetts, but there was the other side, the strange and paranoid attitudes toward those different from the Elect.

13   The cultural attitudes of that early Elect continue to be voiced in everyday life in the United States: the president of a distinguished university, writing a letter to the *Times,* belittling the study of African civilizations; the television network that promoted its show on the Vatican art with the boast that this art represented "the finest achievements of the human spirit." A modern up-tempo state of complex rhythms that depends upon contacts with an international community can no longer behave as if it dwelled in a "Zion Wilderness" surrounded by beasts and pagans.

14   When I heard a schoolteacher warn the other night about the invasion of the American educational system by foreign curriculums, I wanted to yell at the television set, "Lady, they're already here." It has already begun because the world is here. The world has been arriving at these shores for at least ten thousand years from Europe, Africa, and Asia. In the late nineteenth and early twentieth centuries, large numbers of Europeans arrived, adding their cultures to those of the European, African, and Asian settlers who were already here, and recently millions have been entering the country from South America and the Caribbean, making Yale Professor Bob Thompson's bouillabaisse richer and thicker.

15   One of our most visionary politicians said that he envisioned a time when the United States could become the brain of the world, by which he meant the repository of all of the latest advanced information systems. I thought of that remark when an enterprising poet friend of mine called to say that he had just sold a poem to a computer magazine and that the editors were delighted to get it because they didn't carry fiction or poetry. Is that the kind of world we desire? A humdrum homogenous world of all brains but no heart, no fiction, no poetry; a world of robots with human attendants bereft of imagination, of culture? Or does North America deserve a more exciting destiny? To become a place where the cultures of the world crisscross. This is possible because the United States is unique in the world: The world is here.

WHAT DID THE WRITER SAY AND WHAT DID YOU THINK? _____

1. What is Reed's thesis?
2. Where is the thesis first stated?
3. Why does the author have difficulty accepting the traditional definition of "Western Civilization?"

4. Who, according to the author, forms the "Cultural Elect?"
5. What, according to Reed, is offensive about the statement, "Western civilization is the greatest creation of mankind"?
6. Does Reed like or dislike the American Puritans? Does he have mixed feelings?

HOW DID THE WRITER SAY IT? _____

1. Why does Reed frequently cite other people in order to support his points?
2. Why does the author emphasize the good qualities of the Puritans as well as the bad?
3. How does the tone of the last paragraph differ from the tone in the rest of the essay?

═══════════════WHAT ABOUT *YOUR* WRITING?═══════════

In his last paragraph, Ishmael Reed asks a series of *rhetorical questions:* "Is that the kind of world we desire? A humdrum homogenous world of all brains but no heart, no fiction, no poetry; a world of robots with human attendants bereft of imagination, of culture? Or does North America deserve a more exciting destiny?"

A rhetorical question is a question that either expects no reply or clearly calls for one desired reply. It is not a genuine inquiry like "Who was the thirteenth president of the USA?" Reed is confident that he has proven his case that cultural, racial, and ethnic diversity is one of America's greatest glories. Nevertheless, a flat statement to this effect may simply sound too flat—a dull summary, a bit of needless repetition. Rhetorical questions, in this case, can help remind us of the main point without needing to repeat it.

As long as they are not overused, rhetorical questions can also be a powerful device for establishing a dramatic atmosphere, particularly in conclusions. Rhetorical questions of this kind must be handled with restraint or they become forced and artificial, but a good writer should feel free to use them.

> Can all these blunders really be honest mistakes? Isn't it possible that we've let ourselves be duped again? And isn't it time to act?

Doctors get paid only for their patients' being ill, not for their patients' staying healthy. Is that practical? Is that smart? Is that even sane?

Is life so dear, or peace so sweet, as to be purchased at the price of chains and slavery? Forbid it, Almighty God! I know not what course others may take; but as for me, give me liberty, or give me death.

5

PROCESS

*I*n its most familiar form, writing about a process provides instructions. This kind of process paper tells readers the series of steps they must perform to achieve a particular result. At its simplest level, the process paper is a "how-to-do-it" paper: how to cook Beef Wellington, how to drive from town to Camp Wilderness (see p. 15), how to install wall paneling, how to operate a home computer, how to put together a child's bike on Christmas morning. Writing simple, clear instructions makes many demands on a writer, and people who are good at it often earn excellent salaries. Ask any parents struggling with the bike on Christmas morning how many dollars they would offer for easy-to-read and easy-to-follow instructions.

The conventional how-to-do-it paper sometimes can lend itself to humor, as when a writer deliberately gives instructions on what no one wants to learn: how to flunk out of school, how to have a heart attack, and so forth. Besides drawing on the appeal of humor, such papers can also have serious instructional purposes by telling the reader, between the lines, how to do well in school or how to avoid coronaries. Other humorous pieces give instructions on what many people *do* want to learn but don't usually want to acknowledge: *How to Succeed in Business Without Really Trying* and *Gamesmanship, or The Art of Winning Games Without Actually Cheating* are titles of two successful books.

Several other variations on the how-to-do-it paper are also fairly common. A "how-it-works" paper explains the functioning of anything from an electric toothbrush to the system for ratifying a new constitutional amendment.

115

A "how-it-*was*-done" paper might trace the process by which Stonehenge or the Pyramids were built or of how the chase scenes in the old Keystone Kops movies were filmed. A "how-*not*-to-do-it" paper might trace the process by which the writer did everything wrong in reshingling the roof or buying a used car.

At a more advanced level, process papers can study the course of social, political, scientific, and cultural developments: the process that led to the discovery of the smallpox vaccine, the decision of Napoleon to invade Russia, the spread of Christianity, Franklin D. Roosevelt's proposal to increase the membership of the Supreme Court. Process writing can also be a powerful instrument of literary analysis: the process by which Frederic Henry in *A Farewell to Arms* comes to desert the army, or Captain Ahab in *Moby-Dick* associates the white whale with evil, or Iago persuades Othello that Desdemona has been unfaithful.

How does the persuasive principle apply to process writing? If you're writing a straightforward how-to-do-it paper, for example, why not simply list the steps and forget about a thesis? You don't have a "point" to make as such, do you? Aren't you saying only that here are the things one must do to paint a room or change a flat tire or study for an exam? So why not just list them?

These questions are legitimate, and it's certainly possible to write a process paper without a thesis. In most cases, though, the paper won't be as good as it could be and ought to be. Apart from the advantages of writing with a thesis as described in Chapter 1, you're writing a how-to-do-it paper, after all, for people who don't yet know "how to do it." (If they knew, they'd have no reason to read the paper.) A mere long list of things to do, each step considered separately, can both madden readers with boredom and overwhelm them with confusion. A thesis helps readers get solidly oriented at the outset and enables them to see each separate step as part of a coherent pattern.

But what kind of thesis makes sense in the humble little paper on how to paint a room? All kinds.

Painting a room is much easier than it seems.

Painting a room is much harder than it seems.

Painting a room is great fun.

Painting a room is horrible drudgery.

Painting a room is easy compared to preparing the room to be painted.

Painting a room takes less time than most people suppose.

Painting a room takes more time than most people suppose.

Any one of these ideas, not to mention many more imaginative ones, could give unity and interest to a how-to-do-it paper. The writer, in addition to making each step convey the necessary raw information, would connect each step or group of related steps to the thesis.

> ¶ 1—Presentation of thesis: Painting a room is much easier than it seems.
>
> Start of ¶ 2—To prepare the room, you need only a dust cloth, lots of masking tape, spackling paste . . .
>
> Start of ¶ 3—If preparing the room was easy, the painting itself is child's play . . .
>
> Start of ¶ 4—Cleaning up is the easiest part of all . . .

With the desirability of a thesis in mind, it's no massive project to think up promising theses for some of the other subjects already mentioned.

Every step of the way, Napoleon's decision to invade Russia was based on foolish overconfidence.

Franklin D. Roosevelt's proposal to pack the Supreme Court came in response to a long series of legislative frustrations.

Frederic Henry's desertion of the army in *A Farewell to Arms* is the last step in a gradually accelerating process of disillusionment.

The dramatic discovery of the smallpox vaccine came as the result of a coldly logical, totally undramatic scientific process.

The seemingly spontaneous, mad chase scenes in Keystone Kops movies were actually the product of careful planning of every detail.

The process by which the Pyramids were built shows an astonishing knowledge of the laws of modern physics.

Once you set up a thesis, the significant issues are the mechanics of writing about the process itself.

Be Sure You Are Writing About a Process. The words "How to" or "How" in your title guarantee nothing. A process is a series, a sequence, an orderly progression. One step or event follows another: first this, then that, then something else. A happy-go-lucky collection of handy hints is not a process. Chapter 1 of this book followed a necessary sequence in the description of the process of *first* starting with a general subject, *then* limiting the subject, *then* devising a thesis and thesis statement, *then* incorporating the thesis into the whole paper. Chapter 4, on the other hand, while telling "how to" write an example paper, presented a bundle of miscellaneous suggestions on what to think about in looking over the examples; the suggestions were in no particularly rigid order and therefore did not constitute a real process.

Follow Strict Chronological Order. The rule to follow strict chronological order seems obvious, but in fact it is unique to process writing. In other patterns, you try to begin with your most important or dramatic or amusing material. In process writing, you begin with step one. You try to make all the steps of the process as interesting as possible to your reader, but you have no choice about the order in which you discuss them.

Before Describing the First Step of the Process, Indicate Any Special Ingredients or Equipment That Will Be Needed. Recipes, for example, almost always begin with a list of ingredients.

Be Sure the Process Is Complete. In a how-to-do-it paper, you're describing a process that you probably can do automatically, and it's easy to omit some obvious steps because you don't consciously think about them at all. They are not so obvious to your reader. If you're telling the reader how to stop a leak in the kitchen sink, for instance, don't forget to have the poor soul shut off the water supply before removing the faucet and replacing the washer.

Try to Anticipate Difficulties. First, warn the reader in advance if a notably tough step is coming up:

Now comes the hard part.

The next step is a bit tricky.

Be extremely careful here.

Second, advise the reader of what can be done to make the process easier or more pleasant. You're an insider, and you have an insider's information. The process of changing a flat tire does not require anyone to put the lugs into the inverted hubcap so they won't get lost, but it's a technique insiders use to head off trouble before it starts. Painting a room does not require anyone to wear an old hat, but your mentioning the advisability of an old hat might be appreciated.

Third, tell the reader what to do if something goes wrong. Don't terrify the reader, but be frank about common foul-ups:

If any paint should get onto the window . . .

If the hubcap is hard to replace . . .

If You Need to Handle Many Separate Steps, Arrange Them into Groups When Possible. Even a simple process may involve a large number of steps. The process paper is far less intimidating if the steps are presented in manageable bunches. On page 117 the writer divided the process of painting a room into preparation, painting, and cleaning up. Each division received a paragraph, and the reader got the impression of having only three major areas to worry about instead of fifty separate steps. Even as uninspired a grouping of steps as Phase I, Phase II, Phase III, or Beginning, Middle, End, is preferable to none at all. The more steps in the process, of course, the more essential it becomes to collect them into groups.

Define Unfamiliar Terms. Definitions of unfamiliar terms are needed in all writing, but they're especially important in the how-to-do-it paper because the instructions are for an audience that must be assumed to know nothing about the subject.

Two final recommendations about your choice of topics are worth brief notes:

Avoid Highly Technical Processes. Because you must define all unfamiliar terms, you don't want to choose an obscure scientific subject with such a specialized vocabulary that most of your energies will be spent providing definitions rather than presenting a process.

Avoid Subjects for Which Pictures Work Better Than Words. Some processes, often but not always the highly technical ones, can best be explained with a few diagrams and almost as few words. Depending solely or almost solely on words would create pointless trouble for the writer and confusion for the reader. Since you are in a writing class, not an art class, you should avoid such processes.

WRITING SUGGESTIONS
FOR PROCESS ESSAYS

Many topics have already been mentioned in this chapter. The suggestions here are designed to provide some further inspiration. Suggestions have been grouped into two categories: general areas for exploration (with examples) and specific topics.

General Areas For Exploration

1. Do-it-yourself repairs: bikes, cars, radios, television sets, broken windows.
2. Routine chores: gardening, cooking, shopping.
3. School and business: studying, taking notes, registering, applying to colleges, applying for jobs, creating a good impression at job interviews.
4. Sports, games, and other recreational activities: how to win at poker, bridge, Monopoly; how to watch a football game, throw Frisbees, water-ski; how to plan a trip.
5. Finances: budgeting, borrowing, investing.
6. Hobbies: how to start a stamp, coin, tropical fish collection; how to work at a particular art or craft; how a magic trick is performed.
7. Children and pets: baby-sitting, toilet training, safety, housebreaking, traveling.
8. Personal care: grooming, breaking a bad habit, treating a cold, curing a hangover.
9. Humor: how to be a bore, worrywart, nag; how to get out of housework, butter up teachers, call in sick; how to die at thirty.
10. How it works: power steering, air conditioning, instant photography, zippers.
11. The past: how a battle was fought, a crime was committed, a structure was built, a law was passed, a disease was conquered.
12. Literature: how an author prepares the reader for a surprise ending, how a character makes a crucial decision, and so on.

Specific Topics

1. What to do if arrested.
2. What to do in a car accident.
3. How to find a rich husband or wife.
4. How to diet.
5. How to exercise.
6. How to drive defensively.
7. How to apply first aid for snake bites.
8. How to protect oneself in a natural disaster (tornado, hurricane, flood).
9. How to waste time.
10. How to plan for a holiday or other special occasion: Thanksgiving dinner, Passover seder, birthday party, bar mitzvah or confirmation party, Easter egg hunt, wedding.

11. How to live on nothing a year.
12. How to pack a suitcase.
13. How to stop smoking.
14. How to hitch a ride.
15. How to give oneself a perfect shave.

How to Trim Your Kids

Roberta Larsen (student)

Thesis: Trimming your kids' bangs is easy . . . if you know my mom's method.

    I.   Preparation
        A. Table
        B. Tools

   II.   The Beginnings
        A. Cutting the tape
        B. Taping each child

 III. The Trim
        A. Trimming the children
        B. Appreciating the trim's neatness

Conclusion: Mom's method can help almost everyone give almost anyone a quick and tidy trim.

My mom has three kids, and when we were little we were as wiggly and as impatient as any kids on the planet. So, when it got to be time for Mom to trim our bangs, she had three wiggly, impatient, long-haired kids on her hands. Being a bright woman, Mom realized that any successful trimming method would have to be brief—to compensate for our constant motion and lack of patience—and neat—to maintain her sanity. So either from some ancient family tradition, some now-yellowing magazine, or from that secret storehouse of Mom Knowledge, my mother devised the perfect way to trim her kids. I pass it on to anyone else whose kids get a bit ornery at trimming time.

First, you should seat your kids comfortably at a table. Mom always used the kitchen table, but any outside picnic table or gold leaf Louis XVI table will do just fine. The table gives you a place to put your tools—Scotch tape and scissors—and gives your kids something to lean on when they whine about having to get a haircut.

Once the kids are stationary, you should cut one four-inch-long piece of Scotch tape for each child. Stick the pieces of tape onto the edge of the table until you are ready for them. Then, gently place one hand on top of one kid's head to flatten down the bangs and reveal their true length. Draw an imaginary line across your kid's bangs to indicate how much you want to trim. Now, carefully take one of those pieces of tape and stick it on your kid's hair (really!), lining up the top edge of the tape with your imaginary hair cutting line. Do this for each child.

At this point, you have a bunch of kids with tape on their heads. To finish up the trim, have the kids shut their eyes while you carefully cut along the top edge of the tape. It should be quite easy to cut in a straight and accurate line, as the edge of the tape will act as a cutting guide. Once again, do this for each kid.

Now that your kids are trimmed and you can see their faces you can begin to appreciate the best part of Mom's trimming method. It's practically mess-free! The Scotch tape not only keeps the trimmed hair out of your kids' eyes, it also keeps it from falling all over the carpet and chair. Neat trick, eh?

That's Mom's hair-cut trick. I've been using it for ages, and it works on small wiggly children, large cranky adults, and even on yourself. Give it a try, and thank my mom for it. And, by the way, you should see what she can do with pipe cleaners!

CORN BREAD WITH CHARACTER

RONNI LUNDY

Ronni Lundy works as a feature writer for the *Louisville Courier Journal* where her special interests in bluegrass and traditional music often appear in her commentary. She has also done free-lance writing for such national magazines as *Esquire* in which "Corn Bread with Character" was first published in 1983.

Words to check:

homogenized (paragraph 2)	heady (8)
cracklings (2)	throes (8)
forebear (3)	pulverize (11)
wield (3)	scotch (11)
facet (5)	instinctive (12)
impart (7)	facsimile (14)
improvise (7)	

1   There are those who will tell you that real corn bread has just a little sugar in it. They'll say it enhances the flavor or that it's an old tradition in the South. Do not listen to them. If God had meant for corn bread to have sugar in it, he'd have called it cake.

2   *Real* corn bread is not sweet. Real corn bread is not homogenized with the addition of flour or puffed up with excessive artificial rising agents. Real corn bread rises from its own strength of character, has substance, crust, and texture. Real corn bread doesn't depend on fancy cornmeal, buttermilk, or cracklings for its quality. Real corn bread is a forthright, honest food as good as the instincts of its cook and the pan it is baked in.

3   That pan had best be a cast-iron skillet, preferably one inherited from a forebear who knew how to wield it. My mother, who made real corn bread almost every day of my growing-up life, has a great pan, a square cast-iron skillet given by a great aunt. She also has an eight-slot corn stick pan I would be satisfied to find as my sole inheritance someday. In the meantime, I bake corn bread in a nine-inch round cast-iron skillet I grabbed up in a second-hand store because it already had a black, nasty crust on the outside and the proper sheen of seasoning within.

4   If you have to start with a pan fresh from the store, season it according to the instructions for cast iron, then fry bacon in it every morning for a month to add a little flavor. Pour the leftover bacon grease into an empty one-pound coffee can and refrigerate it. Wipe your pan clean with a paper towel and don't ever touch it with anything as destructive as soap and water. When the inside starts to turn black and shiny, you're ready to start making corn bread.

5   It's not enough to have the right pan, however; you also need to know how to heat it properly. Heating right is the most important facet of the art of making corn bread, because if you have your skillet and drippings just hot enough, you'll consistently turn out corn bread with a faultless brown and crispy crust.

6   "Just what are drippings?" you may ask here, thereby revealing that you have never been closer than a pig's eye to a country kitchen.

7   In my family, drippings were the bacon grease my mother saved every morning in coffee cans. If you've followed the directions for seasoning a new pan, you're in good shape here. But what if you've inherited a well-seasoned pan and want to start baking corn bread before your next breakfast? Or what if you've never eaten bacon in your life? Don't despair. You will learn, as I did during a brief flirtation with vegetarianism, that while bacon drippings impart a distinctive taste to corn bread cooked with them, they aren't essential to baking great corn bread. You can improvise a lot with grease.

8   If you feel extravagant, you can use half a stick of butter, but if you need to conserve, you can use some not too flavorful oil with a teaspoon or two of butter for effect. If you like the taste, you can use peanut oil or the thick, golden corn oil sold in health food stores that tastes like Kansas in the heady throes of late August. But you can't use olive oil or sesame oil (too strong and foreign), and margarine won't heat right.

9   To heat the pan correctly, you must leave it in the oven until it and the drippings are really hot but not smoking. Knowing just how long that takes is a trick you'll learn with time. A good rule of thumb: Leave the pan in the oven while you mix the other ingredients, but don't stir too slowly. A good precaution, in the early stages of making corn bread, is to check the pan frequently.

10   A final secret on the art of heating: It does not work to heat the corn bread skillet on top of the stove. Doing so may save you from setting off the smoke alarm, but the burner will create circular hot spots in your skillet and when you flip it to get the corn bread out, the middle crust will stay behind, clinging to those spots.

11   You will need cornmeal, of course. You may want to invest in a sturdy little grinder and pulverize the kernels yourself at home. Or you may want to cultivate a dark and narrow little store somewhere that sells only stone-ground cornmeal in expensively priced brown paper bags. Either method is fine. Both will bake up just as nicely as the commercially ground white cornmeal you can find in bags on any supermarket shelf. That's what my mother always used, and years of sampling gourmet grinds have given me no reason to scotch her preference.

12   In my mother's kitchen, where I learned to make corn bread, there were two kinds of measurements: enough and not enough. If we owned anything as fancy as a measuring cup, I'm sure it was not taken down for an occurrence so everyday as the baking of dinner corn bread. I do know that we had a set of four measuring spoons in primary colors, because it made a dandy toy for visiting children, but I don't remember ever seeing it in my mother's hand as she sprinkled salt, baking powder, or soda into the corn

bread mixing bowl. In the interest of science, however, and for those unable to visit my mother's kitchen, her instinctive art is converted here to teaspoons, tablespoons, and cups. What follows is a recipe for real corn bread, enough to accompany dinner for six:

13 Turn on your oven to 450 degrees.

14 In a nine-inch round cast-iron skillet or a reasonable facsimile thereof, place four tablespoons of the grease of your choice. Place the skillet in the oven and heat it until the grease pops and crackles when you wiggle the pan.

15 While the grease heats, mix together in a medium-sized bowl two cups of fairly finely ground white cornmeal with one teaspoon of salt, one-half teaspoon of baking soda, and one-half teaspoon of baking powder. Use your fingers to blend them together well.

16 Crack one big egg or two little ones into the meal mixture.

17 Add one and a half cups of milk or buttermilk.

18 Stir until just blended.

19 Remove the skillet from the oven and swirl it carefully so the grease coats most of the inside edges of the pan but not your hand. Pour the grease into the corn bread mixture, and if everything is going right, it will crackle invitingly. Mix together well with a big wooden spoon, using about twenty-five strokes.

20 Pour the mixture back into the hot skillet and return it to the oven for twenty minutes. Run the pan under the broiler for a few seconds to get a light-brown top crust, then remove it from the oven and turn it upside down onto a large plate. If your skillet is seasoned right, the bread will slide out in a hot brown slab. If not, then just serve it straight from the pan. It will taste every bit as good. (This recipe can also be baked in a corn stick pan, but the baking time is cut in half.)

21 Serve the bread with fresh sweet butter, or crumble it in a bowl and cover with hot pinto beans, a green onion, and sweet pickle on the side. Now, that's real corn bread.

WHAT DID THE WRITER SAY AND WHAT DID YOU THINK?

1. What is Lundy's thesis?
2. How does this recipe differ from most recipes?
3. How does the author's use of personal background affect the essay?
4. Why does Lundy use more than half the essay to explain the seasoned tools?

5. Why does she use the overworked "If God had meant . . ." in paragraph 1?

HOW DID THE WRITER SAY IT? _____

1. How do the essay title and paragraph 2 relate?
2. Are the obvious repetitions in paragraph 2 effective? Why or why not?
3. What is the overall tone of the essay? Is it unusual for a recipe? Explain.
4. Is Lundy's conclusion typical for a recipe? Why or why not?
5. Where does Lundy begin citing the actual recipe? Why so late?

═══════════════WHAT ABOUT *YOUR* WRITING?═══════════════

Your instructors are captive audiences. They may often enjoy their captivity and be eager to read your work, but in fact they have no choice. In the mood or not, they have to read it. That's their job. Fret all you want about their grading—you'll never find such soft touches again. Your future, non-captive audiences will be infinitely tougher. They don't use red ink, but they don't need any. All they need is a wastebasket. And every good writer respects and fears wastebaskets.

Like Ronni Lundy in "Corn Bread with Character," the professional writer of a magazine article or advertisement suffers from, and benefits tremendously from, one problem that more writers ought to feel. *How do I get my reader's attention?* Nobody starts to read a magazine wondering what Lundy or the Jones and Smith Company has to say that day. The author or the company has to make the reader stop turning the pages. The soft-touch instructor may sometimes comment, "This essay starts slowly but gets better as it goes along." The other folks out there just keep turning the pages.

Think about your readers. They're rooting strongly for you, if only because they want their own reading experience to be pleasurable, but they need your help. Here are three specific suggestions for making a good start.

First, try for a strong title. You don't normally personify food as Lundy does in her title, "Corn Bread with Character." But it is original and catchy, a title that can easily stimulate a reader's curiosity. (For a more detailed discussion of titles, see p. 5.)

Second, spare the reader such unpromising first sentences as "In this composition I will try to show . . ." or "My paper has as its thesis . . ." or "According to Webster's Dictionary . . ." You needn't go overboard—there's no virtue in being self-consciously cute or eccentric. (Lundy's opening sentence, for example, is mostly a simple, straightforward statement.) Still, a well-calculated touch of show biz now and then never hurt anyone and can sometimes work miracles. Consider these first sentences from three essays by George Orwell:

> As I write, highly civilised human beings are flying overhead, trying to kill me.

> Soon after I arrived at Crossgates (not immediately, but after a week or two, just when I seemed to be settling into the routine of school life) I began wetting my bed.

> In Moulmein, in Lower Burma, I was hated by large numbers of people—the only time in my life that I have been important enough for this to happen to me.

Third, and most important, remember that there's a real person reading what you've written. Writing isn't just self-expression—it's communication. If self-expression were the whole story, you'd be better off doodling or singing in the shower or making funny noises while you run through the nearest meadow. Whenever you can—and that will be most of the time—give your reader an immediate reason for paying attention to you. In "Corn Bread with Character," the author employs the oldest, and still most effective, technique in the writer's trade: from the first sentence on, she appeals to the reader's self-interest. "Do what I tell you, and you will soon be enjoying the world's best corn bread." Not all of your writing will deal with life and death issues, but you can almost always give your reader a reason to care—even about family recipes.

A writer is at one end and a reader at the other, and unless the reader is your instructor, that reader has a wastebasket.

HOW TO TAKE A JOB INTERVIEW

KIRBY W. STANAT

Author of *Job Hunting Secrets and Tactics* (1977) and one-time recruiter and placement officer for the University of Wisconsin—Milwaukee, Kirby W. Stanat clearly writes with authority about job interviews. As you read, note the versatility of how-to-do-it writing. Instructions aren't always about straightforward physical activities like giving haircuts (see page 121) or making bread (see page 122): they can also involve psychological complexities like making good impressions.

Words to check:

adamant (paragraph 35)

1   To succeed in campus job interviews, you have to know where that recruiter is coming from. The simple answer is that he is coming from corporate headquarters.

2   That may sound obvious, but it is a significant point that too many students do not consider. The recruiter is not a free spirit as he flies from Berkeley to New Haven, from Chapel Hill to Boulder. He's on an invisible leash to the office, and if he is worth his salary, he is mentally in corporate headquarters all the time he's on the road.

3   If you can fix that in your mind—that when you walk into that bare-walled cubicle in the placement center you are walking into a branch office of Sears, Bendix or General Motors—you can avoid a lot of little mistakes and maybe some big ones.

4   If, for example, you assume that because the interview is on campus the recruiter expects you to look and act like a student, you're in for a shock. A student is somebody who drinks beer, wears blue jeans and throws a Frisbee. No recruiter has jobs for student Frisbee whizzes.

5   A cool spring day in late March, Sam Davis, a good recruiter who has been on the college circuit for years, is on my campus talking to candidates. He comes out to the waiting area to meet the student who signed up for an 11 o'clock interview. I'm standing in the doorway of my office taking in the scene.

6   Sam calls the candidate: "Sidney Student." There sits Sidney. He's at a 45 degree angle, his feet are in the aisle, and he's almost lying down. He's wearing well-polished brown shoes, a tasteful pair of brown pants, a light brown shirt, and a good looking tie. Unfortunately, he tops off this well-coordinated

outfit with his Joe's Tavern Class A Softball Championship jacket, which has a big woven emblem over the heart.

7   If that isn't bad enough, in his left hand is a cigarette and in his right hand is a half-eaten apple.

8   When Sam calls his name, the kid is caught off guard. He ditches the cigarette in an ashtray, struggles to his feet, and transfers the apple from the right to the left hand. Apple juice is everywhere, so Sid wipes his hand on the seat of his pants and shakes hands with Sam.

9   Sam, who by now is close to having a stroke, gives me that what-do-I-have-here look and has the young man follow him into the interviewing room.

10   The situation deteriorates even further—into pure Laurel and Hardy. The kid is stuck with the half-eaten apple, doesn't know what to do with it, and obviously is suffering some discomfort. He carries the apple into the interviewing room with him and places it in the ashtray on the desk—right on top of Sam's freshly lit cigarette.

11   The interview lasts five minutes. . . .

12   Let us move in for a closer look at how the campus recruiter operates.

13   Let's say you have a 10 o'clock appointment with the recruiter from the XYZ Corporation. The recruiter gets rid of the candidate in front of you at about 5 minutes to 10, jots down a few notes about what he is going to do with him or her, then picks up your résumé or data sheet (which you have submitted in advance). . . .

14   Although the recruiter is still in the interview room and you are still in the lobby, your interview is under way. You're on. The recruiter will look over your sheet pretty carefully before he goes out to call you. He develops a mental picture of you.

15   He thinks, "I'm going to enjoy talking with this kid," or "This one's going to be a turkey." The recruiter has already begun to make a screening decision about you.

16   His first impression of you, from reading the sheet, could come from your grade point. It could come from misspelled words. It could come from poor erasures or from the fact that necessary information is missing. By the time the recruiter has finished reading your sheet, you've already hit the plus or minus column.

17   Let's assume the recruiter got a fairly good impression from your sheet.

18   Now the recruiter goes out to the lobby to meet you. He almost shuffles along, and his mind is somewhere else. Then he calls your name, and at that instant he visibly clicks into gear. He just went to work.

19   As he calls your name he looks quickly around the room, waiting for somebody to move. If you are sitting on the middle of your back, with a book open

and a cigarette going, and if you have to rebuild yourself to stand up, the interest will run right out of the recruiter's face. You, not the recruiter, made the appointment for 10 o'clock, and the recruiter expects to see a young professional come popping out of that chair like today is a good day and you're anxious to meet him.

20   At this point, the recruiter does something rude. He doesn't walk across the room to meet you halfway. He waits for you to come to him. Something very important is happening. He wants to see you move. He wants to get an impression about your posture, your stride, and your briskness.

21   If you slouch over to him, sidewinderlike, he is not going to be impressed. He'll figure you would probably slouch your way through your workdays. He wants you to come at him with lots of good things going for you. If you watch the recruiter's eyes, you can see the inspection. He glances quickly at shoes, pants, coat, shirt; dress, blouse, hose—the whole works.

22   After introducing himself, the recruiter will probably say, "Okay, please follow me," and he'll lead you into his interviewing room.

23   When you get to the room, you may find that the recruiter will open the door and gesture you in—with him blocking part of the doorway. There's enough room for you to get past him, but it's a near thing.

24   As you scrape past, he gives you a closeup inspection. He looks at your hair; if it's greasy, that will bother him. He looks at your collar; if it's dirty, that will bother him. He looks at your shoulders; if they're covered with dandruff, that will bother him. If you're a man, he looks at your chin. If you didn't get a close shave, that will irritate him. If you're a woman, he checks your makeup. If it's too heavy, he won't like it.

25   Then he smells you. An amazing number of people smell bad. Occasionally a recruiter meets a student who smells like a canal horse. That student can expect an interview of about four or five minutes.

26   Next the recruiter inspects the back side of you. He checks your hair (is it combed in front but not in back?), he checks your heels (are they run down?), your pants (are they baggy?), your slip (is it showing?), your stockings (do they have runs?).

27   Then he invites you to sit down.

28   At this point, I submit, the recruiter's decision on you is 75 to 80 percent made.

29   Think about it. The recruiter has read your résumé. He knows who you are and where you are from. He knows your marital status, your major and your grade point. And he knows what you have done with your summers. He has inspected you, exchanged greetings with you and smelled you. There is

very little additional hard information that he must gather on you. From now on it's mostly body chemistry.

30   Many recruiters have argued strenuously with me that they don't make such hasty decisions. So I tried an experiment. I told several recruiters that I would hang around in the hall outside the interview room when they took candidates in.

31   I told them that as soon as they had definitely decided not to recommend (to department managers in their companies) the candidate they were interviewing, they should snap their fingers loud enough for me to hear. It went like this.

32   First candidate: 38 seconds after the candidate sat down: Snap!

33   Second candidate: 1 minute, 42 seconds: Snap!

34   Third candidate: 45 seconds: Snap!

35   One recruiter was particularly adamant, insisting that he didn't rush to judgment on candidates. I asked him to participate in the snapping experiment. He went out in the lobby, picked up his first candidate of the day, and headed for an interview room.

36   As he passed me in the hall, he glared at me. And his fingers went "Snap!"

WHAT DID THE WRITER SAY AND WHAT DID YOU THINK?

1. What is the thesis? When is it stated?
2. What point is established by the "snap" experiment?
3. What personal physical details will make an interviewer take an instant dislike to an applicant?
4. Does Stanat's advice apply to all job seekers, or only to those who have just left college? Why?
5. What is so important about a resume or data sheet?
6. Why would an interviewer want to watch an applicant walk?

HOW DID THE WRITER SAY IT?

1. What specific details about "Sidney Student" accent his unacceptability as a job applicant?
2. This essay concentrates almost entirely on what happens before the actual job interview. With this in mind, is the title really appropriate? Why or why not?

3. The essay has no normal concluding paragraph. Does it need one? Why or why not?

==================WHAT ABOUT *YOUR* WRITING?==================

Countless thousands of students have been told never to write *you*. They were misinformed. *You* is a tricky word, and it's easy enough to understand how some teachers, distraught at seeing the word so frequently mismanaged, might invent a rule that outlaws it—but no such rule exists in standard English.

The tricky part is that *you* is both a pronoun of direct address, aimed at a specific person or group, and an indefinite pronoun meaning something like *people* or *one* or *everybody*. When it's used in writing aimed at a general audience—like most freshman English writing—it can be taken in both ways and can often turn out to be unintentionally confusing, insulting, or funny. Imagine a casual reader coming across sentences like

When you catch syphilis you must consult your doctor immediately.

Your paranoid concern with what others think of you makes you a likely candidate for suicide.

The new night school program should give you fresh hope for overcoming your illiteracy.

Those sentences demand immediate revision:

Victims of syphilis must consult their doctors immediately.

Paranoid concern with what others think increases the likelihood of suicide.

The new night school program should give fresh hope for overcoming illiteracy.

To be fair to the inventors of imaginary rules, then, it's wise in most classroom writing to be extremely conservative with you as an indefinite pronoun. The assumed audience is a general one of mixed ages, sexes, backgrounds, and interests; using *you* for this audience is nearly always asking for trouble.

There nothing wrong with *you,* however, in writing that does address itself to a specific audience: the purchaser of a bike who now has to put it together, the new employee who wants information on the pension plan and hospitalization program, the college student worried about a job interview, as in this reading selection by Kirby W. Stanat. This book addresses itself to college freshmen taking a course in English composition, each of whom receives similar reading and writing assignments every day. An audience can't get much more specific than that, and therefore this book feels free to make frequent use of *you*. You must have noticed.

See pages 169–170 for comments on the use of *I*.

DITCH DIVING

TOM BODETT

The author lives in Homer, Alaska, and may—or may not—be drawing on personal experience for his subject. Tom Bodett has made numerous recordings, and some readers may be familiar with him through his commentaries on NPR on "All Things Considered." His published books include *The End of the Road* (1989) and *Growing Up, Growing Old and Going Fishing at the End of the Road* (1990). Process writing presents many opportunities for humor, and "Ditch Diving" can serve as a prime example.

Words to check:

aesthetics (paragraph 1)	piker (7)
panache (5)	berm (8)
gawk (5)	

1   The graceful winter sports of skiing, skating and dog-sledding get a lot of attention around Alaska, but there's another winter activity that nobody seems to appreciate for the art that it actually is—ditch diving. We all become practitioners of this art at one time or another, but none of us seems to hold proper appreciation of what we're doing, perhaps because its aesthetics have never been fully defined for us. Allow me.

2   To dive you need a road, a ditch, some snow on the ground, and any licensed highway vehicle or its equivalent. Nothing else is required, but a good freezing rain will speed up the process.

3   The art of the dive is in the elegance with which you perform three distinct actions. The first one, of course, is that you and your car *leave the roadway*. Not so fast there, hotshot—remember, this is an art. The manner and theme of your dive are weighed heavily in this maneuver.

4   For instance, the "I wasn't looking and drove into the ditch" dive will gain you nothing with the critics. The "He wasn't looking and drove me into the ditch" dive is slightly better, but lacks character. The "It sucked me into the ditch" dive shows real imagination, and the "We spun around three times, hit the ditch going backwards, and thought we were all going to die" dive will earn you credits for sheer drama. The "I drove in the ditch rather than slide past the school bus" dive might win the humanitarian award, but only if you can explain to the police why you were going that fast in the first place.

5   Okay, so now you've left the road. Your second challenge is to *place the vehicle.* Any dumbbell can put a car in a ditch, but it takes an artist to put one there with panache. The overall appeal of your installation is gauged by how much the traffic slows down to gawk at it.

6   Nosed-in within ten degrees of level won't even turn a head. Burrowed into a snowbank with one door buried shut is better, and if you're actually caught in the act of climbing out a window, you're really getting somewhere. Letting your car sit overnight so the snowplows can bury it is a good way of gaining points with the morning commuter traffic. Any wheel left visibly off the ground is good for fifty points each, with a hundred-point bonus for all four. Caution: Only master-class ditch divers should endeavor to achieve this bonus positioning.

7   All right, there you are, nicely featured alongside your favorite roadway. The third part of your mission is to *ask for assistance.* Simply walking to a phone and calling a tow truck will prove you a piker and not an artist at all. Hit the showers, friend. The grace and creativity you display getting back on the road must at least equal those you employed while leaving it.

8   Let's say you were forced into the ditch and are neatly enshrined with one rear wheel off the ground and the hood buried in the berm. Wait until any truck bigger than your bathroom happens along and start walking in that direction with a pronounced limp. Look angry but not defeated, as if you'd walk all night to find the guy who ran you off the road. Look the driver in the eye like it would have been him if he'd been there sooner. This is a risky move, but it's been proven effective. If the truck has personalized license plates and lights mounted all over it, you're in good shape. Those guys love to show how hard their trucks can pull on things.

9   I prefer, however, to rely on the softer side of human nature. Addle-brained people hold a special place in our hearts, and I like to play on these protective instincts. If my car is buried beyond hope, I'll display my tongue in the corner of my mouth and begin frantically digging at the snow drift

with my hands until someone stops to talk me out of it. If my hands get cold and still nobody's stopped, I'll crawl head-first into the hole I've dug and flail my legs around like I was thrown clear of the wreck. This works every time and has won me many a ditch-diving exhibition over the years.

10   I certainly hope I've enlarged your appreciation of this undervalued creative medium. I warn against exercising this art to excess, but when the opportunity arises, remember: Hit 'er hard, sink 'er deep, get 'er out, and please, dive carefully.

WHAT DID THE WRITER SAY AND WHAT DID YOU THINK? _____

1. What is the thesis? Is it stated or unstated?
2. What are the three steps in the process?
3. What are the main differences between a poor ditch dive and a superior one?
4. Where and how does Bodett summarize his essay?

HOW DID THE WRITER SAY IT? _____

1. When does the humorous purpose of this essay first become apparent?
2. What common phrase is echoed by the author's last words: "dive carefully"? How seriously are we intended to take those words?
3. What sports terminology does Bodett use in his essay, and why?

════════════WHAT ABOUT *YOUR* WRITING?════════════

"Please, dive carefully." This phrase, a pun or play on words, takes a standard expression—please drive carefully—and reworks it to make a special point, to fit in with a particular purpose. Opinions may differ, of course, on how successful this phrase is. Some people, too, probably still accept unthinkingly the tired old cliché that puns and word plays are the lowest form of literature. In fact, however, writers as diverse as Shakespeare and Thoreau have been entranced by the exciting stylistic possibilities of word plays.

E. E. Cummings, the American poet, once wrote that poetry should do to you what the old burlesque gag does:

> Question: Would you hit a woman with a baby?
>
> Answer: No, I'd hit her with a brick.

Cummings's view is that poetry should fool around with words, should try to astonish and delight the reader by revealing previously unnoticed possibilities of language. Although prose is ordinarily more sedate than poetry, it too can profit from the touch of originality, the fresh slant, the new twist that fooling around with words can sometimes contribute.

Most frequently, of course, word plays provide a welcome note of humor. "The orchestra played Beethoven last night. Beethoven lost." A *Time* magazine movie review once described a wagon train surrounded by Indians as being "in the Siouxp."

Word plays lend themselves to satire, too. In Shakespeare's *Henry IV, Part I,* Glendower, a braggart with mystical inclinations, is talking to Hotspur, an honest, downright soldier:

> GLENDOWER: I can call spirits from the vasty deep.
>
> HOTSPUR: Why, so can I . . . But will they come when you do call for them?

Other word plays can be entirely serious. In *Walden,* Thoreau simply treats a common figurative expression with unexpected literalness:

> If you have built castles in the air, your work need not be lost; that is where they should be. Now put the foundations under them.

There's no compulsion to experiment with word plays. They're risky. Unsuccessful word plays are always damaging because they call attention to themselves. They should generally be used in moderation; the writer wants to give an impression of being clever, but not of being a show-off. If you have neither the temperament nor the knack for word plays, you should avoid them completely. With all these cautions, however, a distinctive style helps capture your reader's attention, and skillful fooling around with words can help create a distinctive style.

PORTRAITS OF A COP

N. R. KLEINFIELD

Though not a how-to-do-it selection, "Portraits of a Cop" is decidedly a process essay. Here we are told how a highly specialized task is performed, but we are neither expected to do it ourselves, nor are we given any direct instructions. The author provides us with a fascinating, factual account of an art frequently dramatized in movies and television shows—and never taught in art school.

Words to check:

embellishment (paragraph 3)   befuddle (5)

1   A pencil poking out from behind his ear, Arthur Hagenlocher fidgets on his high-legged chair in his box-like office in the old Loft's candy factory at 400 Broome St. in the New York City Hall area. Staring at him are an uncompleted sketch and all manner of pencils and soft erasers. Tacked up on the walls are sketches he and his colleagues have drawn. Except for one of Richard Nixon and another of Alfred E. Newman ("What, me worry?"), the sketches resemble no one recognizable, and Mr. Hagenlocher himself doesn't have any idea who they are supposed to be.

2   "They're just faces to me," he says. "I don't know what their names are, what their occupations are, where they live. To be frank, I haven't any notion who they are. With most of them, I never will."

3   Arthur Hagenlocher makes a career of sketching people he has never met. Told by other people what they look like, he sketches them plainly, without much fine detail or embellishment. When he sketches them well enough, they will look, at best, like any one of several thousand or several million people; at worst, they will look like no one. Every so often, however, his sketches lead to the apprehension of a criminal, which, in fact, is what they are intended to do. Arthur Hagenlocher is a police artist, and everyone he draws is a suspected criminal. . . .

4   When a crime that it witnessed occurs and a detective wishes a sketch, he calls an artist as quickly as possible (one artist is always on call). Either the detective will bring witnesses to the artist's office, or else the artist will hustle to the scene of the crime and work there.

5   First off, Mr. Hagenlocher buttonholes all available witnesses, and weeds out those who, by his judgment, are unreliable. Almost always, Mr. Hagenlocher prefers to deal with just one reliable witness, rather than with many

conflicting voices that simply befuddle him. All too often when he works with several witnesses, there is a clash of facts. "The more witnesses there are, the more confusing it gets," the artist says.

6   Determining who makes the most reliable witness involves perception, interrogation and luck. "There's a lot of psychology involved," Mr. Hagenlocher says. "You can sort of feel a good witness. If someone hesitates, or changes his mind, he's no good. If you have to pull things out of someone, he's no good. If the person just starts telling you about mouths and ears right away, then he's good."

7   Usually, the younger the witness, the better. "Fourteen-year-old kids make great witnesses," Mr. Hagenlocher says. "They remember everything. Old ladies make terrible witnesses. They can't remember anything. You ask a child about a nose, and he'll start telling you about a nose. You ask an adult about a nose, and he'll start telling you about the color of the person's socks." Youngsters also tend to draw their own sketches to help out.

8   Initially, Mr. Hagenlocher tries to put witnesses at ease so they trust him, rather than barging up and identifying himself as a police officer. When questioning someone, the artist tries to exact as much detail as possible about the suspect, though he can get by on remarkably few facts. As a rule, he looks for five features: shape of face, hair, eyes, ears, and mouth. Distinguishing scars, birthmarks, beards, and mustaches are an artist's dream for producing a useful sketch, but they don't often crop up.

9   Mr. Hagenlocher always carts along 150 to 200 of the 900,000 mug shots the police force keeps. Witnesses are asked to leaf through these to try to find a similar face, and then subtle changes can be made in the sketch. "You could use just one photo and work from that," Mr. Hagenlocher says. "Using that as a base, you have the witness compare the hair—is it longer or shorter?—the mouth—is it thinner or wider?—and so forth. But that's harder and takes more time. It's usually much quicker to show him a lot of photos and have them pick one that's close."

10   "But I remember one time," the artist goes on, "when a girl flipped through a mess of photos and finally picked one. 'That looks exactly like him,' she said, 'except the hair was longer, the mouth was wider, the eyes were further part, the nose was smaller and the face was rounder.' She was a big help."

11   Besides the five basic features, Mr. Hagenlocher also questions witnesses about a suspect's apparent nationality and the nature of the language he used. This can be of subtle assistance in sketching the suspect, but it can also sometimes link several sketches together. For instance, if over a short period of time three suspects are described as soft-spoken, in addition to having other similar traits, then chances are they are the same

person. It is also a good idea to ask a witness if a suspect resembled a famous person. Suspects have been compared to Marlon Brando, Rod Steiger, Winston Churchill, Nelson Eddy, Jack Palance, Jackie Gleason, Mick Jagger and a Greek god.

12   After Mr. Hagenlocher completes a sketch, he shows it to the witness or witnesses for their reaction. Usually, there will be lots of minor, and sometimes not too minor, changes to be made. When it's finished, the sketch isn't intended to approach the polished form of a portrait. "We're just trying to narrow down the possibilities," Mr. Hagenlocher says. "If you've just got a big nose and a thin mouth to go with, then at least you've ruled out all the people with small noses and thick mouths. There are still millions of people still in the running, but millions have also been eliminated."

13   From time to time, Mr. Hagenlocher produces no sketch at all. This happens when he receives too many conflicting reports from witnesses, or when a witness can't make up his mind or can't supply sufficient detail. "The whole point is to completely satisfy the witness," Mr. Hagenlocher says. "If the witness isn't satisfied, then I don't turn in a sketch. Some women have cried when they saw my sketch. Others have said, 'No way, no way. That's nothing like him.'" . . .

14   Once a sketch is completed, two photographs are taken of it. These go to the detective who requested the sketch, who can then order copies that can be distributed among police precincts and other forces and departments. The sketch itself, designated by an identification number, the case number, the date drawn and the artist's initials, is filed away in the sketching room. When a suspect is apprehended, the sketch is filed in a different place. Though they are supposed to, detectives don't always notify artists when culprits are caught because they are tied down with new cases. . . .

15   For the time being, Mr. Hagenlocher is content with turning out sketches of people he doesn't know. "There's a tremendous satisfaction," he says. "If you can take a picture of a person after he's apprehended and have it look like your sketch, you say, 'Wow, I can't believe I did that.' But you did."

WHAT DID THE WRITER SAY AND WHAT DID YOU THINK?

1. What do Mr. Hagenlocher's subjects have in common besides being suspected criminals?
2. What does Mr. Hagenlocher need to do before he can begin drawing?
3. What is the major practical value of the pictures?

4. What is the test for whether a picture is ready to be turned over to a detective?

HOW DID THE WRITER SAY IT? _____

1. Is there a clearly stated thesis? If not, is a thesis implied?
2. The author's main concern is to describe how Mr. Hagenlocher does his job. What details in the essay also add human interest by helping us see the artist as an individual?

=============WHAT ABOUT *YOUR* WRITING?=============

Unfortunately, interviews have started to get a bad name. Many people understandably associate interviews with the more sordid side of television journalism. A microphone-wielding busybody asks a mother whose three children have just died in a fire if she feels sad. A scandalmonger, already sure of the identity of the good guys and bad guys, asks prepared—and loaded—questions of a surprised public figure whose possibly honest hesitations and uncertainties are made to appear shifty evasions.

Interviews need not be that way. In "Portraits of a Cop," Kleinfield has used an interview to present a lively and informative account of an unusual profession, much of the account in the interviewed person's own words.

You are unlikely, outside of a journalism class, to be asked to write up an interview, but you can sometimes use interviews to add life and authenticity to more common writing assignments. Are you planning to sound off about food in the school cafeteria? Why not start with a few real quotes from people you've spoken to? Are you thinking about a paper that suggests that tastes in sports reveal a great deal about a person's character? Why rely on a few memories? Why not ask around? Some people will tell you they don't want to be bothered, but most will probably feel mildly flattered and be eager to cooperate. Remember that for a short paper you're usually looking only for interesting tidbits and a few good lines; you're not going to write a four-part report to the nation, and many interviews may take just a minute or two. Name names and quote directly whenever you can. A little material gathered from interviews can add a strong touch of fact to an otherwise purely personal essay.

THE SPIDER AND THE WASP

ALEXANDER PETRUNKEVITCH

Alexander Petrunkevitch (1875–1964) was one of the world's leading authorities on spiders. Born in Russia, he taught at various American universities. His wide range of skills and interests is suggested by his translation of English (to Russian) and Russian (to English) poetry and by such titles as *Index Catalogue of Spiders of North, Central, and South America* (1911). *Choice and Responsibility* (1947), and *Principles of Classification* (1952).

Words to check:

progeny (paragraph 1)	chitinous (9)
archenemy (1)	girth (11)
unwittingly (1)	secretion (13)
tactile (8)	olfactory (14) ˙
nectar (9)	simulating (15)
pungent (9)	

1   In the feeding and safeguarding of their progeny insects and spiders exhibit some interesting analogies to reasoning and some crass examples of blind instinct. The case I propose to describe here is that of the tarantula spiders and their archenemy, the digger wasps of the genus Pepsis. It is a classic example of what looks like intelligence pitted against instinct—a strange situation in which the victim, though fully able to defend itself, submits unwittingly to its destruction.

2   Most tarantulas live in the tropics, but several species occur in the temperate zone and a few are common in the southern U.S. Some varieties are large and have powerful fangs with which they can inflict a deep wound. These formidable looking spiders do not, however, attack man; you can hold one in your hand, if you are gentle, without being bitten. Their bite is dangerous only to insects and small mammals such as mice; for a man it is no worse than a hornet's sting.

3   Tarantulas customarily live in deep cylindrical burrows, from which they emerge at dusk and into which they retire at dawn. Mature males wander about after dark in search of females and occasionally stray into houses. After mating, the male dies in a few weeks, but a female lives much longer and can mate several years in succession. In a Paris museum is a tropical specimen which is said to have been living in captivity for 25 years.

4   A fertilized female tarantula lays from 200 to 400 eggs at a time; thus it is possible for a single tarantula to produce several thousand young. She takes no care of them beyond weaving a cocoon of silk to enclose the eggs. After they hatch, the young walk away, find convenient places in which to dig their burrows and spend the rest of their lives in solitude. The eyesight of tarantulas is poor, being limited to a sensing of change in the intensity of light and to the perception of moving objects. They apparently have little or no sense of hearing, for a hungry tarantula will pay no attention to a loudly chirping cricket placed in its cage unless the insect happens to touch one of its legs.

5   But all spiders, and especially hairy ones, have an extremely delicate sense of touch. Laboratory experiments prove that tarantulas can distinguish three types of touch: pressure against the body wall, stroking of the body hair, and riffling of certain very fine hairs on the legs called trichobothria. Pressure against the body, by the finger or the end of a pencil, causes the tarantula to move off slowly for a short distance. The touch excites no defensive response unless the approach is from above where the spider can see the motion, in which case it rises on its hind legs, lifts its front legs, opens its fangs and holds this threatening posture as long as the object continues to move.

6   The entire body of a tarantula, especially its legs, is thickly clothed with hair. Some of it is short and wooly, some long and stiff. Touching this body hair produces one of two distinct reactions. When the spider is hungry, it responds with an immediate and swift attack. At the touch of a cricket's antennae the tarantula seizes the insect so swiftly that a motion picture taken at the rate of 64 frames per second shows only the result and not the process of capture. But when the spider is not hungry, the stimulation of its hairs merely causes it to shake the touched limb. An insect can walk under its hairy belly unharmed.

7   The trichobothria, very fine hairs growing from disclike membranes on the legs, are sensitive only to air movement. A light breeze makes them vibrate slowly, without disturbing the common hair. When one blows gently on the trichobothria, the tarantula reacts with a quick jerk of its four front legs. If the front and hind legs are stimulated at the same time, the spider makes a sudden jump. This reaction is quite independent of the state of its appetite.

8   These three tactile responses—to pressure on the body wall, to moving of the common hair, and to flexing of the trichobothria—are so different from one another that there is no possibility of confusing them. They serve the tarantula adequately for most of its needs and enable it to avoid most annoyances and dangers. But they fail the spider completely when it meets its deadly enemy, the digger wasp Pepsis.

9   These solitary wasps are beautiful and formidable creatures. Most species are either a deep shiny blue all over, or deep blue with rusty wings. The largest have a wing span of about four inches. They live on nectar. When excited, they give off a pungent odor—a warning that they are ready to attack. The sting is much worse than that of a bee or common wasp, and the pain and swelling last longer. In the adult stage the wasp lives only a few months. The female produces but a few eggs, one at a time at intervals of two or three days. For each egg the mother must provide one adult tarantula, alive but paralyzed. The mother wasp attaches the egg to the paralyzed spider's abdomen. Upon hatching from the egg, the larva is many hundreds of times smaller than its living but helpless victim. It eats no other food and drinks no water. By the time it has finished its single Gargantuan meal and become ready for wasphood, nothing remains of the tarantula but its indigestible chitinous skeleton.

10   The mother wasp goes tarantula-hunting when the egg in her ovary is almost ready to be laid. Flying low over the ground late on a sunny afternoon, the wasp looks for its victim or for the mouth of a tarantula burrow, a round hole edged by a bit of silk. The sex of the spider makes no difference, but the mother is highly discriminating as to species. Each species of Pepsis requires a certain species of tarantula, and the wasp will not attack the wrong species. In a cage with a tarantula which is not its normal prey, the wasp avoids the spider and is usually killed by it in the night.

11   Yet when a wasp finds the correct species, it is the other way about. To identify the species the wasp apparently must explore the spider with her antennae. The tarantula shows an amazing tolerance to this exploration. The wasp crawls under it and walks over it without evoking any hostile response. The molestation is so great and so persistent that the tarantula often rises on all eight legs, as if it were on stilts. It may stand this way for several minutes. Meanwhile the wasp, having satisfied itself that the victim is of the right species, moves off a few inches to dig the spider's grave. Working vigorously with legs and jaws, it excavates a hole 8 to 10 inches deep with a diameter slightly larger than the spider's girth. Now and again the wasp pops out of the hole to make sure that the spider is still there.

12   When the grave is finished, the wasp returns to the tarantula to complete her ghastly enterprise. First she feels it all over once more with her antennae. Then her behavior becomes more aggressive. She bends her abdomen, protruding her sting, and searches for the soft membrane at the point where the spider's legs join its body—the only spot where she can penetrate the horny skeleton. From time to time, as the exasperated spider slowly shifts ground, the wasp turns on her back and slides along with the

aid of her wings, trying to get under the tarantula for a shot at the vital spot. During all this maneuvering, which can last for several minutes, the tarantula makes no move to save itself. Finally the wasp corners it against some obstruction and grasps one of its legs in her powerful jaws. Now at last the harassed spider tries a desperate but vain defense. The two contestants roll over and over on the ground. It is a terrifying sight and the outcome is always the same. The wasp finally manages to thrust her sting into the soft spot and holds it there for a few seconds while she pumps in the poison. Almost immediately the tarantula falls paralyzed on its back. Its legs stop twitching, its heart stops beating. Yet it is not dead, as is shown by the fact that if taken from the wasp it can be restored to some sensitivity by being kept in a moist chamber for several months.

13   After paralyzing the tarantula, the wasp cleans herself by dragging her body along the ground and rubbing her feet, sucks the drop of blood oozing from the wound in the spider's abdomen, then grabs a leg of the flabby, helpless animal in her jaws and drags it down to the bottom of the grave. She stays there for many minutes, sometimes for several hours, and what she does all that time in the dark we do not know. Eventually she lays her egg and attaches it to the side of the spider's abdomen with a sticky secretion. Then she emerges, fills the grave with soil carried bit by bit in her jaws, and finally tramples the ground all around to hide any trace of the grave from prowlers. Then she flies away, leaving her descendant safely started in life.

14   In all this the behavior of the wasp evidently is qualitatively different from that of the spider. The wasp acts like an intelligent animal. This is not to say that instinct plays no part or that she reasons as man does. But her actions are to the point; they are not automatic and can be modified to fit the situation. We do not know for certain how she identifies the tarantula—probably it is by some olfactory or chemo-tactile sense—but she does it purposefully and does not blindly tackle a wrong species.

15   On the other hand, the tarantula's behavior shows only confusion. Evidently the wasp's pawing gives it no pleasure, for it tries to move away. That the wasp is not simulating sexual stimulation is certain, because male and female tarantulas react in the same way to its advances. That the spider is not anesthetized by some odorless secretion is easily shown by blowing lightly at the tarantula and making it jump suddenly. What, then, makes the tarantula behave as stupidly as it does?

16   No clear, simple answer is available. Possibly the stimulation by the wasp's antennae is masked by a heavier pressure on the spider's body, so that it reacts

as when prodded by a pencil. But the explanation may be much more complex. Initiative in attack is not in the nature of tarantulas; most species fight only when cornered so that escape is impossible. Their inherited patterns of behavior apparently prompt them to avoid problems rather than attack them. For example, spiders always weave their webs in three dimensions, and when a spider finds that there is insufficient space to attach certain threads in the third dimension, it leaves the place and seeks another, instead of finishing the web in a single plane. This urge to escape seems to arise under all circumstances, in all phases of life, and to take the place of reasoning. For a spider to change the pattern of its web is as impossible as for an inexperienced man to build a bridge across a chasm obstructing his way.

17   In a way the instinctive urge to escape is not only easier but often more efficient than reasoning. The tarantula does exactly what is most efficient in all cases except in an encounter with a ruthless and determined attacker dependent for the existence of her own species on killing as many tarantulas as she can lay eggs. Perhaps in this case the spider follows its usual pattern of trying to escape, instead of seizing and killing the wasp, because it is not aware of its danger. In any case, the survival of the tarantula species as a whole is protected by the fact that the spider is much more fertile than the wasp.

WHAT DID THE WRITER SAY AND WHAT DID YOU THINK? _____

1. A primary thesis tells why the process is worth discussing. What is the thesis, and where does it appear?
2. A secondary thesis tries to explain why the process happens as it does. What is the thesis, and where does it appear?
3. Does the author acknowledge alternate explanations?
4. What makes the behavior of the spider so puzzling?
5. Where does the author suggest his own emotional reaction to the process?
6. Is the reader meant to take sides, to root for the spider or wasp?
7. People who think they are totally indifferent to nature and science often become deeply involved in "The Spider and the Wasp." Can you suggest why?
8. Can you think of certain types of human beings whose behavior corresponds to the spider's? The wasp's?

HOW DID THE WRITER SAY IT? ————————————————

1. Who is the intended audience for this selection?
2. The description of the process does not begin until paragraph 10, though paragraph 9 presents a summary of the process. What has the author been doing until then?
3. Are all obscure scientific terms defined?
4. Consult the table of contents. What patterns of writing are in this selection besides *process?*
5. Does the author gather the many separate steps into groups? If so, into how many?
6. "The mother wasp goes tarantula-hunting. . . ." Does this phrase seem too informal, almost slangy, for a scientific article? Are there other unusually informal words or phrases? Are they justified?

═══════════════WHAT ABOUT *YOUR* WRITING?═══════════════

Nobody reads "The Spider and the Wasp" as an interesting little essay on the strange behavior of some strange little creatures. Most readers respond because the essay reaches them at a deep emotional level, because it appeals dramatically to some permanent human concerns: in this case, life and death, care of progeny, survival of the fittest, and so on.

You may have read with an amused smile the note at the start of this selection that Petrunkevitch was "one of the world's leading authorities on spiders." But don't you have an esoteric little specialty that you can relate to universal human concerns? If you're an enthusiastic player of video games, you have a beautiful piece on man versus machine that's waiting to be written. If you own tropical fish and have seen adult fish eating their own young, you have the potential for a powerful cruelty-of-nature essay that takes a different approach from Petrunkevitch's. In a sense, you're a specialist on anything that has ever hit you hard. If you ever waited week after week as a child for a "free offer" after you sent in a box top, aren't you "one of the world's leading authorities" on what waiting can do to the soul? Don't shy off from specialties because you're afraid that people won't be interested. Show how the specialty is related to a universal issue, and make them interested.

6

COMPARISON
AND
CONTRAST

A comparison-and-contrast paper is one of the most common kinds of writing assignments because it reflects one of the most common kinds of thinking, the kind of thinking on which most practical decisions are probably based. Comparison and contrast often dominate thought in choosing a college, a major field, a career, a job. We compare and contrast doctors and dentists; husbands and wives (actual and potential) and children; homes, neighborhoods, and cities; breakfast foods, pizza joints, and brands of soda pop. The comparison-and-contrast assignment on an essay exam or composition in an English class is not a remote intellectual exercise but a natural extension of the role played by comparison and contrast in human life.

Just as comparison-and-contrast thinking aims at a decision or judgment— the school I attend, the job offer I accept, the horse I bet on, the toothpaste I buy—so comparison-and-contrast writing must add up to something. Without a thesis, comparison-and-contrast writing is a pointless game in a never-never land where the only activity people engage in is devising elaborate lists of "similarities and differences" or "advantages and disadvantages." The comparison-and-contrast paper must commit itself firmly to the persuasive principle.

Late Dickens novels express a far more pessimistic view of life than early Dickens novels.

Boston is a more exciting city than San Francisco.

The community college can sometimes offer a number of benefits unknown at the four-year college.

The dream and the reality of owning a car are seldom the same.

Sexual discrimination is harder to fight than racial discrimination.

There is no logical way of determining whether Babe Ruth or Henry Aaron was the better home-run hitter.

Three quick pointers:

1. As a matter of common sense and convenience, stick to two units for comparison and contrast. No regulation prohibits three or more units, but two are far easier to manage.

2. Avoid vague, what-else-is-new theses like "There are many similarities between Smith and Jones." The same statement could be made of any two people and is therefore worthless.

3. Don't feel that you need to pay equal attention to comparisons and contrasts. In practice, most papers give much greater weight to similarities (comparisons) *or* to differences (contrasts). Some papers may deal entirely with one or the other; their whole point may be that two seemingly similar items are, in fact, very different or that two seemingly different items are very similar. Check with your instructor whether an all-contrast or all-comparison paper is acceptable. In any event, theses like "Despite obvious differences, drug addiction and alcoholism present strikingly similar psychological problems" are quite common and quite workable. In a paper with that thesis, the "obvious differences" could be taken care of in the introduction, and the rest of the paper would deal solely with the similarities.

PATTERNS

Comparison-and-contrast papers can use one of two patterns, both highly structured. A long paper can sometimes shift patterns from one distinct division of the paper to another, but most papers should stick to one pattern.

BLOCK PATTERN

In the first pattern, the writer discusses one unit in its entirety before going on to the other.

Thesis statement: Boston is a more exciting city than San Francisco.

I. Boston
    A. Cultural opportunities
    B. Recreational opportunities
    C. Sense of history
    D. Physical beauty

II. San Francisco
    A. Cultural opportunities
    B. Recreational opportunities
    C. Sense of history
    D. Physical beauty

Thesis statement: The community college can sometimes offer a number of benefits unknown at the four-year college.

I. Community college
    A. Cost
    B. Convenience
    C. Instructors
    D. Training for a vocation

II. Four-year college
    A. Cost
    B. Convenience
    C. Instructors
    D. Lack of training for a vocation

Notice that in these sample outlines we could easily reverse the order of the major topics. Rather than concluding with negative comments about San Francisco or four-year colleges, some writers may want to stress the positive by ending with praise of Boston or community colleges. Which comes first is up to the writer.

The danger built into the block pattern is that the writer can end up with two separate essays instead of one unified comparison-and-contrast essay. To ensure unity, take note of the following guidelines:

Each Subtopic in Part I Must Also Be Discussed in Part II. Bring up Boston's cultural opportunities only if you have something to say about San Francisco's cultural opportunities or lack of them. Boston's cultural opportunities must be compared with or contrasted to something; in comparison-and-contrast writing, they are not significant in themselves.

Subtopics Should Be Discussed in the Same Order in Both Parts. If cost and convenience are the first two subtopics you consider for community colleges, they should be the first two subtopics when you turn to four-year colleges.

Paragraphing Should Be Similar in Both Parts. A paper with only one or two sentences for each subtopic under "Boston" will probably gather the subtopics together into one good-sized "Boston" paragraph. A paper with a lot to say on each Boston subtopic will probably give a separate paragraph to each. Whatever paragraph arrangement is appropriate for Boston should usually be maintained for San Francisco.

Subtopics in Part II Should Generally Include Reminders of the Point Made About the Same Subtopic in Part I. Since in the block pattern you consider the first unit (Boston, community colleges) before moving on to the second (San Francisco, four-year colleges), your readers may experience some memory lapses by the time they finally reach Part II. Their memories need refreshing. Above all, they should not be allowed to forget that they are reading a single comparison-and-contrast paper rather than two separate essays. In the paragraph outlines that follow, note the italicized reminders:

¶ 1—Presentation of thesis: Boston is a more exciting city than San Francisco.

Start of ¶ 2—Boston's cultural opportunities are unrivaled anywhere in the country . . .

Start of ¶ 3—Recreational opportunities in Boston are every bit as impressive . . .

Start of ¶ 4—The sense of a rich, still vital past adds to the excitement of Boston . . .

Start of ¶ 5—Finally, Boston is a surprising delight to the eye . . .

Start of ¶ 6—When we look at San Francisco, we find a cultural scene that, *in sharp contrast to Boston's* . . .

Start of ¶ 7—San Francisco's recreational opportunities, though plentiful, also *suffer when placed against the something-for-everyone of Boston* . . .

Start of ¶ 8—The sense of a living history in San Francisco *seems bland and shallow when we think of Boston* . . .

Start of ¶ 9—Even in its overwhelming physical beauty, San Francisco *fails to surpass the breathtaking charm of Boston* . . .

Start of ¶ 1—Presentation of thesis: The community college can sometimes offer a number of benefits unknown at the four-
year college.

Start of ¶ 2—First, community colleges are cheap . . .

Start of ¶ 3—Second, they are incredibly convenient . . .

Start of ¶ 4—Third, most instructors are likely to be experienced and
readily available . . .

Start of ¶ 5—Last, community colleges offer the practical education
most students want . . .

Start of ¶ 6—At many four-year colleges, the cost of attending is so
astronomically greater than at community colleges
that . . .

Start of ¶ 7—*Contrasting dramatically to the convenience of a community college,* a four-year college . . .

Start of ¶ 8—*Instead of meeting full-time, professional teachers,* the
beginning student at a four-year college will more
probably . . .

Start of ¶ 9—Finally, many four-year colleges are still fighting against
*the vocational trends in education that the community
colleges have welcomed* . . .

ALTERNATING PATTERN

This pattern can be thought of as a seesaw. It swings back and forth between
its two subjects.

Thesis statement: Boston is a more exciting city than San Francisco.

I.   Cultural opportunities
   A. Boston
   B. San Francisco

II. Recreational opportunities
   A. Boston
   B. San Francisco

III. Sense of history
   A. Boston
   B. San Francisco

IV. Physical beauty
   A. Boston
   B. San Francisco

Thesis statement: The community college can sometimes offer a number of benefits unknown at the four-year college.

I. Cost
   A. Community college
   B. Four-year college
II. Convenience
   A. Community college
   B. Four-year college
III. Instructors
   A. Community college
   B. Four-year college
IV. Training for a vocation
   A. Community college
   B. Four-year college

Most of the principles applicable to the block pattern still hold. You still say something about both subjects for each issue considered; you still use a consistent order (observe how "Boston" and "Community college" always come first); you still make a consistent arrangement of paragraphs. The major difference is that reminders are not nearly as important as in the block pattern. Instead of getting to San Francisco's cultural opportunities one or two pages after dealing with Boston's cultural opportunities, you'll be getting to them in the very next sentences.

WHICH PATTERN?

Both patterns enable you to write what you want. Both patterns cover the same territory, though in different order. In many cases, you can probably do a good job with either pattern, so your decision may be more a matter of taste than anything else. It is possible, however, to make some distinctions between patterns, and for whatever the distinctions are worth, here are a couple to keep in mind:

The Block Pattern Tends to Work Better for Short Papers, Alternating for Long Papers. In short papers, alternating can sometimes bounce back and forth between subjects too frequently to let anything settle in the reader's mind. In long papers, the block pattern can put too much of a burden on the reader's memory: the reader should not have to wonder on page 7 what it was that you said on page 2, and you may be forced to spend a disproportionate amount of time and words on reminders.

The Block Pattern Tends to Work Better with Few Subtopics, Alternating with Many.   With only a few subtopics, the reader should have no difficulty keeping track of them. You can safely make your four points about Boston and then go on to San Francisco. The seesaw, back-and-forth movement of alternating could be somewhat distracting. With many subtopics, alternating is probably safest; if you had a dozen or more elements to consider about Boston and San Francisco, for example, discussing each city one after the other within each element would make the comparison-and-contrast relationship immediately clear. The block pattern could again put a fierce strain on the reader's memory and patience.

WRITING SUGGESTIONS FOR COMPARISON-AND-CONTRAST THEMES

Comparison-and-contrast writing offers almost endless variations in choice of subject. The subjects listed here may be less valuable for themselves than for bringing other subjects to your mind. In any event, don't forget the necessity for a thesis and for sticking to one of the two patterns of organization.

1. Two household chores.
2. Life in a city vs. life in a suburb; life in two cities or two suburbs.
3. Two commercial products: razor blades, hair sprays, tires, breakfast foods.
4. Two department stores or discount stores.
5. Contrasting fates of two married couples.
6. Two sports or two athletes: baseball vs. football, football vs. soccer, Michael Jordan vs. Magic Johnson, and so on.
7. Two clergymen or two churches.
8. Two movies or television programs (should be of same basic type: Westerns, horror movies, situation comedies).
9. Two politicians.
10. Two musicians or singers.
11. Conflicting viewpoints on controversial subjects: capital punishment, abortions, and so on.

12. Two character traits or emotions that can be confused: courage and recklessness, love and infatuation.
13. Two high schools or two colleges; high school versus college.
14. Two teachers with contrasting educational philosophies.
15. Dogs versus cats.
16. Attitude you had as a child versus attitude you have now toward parents, religion, sex, and so on.
17. Contrast between advertising claims and reality.
18. Two "dates."
19. Two tourist attractions.
20. Two employers.

BLOCK PATTERN

Rockin' Beethoven

Tanya Washington (student)

Thesis: I love both classical music and rock and roll.

    I.   Classical music
        A. For quiet and thoughtful moods
           1. Helps creative thought
           2. Helps solve problems
        B. A mental pleasure
           1. Aids concentration
           2. Serves as mental exercise

   II.   Rock and roll
        A. For self-indulgent moods
           1. Puts me in a "party" mood
           2. Wakes me up
        B. A physical pleasure
           1. Makes me dance, not think
           2. Fills my need for power and emotion

Conclusion: Classical music and rock and roll both have much to offer any music fan.

I am a big music fan. I spend all my extra money on tapes and CD's. I go to concerts whenever I can, and I find it almost impossible to drive anywhere without the car stereo going. I confuse a lot of people with my love of music, though, because I'm just as likely to slide a tape of Bach's Goldberg Variations into the player as I am to slap on my newest Replacements album. In fact, it's not even all that unusual to find me blasting Beethoven on the radio while driving to a U2 concert. You see, for very different reasons, but with very great devotion, I love both classical music and rock and roll.

Classical music is what I like best when I'm feeling quiet and thoughtful. Its artistry serves both as a wonderful background for creative thought and as a way to lift me out of and beyond whatever troubles me. I write better when I listen to classical music. I calm my mind and solve my problems by allowing its intricate and delicate constructions to overwhelm and distract me. Classical music soothes me and releases me.

Listening to classical music is also a mental pleasure for me. Something about it stimulates my mind and forces me to pay attention to structure and form with a concentration which surprises me. Discovering how different composers repeat, rework, and revise a musical theme throughout one piece is, for me, as good a mental exercise as analyzing a great poem for English class. Classical music feeds my mind.

But then, of course, there's rock and roll. While classical music suits my solemn moods, rock and roll is for when I feel a little self-indulgent. I listen to rock when I'm getting ready for a party, when I want to feel like life is a party, or when I want to convince myself that, no matter what happens, the party goes on. While classical music calms me, rock wakes me up by making my life shake, rattle, and roll to a solid back beat.

Rock and roll is a physical pleasure. I like my rock so loud I can feel it through the soles of my feet. Rock doesn't ask me to think. It tells me to shut up and dance. So I do. Though they are pleasant surprises when I find them, I don't look for structure, form, or artistry in rock music. I look, instead, for power, emotion, and something that makes me dance 'til I hurt. Classical music is for my mind, but rock is for my blood, bone, and muscle.

If you're a classical fan who has never heard of Peter Gabriel, or if you're a rock fan who has never given Vivaldi a shot, open up your mind. Wander over to a music store and try something new. You just might find a whole new musical world.

ALTERNATING PATTERN
Highs and Lows

Emily Alexander (student)

Thesis: Except for one small similarity, high- and low-maintenance women are completely different.

    I.   Clothing
        A. High maintenance
          1. Fancy clothes
          2. Impractical underwear
          3. Uncomfortable shoes
        B. Low maintenance
          1. Ordinary clothes
          2. Practical underwear
          3. Sneakers

   II.   Lunch
        A. High maintenance
          1. Gourmet food
          2. Pretty drinks and light beer
        B. Low maintenance
          1. Fast food
          2. Hard liquor and anything but light beer

 III. Lifestyles
        A. High maintenance
          1. Boyfriends with fancy names
          2. Glamorous jobs and cars
          3. Perfect nails, hair, and children
        B. Low maintenance
          1. Boyfriends with ordinary names
          2. Messy jobs and cars
          3. Natural nails, hair, and children

Conclusion: Each type secretly wants to be the other.

Some women need two hours to prepare for a trip to the grocery store. Others can get ready to go anywhere in twenty minutes or less. Some women never leave the house without foundation, powder, blusher, lipstick, three shades of eye shadow, eyeliner, and mascara on their faces. Some women slap on a little Chapstick and feel "made-up." Some women are high maintenance. Others are low maintenance. Both types are completely different from the other in all but one way.

When high-maintenance women get dressed, they put on real leather, handmade lace, anything that must be dry-cleaned. Their clothes are in colors like "Sienna," "Atmosphere," and "Aubergine." Their underwear is lacy, filmy, satiny stuff from Victoria's Secret. Their shoes have four-inch heels and are incredibly painful.

Low-maintenance women wear blue jeans, cotton/polyester knits, anything that won't wrinkle, and clothes that don't show stains. They wear white cotton underwear like their mothers did, and pin the ripped elastic with safety pins. They wear sneakers, and in the back of their closet they have one pair of high heels for weddings and funerals.

High-maintenance women "do" lunch. They have avocado, artichoke and palm-heart salad, tossed in a light vinaigrette, followed by a fresh fruit sorbet. They drink white wine or anything that looks pretty. On the weekend they drink light beer, if they drink beer at all.

Low-maintenance women eat lunch. They have hamburgers, fries, or steak sandwiches. They always spill something. Yoo-hoo and Ho-ho's are their favorite desserts. Low-maintenance women drink scotch or vodka. On the weekend, they drink everything but light beer.

High-maintenance women date men named Brad or Colin or Richard. They work in glamorous, air-conditioned jobs and park their dashing sports cars in personalized spaces. Their nails are always manicured, their hair is always combed, and they think little Eloise is a perfect child.

Low-maintenance women date men named Mike or Tony or Fred. They work long, hard, and messy jobs, and their mini-vans and station wagons usually have a week's supply of groceries in the back. Their nails and hair are sensibly short, and they love little Betsy but think she's a brat.

High-maintenance women and low-maintenance women each secretly want to be the other type.

HIS TALK, HER TALK

JOYCE MAYNARD

While a sophomore at Yale, Joyce Maynard published her first book, *Looking Backward: A Chronicle of Growing Up Old in the Sixties* (1973). Currently she is a newspaper columnist. Her other books include *Baby Love* (1981), *New House* (1987), and *To Die For* (1992). "His Talk, Her Talk" first appeared as a newspaper column in 1985.

Words to check:

innate (paragraph 1)	broached (8)
dissolution (7)	savor (9)
capsulize (7)	quantum mechanics (10)

1   It can be risky these days to suggest that there are any innate differences between men and women, other than those of anatomy. Out the window go the old notions about man and aggression, woman and submission (don't even say the word), man and intellect, woman and instinct. If I observe that my infant son prefers pushing a block along the floor while making car noises to cradling a doll in his arms and singing lullabies (and he does)— well, I can only conclude that, despite all our earnest attempts at nonsexist child-rearing, he has already suffered environmental contamination. Some of it, no doubt unwittingly, came from my husband and me, reared in the days when nobody winced if you recited that old saw about what little girls and little boys are made of.

2   I do not believe, of course, that men are smarter, steadier, more high-minded than women. But one or two notions are harder to shake—such as the idea that there is such a thing as "men's talk" or "women's talk." And that it's a natural instinct to seek out, on occasion, the company of one's own sex, exclude members of the other sex and not feel guilty about it.

3   Oh, but we do. At a party I attended the other night, for instance, it suddenly became apparent that all the women were in one room and all the men were in the other. Immediately, we redistributed ourselves, which was a shame. No one had suggested we segregate. The talk in the kitchen was simply, all the women felt, more interesting.

4   What was going on in the kitchen was a particular sort of conversation that I love and that most men I know would wash and wax the car, change the oil filter and vacuum the upholstery to avoid. There is a way women talk

with other women, and, I gather, a way that men talk when in the company of other men. They are not at all the same.

5   I think I know my husband very well, but I have no idea what goes on when he and his male friends get together. Neither can he picture what can keep a woman friend and me occupied for three hours over a single pot of coffee.

6   The other day, after a long day of work, my husband, Steve, and his friend Dave stopped at a bar for a few beers. When he got home, I asked what they had talked about. "Oh, the usual." Like what? "Firewood. Central America. Trucks. The Celtics. Religion. You know."

7   No, not really. I had only recently met with my friend Ann and her friend Sally at a coffee shop nearby, and what we talked about was the workshop Sally would be holding that weekend concerning women's attitudes toward their bodies; Ann's 11-year-old daughter's upcoming slumber party, how hard it is to buy jeans, and the recent dissolution of a friend's five-year marriage. Asked to capsulize our afternoon's discussion, in a form similar to my husband's outline of his night out, I would say we talked about life, love, happiness and heartbreak. Larry Bird's name never came up.

8   I don't want to reinforce old stereotypes of bubble-headed women (Lucy and Ethel), clinking their coffee cups over talk of clothes and diets while the men remove themselves to lean on mantels, puff on cigars and muse about world politics, machines and philosophy. A group of women talking, it seems to me, is likely to concern itself with matters just as pressing as those broached by my husband and his friends. It might be said, in fact, that we're really talking about the same eternal conflicts. Our styles are just different.

9   When Steve tells a story, the point is, as a rule, the ending, and getting there by the most direct route. It may be a good story, told with beautiful precision, but he tells it the way he eats a banana: in three efficient chews, while I cut mine up and savor it. He can (although this is rare) spend 20 minutes on the telephone with one of his brothers, tantalizing me with occasional exclamations of amazement or shock, and then after hanging up, reduce the whole conversation for me to a one-sentence summary. I, on the other hand, may take three quarters of an hour describing some figure from my past while he waits—with thinly veiled impatience—for the point to emerge. Did this fellow just get elected to the House of Representatives? Did he die and leave me his fortune?

10   In fairness to Steve, I must say that, for him, not talking about something doesn't necessarily mean not dealing with it. And he does listen to what I have to say. He likes a good story, too. It's just that, given a choice, he'd rather hear about quantum mechanics or the history of the Ford Mustang. Better yet, he'd rather play ball.

WHAT DID THE WRITER SAY AND WHAT DID YOU THINK?

1. What is Maynard's thesis? Does she state it or imply it?
2. What do you think Maynard means when she writes in paragraph 2, "But one or two notions are harder to shake—. . . ."
3. Does Maynard indicate why, as she puts it, this "natural instinct" remains entrenched? Does she see the difference as a problem? Explain your answer.
4. Are the different topics which Maynard cites for men and women realistic? Do you believe her observations are accurate?
5. In paragraphs 3 and 4, Maynard mentions that the women were talking in the kitchen. Do you think that the place of conversation is significant? Why or why not?
6. Does Maynard indicate any similarities between "men's talk" and "women's talk"? If so, what are they?

HOW DID THE WRITER SAY IT?

1. How long is Maynard's introduction?
2. Maynard uses numerous examples to illustrate the types of "talk." Why are such examples essential to the essay's purpose?
3. What organizational pattern(s) does the author use?
4. How does the "banana" symbolism in paragraph 9 show both difference and similarity between "men's talk" and "women's talk"?
5. How does Maynard's use of first-person experience affect the essay? Would the third-person formal point of view have been a better choice? Why or why not?

WHAT ABOUT *YOUR* WRITING?

"Never begin a sentence with *and.*" The only real problem with that rule is that it shouldn't be a rule at all. It's good enough *advice,* as far as it goes. When readers see *and* at the start of a sentence, their first thought is likely to be that the word introduces a tacked-on idea that logically should be part of the previous sentence. More often than not, they are right.

Still, there's no rule. Precisely because most sentences don't and shouldn't begin with *and,* many good writers sometimes use the word to single out a sentence for special notice and dramatic emphasis. Joyce Maynard does it in the third sentence of paragraph 2 of "His Talk, Her Talk." Abraham Lincoln does it in his "Second Inaugural Address":

> Both parties deprecated war; but one of them would make war rather than let the nation survive; and the other would accept war rather than let it perish. And the war came.

In the powerful last paragraph of Edgar Allan Poe's "The Masque of the Red Death," we find a virtual festival of *ands,* here used not only for dramatic force, but to suggest the eloquence of the King James version of the Bible— many sentences of which also begin with *and.*

> And now was acknowledged the presence of the Red Death. He had come like a thief in the night. And one by one dropped the revellers in the blood-bedewed halls of their revel, and died each in the despairing posture of his fall. And the life of the ebony clock went out with that of the last of the gay. And the flames of the tripods expired. And Darkness and Decay and the Red Death held illimitable dominion over all.

The moral is simple: Sentences shouldn't begin with *and* except in special circumstances. In special circumstances, *and* can be effective. When it is effective—clearly effective—use it. There's no rule.

TWO VARIETIES OF KILLERS

ELLEN CURRIE

Ellen Currie's novel *Available Light* was published in 1986, the same year "Two Varieties of Killers" appeared in the *New York Times.* As you read, note that Currie contrasts not only the crimes and the killers, but also the responses of the public.

Words to check:

decorous (paragraph 1)   indicted (8)
portentous (4)   antics (10)
bounden (4)   mediagenic (10)
pathology (7)   glib (12)
savaged (8)   caddish (13)

1   Henry James,[1] like many decorous and respectable people, entertained a lively interest in murder. He was a fan of the Scottish solicitor William Roughead, who wrote about real-life crime for the first 40 years of this century; James once told Mr. Roughead he was interested in crime because through it "manners and morals become clearly disclosed." He urged Mr. Roughead to write about "the dear old human and sociable murders and adulteries and forgeries in which we are so agreeably at home. And don't tell me, for charity's sake, that your supply runs short."

2   Contemporary supplies of murder, adultery and forgery remain abundant. But crime seems to me less sociable these days, if I am right in taking "sociable" to mean human and comprehensible and even sympathetic. The crimes get bigger and more horrible, and yet we are not sufficiently horrified by them; we pay less and less attention to the manners and the morals they disclose.

3   Look at the difference, for example, between the crimes of Madeleine Smith, who stirred arsenic into her lover's cocoa in 1857, and the convicted killer Theodore R. Bundy, who has been linked with the murders of 36 women he didn't even know.

4   Madeleine Smith, whose case greatly interested Henry James (he called her a "portentous young person"), was the daughter of a Glasgow architect. In 1855, when she was 19, she crossed paths with a young Frenchman. He was handsome, Mr. Roughead wrote, but "socially impossible." They met in secret and wrote to each other constantly. When they became lovers Miss Smith's letters took on what Mr. Roughead described as "a tropical and abandoned tone." They were indelicate letters, naive and outspoken. Another scholar of crime has pointed out that in a day when sex was supposed to be no more than a woman's bounden duty, Madeleine Smith found it a pagan festival.

5   Her lover kept her letters, 198 of them. When she accepted an older, richer and more settled suitor, she asked for the letters' return. Wild with jealousy, her lover claimed he would return them only to her father. That prospect drove Miss Smith mad with shame and fear. She bought arsenic. Her lover soon died of arsenic poisoning. She was brought to trial and conducted herself with great dignity. The verdict: not proven.

6   These people are not admirable, but they are real. Their awful situation is comprehensible; a blown-up, highly colored version of the kind of dilemma ordinary people face. Madeleine Smith's crime was personal. It was a crime of passion.

[1] American/British writer (1843–1916).

7   The case of Ted Bundy is different. To me, it is not "sociable," not comprehensible on any human scale. It is peculiarly impersonal. He didn't even
know his victims; they represented an abstraction—women. His are crimes
not of passion but pathology. Our reaction to them seems to me to partake of
pathology too.

8   According to the reports I have read, some law enforcement officials say
Mr. Bundy may have killed more than 36 young women in sexual crimes
across the country. (Like Madeleine Smith, Ted Bundy says he is innocent of
any crime.) He has been convicted of battering to death, early on Super Bowl
Sunday 1978 in the Chi Omega sorority house at Florida State University, two
young women. He hideously beat two more young women in the same house
and, blocks away, savaged another young woman. He didn't know any of
them. Captured and charged, Mr. Bundy was also indicted in the kidnapping
and murder of a 12-year-old girl. He didn't know her, either. He was convicted of all charges. His execution, scheduled for July 3, was indefinitely
postponed to give his lawyers time to frame an appeal.[2]

9   The young women Ted Bundy has been convicted of killing, and is suspected of killing, resemble, an investigator said, "everyone's daughter."
Their photographs show the sweet faces of their youth, the long hair of their
period. Except for those who loved them, their identities overlap now, and
blur. These women are not vivid and defined because they did nothing to
bring about their deaths. They were not Ted Bundy's angry and discarded
lovers. They did not refuse to return his disastrous, impassioned letters.
They didn't know him.

10   At first all these deaths of pretty young women attracted wide public notice. But once Mr. Bundy was apprehended, the attention was all on his antics and not on the innocent dead. Bundy is a 20th century phenomenon. He
is mediagenic. He is handsome, usually described as a former law student
and witty, brilliant, charming, polished. Oddly, these latter qualities do not
come through in any of the several books about him. Mr. Bundy was once
active in Republican politics; there are those who profess to believe that he
might ultimately have been elected to high public office had he stayed the
course. He has twice made dramatic escapes from custody. He has acted as
his own counsel in sensational televised trials. He has been the subject of a
television movie. Ted Bundy T-shirts, for, against, and smart aleck ("Ted
Bundy is a one-night stand"), have enjoyed popularity. So have jingles: "Let's
salute the mighty Bundy / Here on Friday, gone on Monday / All his roads
lead out of town / It's hard to keep a good man down." Bundy Burgers and a

---

[2] Bundy was executed in 1989.

Bundy cocktail had some play in a Colorado bar. Groupies have gathered at his trials. He gets a lot of mail.

11   Theodore Bundy is said by psychiatrists to be an antisocial personality, a man without conscience. In a strange, third-person meditation on the killings, Mr. Bundy described the rapes and murders as "inappropriate acting out."

12   Perhaps Ted Bundy doesn't labor under a conscience. But how about the rest of us? Shouldn't we feel more revulsion, more grief for those young lives? Something vile has happened to our ideas of what is valuable and what is waste. Perhaps we have seen too much evil and on too grand a scale. We are glib and dismissive of the moral issues. We think Mr. Bundy is good for a laugh. We made him a celebrity. (Richard Schickel, in his book "Intimate Strangers," about the nature of celebrity in modern society, contends that multiple murderers have grasped the essentials of the celebrity system better than normal people.)

13   Crime does disclose on manners and on morals. If people must kill people, I have to put my dollar down on wicked Madeleine Smith. With her sexy letters, poisoned cocoa, caddish lover, she dealt in death. But she is piercingly familiar. Ted Bundy's unspeakable crimes and our cheap reaction to them reveal us to ourselves in a strange and deathly light.

WHAT DID THE WRITER SAY AND WHAT DID YOU THINK?

1. What is the thesis?
2. Define "sociable crime" in your own words.
3. What similarities exist between Madeleine Smith and Ted Bundy?
4. What does Currie think modern crime says about modern society?
5. What do you think made Bundy so "popular" with the public?
6. Why is Madeleine Smith "piercingly familiar?"

HOW DID THE WRITER SAY IT?

1. Which comparison-contrast pattern is used in this essay?
2. The phrase "wicked" describes Madeleine Smith in the last paragraph. What word or words could describe Ted Bundy?
3. Comment on Bundy's description of his behavior as "inappropriate acting out." What behavior would such a comment usually refer to?
4. Is there a specific thesis statement? If so, where?

===============WHAT ABOUT *YOUR* WRITING?===============

Note how many words of qualification and caution are spread through the Currie essay. The author needs to demonstrate her awareness that she is dealing with matters of speculation, not scientific and mathematical truths. She can't prove her points; she can only make them seem plausible. The persuasive power of the essay depends in part on whether Currie strikes the reader as reliable, a sensible person studying complex phenomena and trying to draw reasonable inferences from them.

In the second paragraph alone we find the phrases "seems to me" and "if I am right." In paragraph 7 we find "To me" and "seems to me." In the next paragraph we find "According to the reports I have read." Currie establishes a tone of reason; more, she establishes herself as a person of reason, a person with a fitting hesitation about insisting on the absolute truth of her own ideas. When you, like Currie, are presenting ideas that are necessarily speculative and subjective, it's good policy to use Currie's techniques of qualification and caution.

Don't go overboard, of course. Don't write *in my opinion* in every other sentence. Don't confuse being reasonable with being timid. Don't write cowardly nonsense like *I think that George Washington played an important part in the American Revolution* or *It seems to me that heroin is a dangerous drug.* Present the strongest case you can as strongly as you can. Currie goes all out in presenting her case, too, once she's laid the foundations. The foundations are important, however, and the wise writer will not neglect them.

CONVERSATIONAL BALLGAMES

NANCY MASTERSON SAKAMOTO

This frequently anthologized selection from Nancy Sakamoto's textbook *Polite Fictions* (1982) is considered something of a modern classic in using comparison-and-contrast techniques to explain elusive and difficult issues. Sakamoto, coauthor of *Mutual Understanding of Different Cultures* (1981) is professor of American Studies at Shitennoji Gakuen University.

1   After I was married and had lived in Japan for a while, my Japanese gradually improved to the point where I could take part in simple conversations with

my husband and his friends and family. And I began to notice that often, when I joined in, the others would look startled, and the conversational topic would come to a halt. After this happened several times, it became clear to me that I was doing something wrong. But for a long time, I didn't know what it was.

2   Finally, after listening carefully to many Japanese conversations, I discovered what my problem was. Even though I was speaking Japanese, I was handling the conversation in a western way.

3   Japanese-style conversations develop quite differently from western-style conversations. And the difference isn't only in the languages. I realized that just as I kept trying to hold western-style conversations even when I was speaking Japanese, so my English students kept trying to hold Japanese-style conversations even when they were speaking English. We were unconsciously playing entirely different conversational ballgames.

4   A western-style conversation between two people is like a game of tennis. If I introduce a topic, a conversational ball, I expect you to hit it back. If you agree with me, I don't expect you simply to agree and do nothing more. I expect you to add something—a reason for agreeing, another example, or an elaboration to carry the idea further. But I don't expect you always to agree. I am just as happy if you question me, or challenge me, or completely disagree with me. Whether you agree or disagree, your response will return the ball to me.

5.   And then it is my turn again. I don't serve a new ball from my original starting line. I hit your ball back again from where it has bounced. I carry your idea further, or answer your questions or objections, or challenge or question you. And so the ball goes back and forth, with each of us doing our best to give it a new twist, an original spin, or a powerful smash.

6   And the more vigorous the action, the more interesting and exciting the game. Of course, if one of us gets angry, it spoils the conversation, just as it spoils a tennis game. But getting excited is not at all the same as getting angry. After all, we are not trying to hit each other. We are trying to hit the ball. So long as we attack only each other's opinions, and do not attack each other personally, we don't expect anyone to get hurt. A good conversation is supposed to be interesting and exciting.

7   If there are more than two people in the conversation, then it is like doubles in tennis, or like volleyball. There's no waiting in line. Whoever is nearest and quickest hits the ball, and if you step back, someone else will hit it. No one stops the game to give you a turn. You're responsible for taking your own turn.

8   But whether it's two players or a group, everyone does his best to keep the ball going, and no one person has the ball for very long.

9   A Japanese-style conversation, however, is not at all like tennis or volley-ball. It's like bowling. You wait for your turn. And you always know your place in line. It depends on such things as whether you are older or younger, a close friend or a relative stranger to the previous speaker, in a senior or junior position, and so on.

10   When your turn comes, you step up to the starting line with your bowling ball, and carefully bowl it. Everyone else stands back and watches politely, murmuring encouragement. Everyone waits until the ball has reached the end of the alley, and watches to see if it knocks down all the pins, or only some of them, or none of them. There is a pause, while everyone registers your score.

11   Then, after everyone is sure that you have completely finished your turn, the next person in line steps up to the same starting line, with a different ball. He doesn't return your ball, and he does not begin from where your ball stopped. There is no back and forth at all. All the balls run parallel. And there is always a suitable pause between turns. There is no rush, no excitement, no scramble for the ball.

12   No wonder everyone looked startled when I took part in Japanese conversations. I paid no attention to whose turn it was, and kept snatching the ball halfway down the alley and throwing it back at the bowler. Of course the conversation died. I was playing the wrong game.

13   This explains why it is almost impossible to get a western-style conversation or discussion going with English students in Japan. I used to think that the problem was their lack of English language ability. But I finally came to realize that the biggest problem is that they, too, are playing the wrong game.

14   Whenever I serve a volleyball, everyone just stands back and watches it fall, with occasional murmurs of encouragement. No one hits it back. Everyone waits until I call on someone to take a turn. And when that person speaks, he doesn't hit my ball back. He serves a new ball. Again, everyone just watches it fall.

15   So I call on someone else. This person does not refer to what the previous speaker has said. He also serves a new ball. Nobody seems to have paid any attention to what anyone else has said. Everyone begins again from the same starting line, and all the balls run parallel. There is never any back and forth. Everyone is trying to bowl with a volleyball.

16   And if I try a simpler conversation, with only two of us, then the other person tries to bowl with my tennis ball. No wonder foreign English teachers in Japan get discouraged.

17   Now that you know about the difference in the conversational ballgames, you may think that all your troubles are over. But if you have been trained all your life to play one game, it is no simple matter to switch to another, even if you know the rules. Knowing the rules is not at all the same thing as playing the game.

18   Even now, during a conversation in Japanese I will notice a startled reaction, and belatedly realize that once again I have rudely interrupted by instinctively trying to hit back the other person's bowling ball. It is no easier for me to "just listen" during a conversation, than it is for my Japanese students to "just relax" when speaking with foreigners. Now I can truly sympathize with how hard they must find it to try to carry on a western-style conversation.

19   If I have not yet learned to do conversational bowling in Japanese, at least I have figured out one thing that puzzled me for a long time. After his first trip to America, my husband complained that Americans asked him so many questions and made him talk so much at the dinner table that he never had a chance to eat. When I asked him why he couldn't talk and eat at the same time, he said that Japanese do not customarily think that dinner, especially on fairly formal occasions, is a suitable time for extended conversation.

20   Since westerners think that conversation is an indispensable part of dining, and indeed would consider it impolite not to converse with one's dinner partner, I found this Japanese custom rather strange. Still, I could accept it as a cultural difference even though I didn't really understand it. But when my husband added, in explanation, that Japanese consider it extremely rude to talk with one's mouth full, I got confused. Talking with one's mouth full is certainly not an American custom. We think it very rude, too. Yet we still manage to talk a lot and eat at the same time. How do we do it?

21   For a long time, I couldn't explain it, and it bothered me. But after I discovered the conversational ballgames, I finally found the answer. Of course! In a western-style conversation, you hit the ball, and while someone else is hitting it back, you take a bite, chew, and swallow. Then you hit the ball again, and then eat some more. The more people there are in the conversation, the more chances you have to eat. But even with only two of you talking, you still have plenty of chances to eat.

22   Maybe that's why polite conversation at the dinner table has never been a traditional part of Japanese etiquette. Your turn to talk would last so long without interruption that you'd never get a chance to eat.

WHAT DID THE WRITER SAY AND WHAT DID YOU THINK?

1. What is the thesis?
2. What are the sports to which conversations are compared?
3. What specifically makes class discussions so difficult for an English-speaking teacher in Japan?
4. What determines a person's "place in line" in a Japanese conversation?
5. Why does Sakamoto describe her husband's difficulty with dinner-table conversation? How well does this section of the essay fit with the rest?
6. Does the author prefer one form of conversation to another? How can you tell?

HOW DID THE WRITER SAY IT?

1. In which pattern is the essay written? Is more than one pattern used?
2. Do the sports analogies make the author's points more interesting? Easier to understand?
3. How do humorous touches contribute to the success of this essay?
4. Is the thesis ever stated specifically? If so, where?

WHAT ABOUT *YOUR* WRITING?

At one time or another, nearly every English teacher starts chatting with a student about writing, and more often than seems possible, this kind of scene takes place.

"You write well enough," says the teacher. "But I wonder if you can't try for a little more life in your writing. Don't be so stiff, so formal. Drop in a personal touch now and then."

"A personal touch?" asks the student.

"Well, yes. If you're writing about the generation gap or something like that, don't just come on like a professional sociologist. Start out with an argument you once had with your parents. Then get into the sociology, if you have to."

"You mean I can use *I* if I want to?"

"?"

"We were never allowed to use *I.* "

"?"

It seems that a lot of students had high school teachers who understandably got upset with weasel sentences like "I think that Abraham Lincoln was an important figure in American history" and personal letters like "I remember last week you said in class that Hemingway started his writing career as a newspaper reporter, and I wonder what you think of this idea I came up with." So the teacher made up a rule that prohibited the use of *I.* It's possible to sympathize with the teacher, but the rule has nothing to do with the realities of writing.

Sakamoto's essay successfully breaks the ice by using the "I" approach. The author has some serious discussion of complex social and cultural differences in store for her audience, and it makes good sense to do what she can to create a reader-friendly atmosphere. Using *I* in your writing is neither good nor bad in itself, but when *I* works, go ahead.

You're allowed.

THE LOWEST ANIMAL

MARK TWAIN

"All modern American literature comes from one book by Mark Twain called *Huckleberry Finn,*" Ernest Hemingway once wrote. "There was nothing before. There has been nothing as good since." Mark Twain was the pen name used by Samuel L. Clemens (1835-1910). Mississippi steamboat pilot, Nevada newspaperman, novelist, publisher, lecturer, scathing social critic, brooding philosopher—Mark Twain is one of the giants.

"The Lowest Animal" is one of a group of essays, unpublished during Mark Twain's lifetime, that has been collectively entitled *The Damned Human Race.* It was written between 1905 and 1909. The author felt that this selection was too controversial and too bitter to be accepted by the public. Do you agree?

Words to check:

conjectured (paragraph 2)	concubines (10)
postulate (2)	atrocious (10)
quadrupeds (5)	prior (13)
anaconda (7)	zealot (13)
scrupled (8)	multitudinous (17)
chicane (8)	ineradicable (22)

1   I have been studying the traits and dispositions of the "lower animals" (so-called), and contrasting them with the traits and dispositions of man. I find the result humiliating to me. For it obliges me to renounce my allegiance to the Darwinian theory of the Ascent of Man from the Lower Animals; since it now seems plain to me that that theory ought to be vacated in favor of a new and truer one, this new and truer one to be named the Descent of Man from the Higher Animals.

2   In proceeding toward this unpleasant conclusion I have not guessed or speculated or conjectured, but have used what is commonly called the scientific method. That is to say, I have subjected every postulate that presented itself to the crucial test of actual experiment, and have adopted it or rejected it according to the result. Thus I verified and established each step of my course in its turn before advancing to the next. These experiments were made in the London Zoological Gardens, and covered many months of painstaking and fatiguing work.

3   Before particularizing any of the experiments, I wish to state one or two things which seem to more properly belong in this place than further along. This in the interest of clearness. The massed experiments established to my satisfaction certain generalizations, to wit:

4   1. That the human race is of one distinct species. It exhibits slight variations—in color, stature, mental caliber, and so on—due to climate, environment, and so forth; but is a species by itself, and not to be confounded with any other.

5   2. That the quadrupeds are a distinct family, also. This family exhibits variations—in color, size, food preferences and so on; but it is a family by itself.

6   3. That the other families—the birds, the fishes, the insects, the reptiles, etc.—are more or less distinct, also. They are in the procession. They are links in the chain which stretches down from the higher animals to man at the bottom.

7   Some of my experiments were quite curious. In the course of my reading I had come across a case where, many years ago, some hunters on our Great Plains organized a buffalo hunt for the entertainment of an English earl—that, and to provide some fresh meat for his larder. They had charming sport. They killed seventy-two of those great animals; and ate part of one of them and left the seventy-one to rot. In order to determine the difference between an anaconda and an earl—if any—I caused seven young calves to be turned into the anaconda's cage. The grateful reptile immediately crushed one of them and swallowed it, then lay back satisfied. It showed no further interest in the calves, and no disposition to harm them.

I tried this experiment with other anacondas; always with the same result. The fact stood proven that the difference between an earl and an anaconda is that the earl is cruel and the anaconda isn't; and that the earl wantonly destroys what he has no use for, but the anaconda doesn't. This seemed to suggest that the anaconda was not descended from the earl. It also seemed to suggest that the earl was descended from the anaconda, and had lost a good deal in the transition.

8   I was aware that many men who have accumulated more millions of money than they can ever use have shown a rabid hunger for more, and have not scrupled to cheat the ignorant and the helpless out of their poor servings in order to partially appease that appetite. I furnished a hundred different kinds of wild and tame animals the opportunity to accumulate vast stores of food, but none of them would do it. The squirrels and bees and certain birds made accumulations, but stopped when they had gathered a winter's supply, and could not be persuaded to add to it either honestly or by chicane. In order to bolster up a tottering reputation the ant pretended to store up supplies, but I was not deceived. I know the ant. These experiments convinced me that there is this difference between man and the higher animals: he is avaricious and miserly, they are not.

9   In the course of my experiments I convinced myself that among the animals man is the only one that harbors insults and injuries, broods over them, waits till a chance offers, then takes revenge. The passion of revenge is unknown to the higher animals.

10   Roosters keep harems, but it is by consent of their concubines; therefore no wrong is done. Men keep harems, but it is by brute force, privileged by atrocious laws which the other sex were allowed no hand in making. In this matter man occupies a far lower place than the rooster.

11   Cats are loose in their morals, but not consciously so. Man, in his descent from the cat, has brought the cat's looseness with him but has left the unconsciousness behind—the saving grace which excuses the cat. The cat is innocent, man is not.

12   Indecency, vulgarity, obscenity—these are strictly confined to man; he invented them. Among the higher animals there is no trace of them. They hide nothing; they are not ashamed. Man, with his soiled mind, covers himself. He will not even enter a drawing room with his breast and back naked, so alive are he and his mates to indecent suggestion. Man is "The Animal that Laughs." But so does the monkey, as Mr. Darwin pointed out; and so does the Australian bird that is called the laughing jackass. No—Man is the Animal that Blushes. He is the only one that does it—or has occasion to.

13   At the head of this article[1] we see how "three monks were burnt to death" a few days ago, and a prior "put to death with atrocious cruelty." Do we inquire into the details? No; or we should find out that the prior was subjected to unprintable mutilations. Man—when he is a North American Indian—gouges out his prisoner's eyes; when he is King John, with a nephew to render untroublesome, he uses a red-hot iron; when he is a religious zealot dealing with heretics in the Middle Ages, he skins his captive alive and scatters salt on his back; in the first Richard's time he shuts up a multitude of Jew families in a tower and sets fire to it; in Columbus's time he captures a family of Spanish Jews and—but *that* is not printable; in our day in England a man is fined ten shillings for beating his mother nearly to death with a chair, and another man is fined forty shillings for having four pheasant eggs in his possession without being able to satisfactorily explain how he got them. Of all the animals, man is the only one that is cruel. He is the only one that inflicts pain for the pleasure of doing it. It is a trait that is not known to the higher animals. The cat plays with the frightened mouse; but she has this excuse, that she does not know that the mouse is suffering. The cat is moderate—unhumanly moderate: she only scares the mouse, she does not hurt it; she doesn't dig out its eyes, or tear off its skin, or drive splinters under its nails—man-fashion; when she is done playing with it she makes a sudden meal of it and puts it out of its trouble. Man is the Cruel Animal. He is alone in that distinction.

14   The higher animals engage in individual fights, but never in organized masses. Man is the only animal that deals in that atrocity of atrocities, War. He is the only one that gathers his brethren about him and goes forth in cold blood and with calm pulse to exterminate his kind. He is the only animal that for sordid wages will march out, as the Hessians did in our Revolution, and as the boyish Prince Napoleon did in the Zulu war, and help to slaughter strangers of his own species who have done him no harm and with whom he has no quarrel.

15   Man is the only animal that robs his helpless fellow of his country—takes possession of it and drives him out of it or destroys him. Man has done this in all the ages. There is not an acre of ground on the globe that is in possession of its rightful owner, or that has not been taken away from owner after owner, cycle after cycle, by force and bloodshed.

16   Man is the only Slave. And he is the only animal who enslaves. He has always been a slave in one form or another, and has always held other slaves in

---

[1] The author had intended to begin the article with excerpts from newspaper reports about religious persecution in Crete.

bondage under him in one way or another. In our day he is always some man's slave for wages, and does that man's work; and this slave has other slaves under him for minor wages, and they do *his* work. The higher animals are the only ones who exclusively do their own work and provide their own living.

17   Man is the only Patriot. He sets himself apart in his own country, under his own flag, and sneers at the other nations, and keeps multitudinous uniformed assassins on hand at heavy expense to grab slices of other people's countries, and keep *them* from grabbing slices of *his*. And in the intervals between campaigns he washes the blood off his hands and works for "the universal brotherhood of man"—with his mouth.

18   Man is the Religious Animal. He is the only Religious Animal. He is the only animal that has the True Religion—several of them. He is the only animal that loves his neighbor as himself, and cuts his throat if his theology isn't straight. He has made a graveyard of the globe in trying his honest best to smooth his brother's path to happiness and heaven. He was at it in the time of the Caesars, he was at it in Mahomet's time, he was at it in the time of the Inquisition, he was at it in France a couple of centuries, he was at it in England in Mary's day, he has been at it ever since he first saw the light, he is at it today in Crete—as per the telegrams quoted above—he will be at it somewhere else tomorrow. The higher animals have no religion. And we are told that they are going to be left out, in the Hereafter. I wonder why? It seems questionable taste.

19   Man is the Reasoning Animal. Such is the claim. I think it is open to dispute. Indeed, my experiments have proven to me that he is the Unreasoning Animal. Note his history, as sketched above. It seems plain to me that whatever he is he is *not* a reasoning animal. His record is the fantastic record of a maniac. I consider that the strongest count against his intelligence is the fact that with that record back of him he blandly sets himself up as the head animal of the lot: whereas by his own standards he is the bottom one.

20   In truth, man is incurably foolish. Simple things which the other animals easily learn, he is incapable of learning. Among my experiments was this. In an hour I taught a cat and a dog to be friends. I put them in a cage. In another hour I taught them to be friends with a rabbit. In the course of two days I was able to add a fox, a goose, a squirrel and some doves. Finally a monkey. They lived together in peace; even affectionately.

21   Next, in another cage I confined an Irish Catholic from Tipperary, and as soon as he seemed tame I added a Scotch Presbyterian from Aberdeen. Next

a Turk from Constantinople; a Greek Christian from Crete; an Armenian; a Methodist from the wilds of Arkansas; a Buddhist from China; a Brahman from Benares. Finally, a Salvation Army Colonel from Wapping. Then I stayed away two whole days. When I came back to note results, the cage of Higher Animals was all right, but in the other there was but a chaos of gory odds and ends of turbans and fezzes and plaids and bones and flesh—not a specimen left alive. These Reasoning Animals had disagreed on a theological detail and carried the matter to a Higher Court.

22   One is obliged to concede that in true loftiness of character, Man cannot claim to approach even the meanest of the Higher Animals. It is plain that he is constitutionally incapable of approaching that altitude; that he is constitutionally afflicted with a Defect which must make such approach forever impossible, for it is manifest that this defect is permanent in him, indestructible, ineradicable.

23   I find this Defect to be *the Moral Sense.* He is the only animal that has it. It is the secret of his degradation. It is the quality *which enables him to do wrong.* It has no other office. It is incapable of performing any other function. It could never have been intended to perform any other. Without it, man could do no wrong. He would rise at once to the level of the Higher Animals.

24   Since the Moral Sense has but the one office, the one capacity—to enable man to do wrong—it is plainly without value to him. It is as valueless to him as is disease. In fact, it manifestly *is* a disease. *Rabies* is bad, but it is not so bad as this disease. Rabies enables a man to do a thing which he could not do when in a healthy state: kill his neighbor with a poisonous bite. No one is the better man for having rabies. The Moral Sense enables a man to do wrong. It enables him to do wrong in a thousand ways. Rabies is an innocent disease, compared to the Moral Sense. No one, then, can be the better man for having the Moral Sense. What, now, do we find the Primal Curse to have been? Plainly what it was in the beginning: the infliction upon man of the Moral Sense; the ability to distinguish good from evil; and with it, necessarily, the ability to *do* evil; for there can be no evil act without the presence of consciousness of it in the doer of it.

25   And so I find that we have descended and degenerated, from some far ancestor—some microscopic atom wandering at its pleasure between the mighty horizons of a drop of water perchance—insect by insect, animal by animal, reptile by reptile, down the long highway of smirchless innocence, till we have reached the bottom stage of development—namable as the Human Being. Below us—nothing. Nothing but the Frenchman.

WHAT DID THE WRITER SAY AND WHAT DID YOU THINK? _____

1. What is Mark Twain's thesis?
2. What meaning of *descent* did Darwin have in mind in his book *The Descent of Man?* What meaning does Twain use?
3. The author attributes human inferiority to the "Moral Sense." How would he define it?
4. Mark Twain delivers a profoundly bleak message about human nature. Why doesn't he seem to be especially depressed?
5. Who are the "uniformed assassins" in paragraph 17?
6. In what sense is the cat "innocent" in its sexual behavior and torturing of the mouse?
7. Are the comments on religion primarily an attack on religion or on human attitudes toward religion? If the latter, can an attack on religion itself be implied?
8. If you wanted to criticize the author's position, would you concentrate on the case he presents or bring up matters he leaves out?
9. Does the author sentimentalize the behavior of animals?
10. What is the point in the last sentence of the remark about the French, or is the remark nothing but an irrelevant wisecrack?

HOW DID THE WRITER SAY IT? _____

1. In paragraph 7 the author uses the example of the earl and the anaconda to establish human cruelty. After discussing some other issues, he uses examples of torture in paragraph 13 to show human cruelty. Is he repeating himself? Is the organization weak? If you think so, how might the author defend himself?
2. Which instances of humor strike you as most successful? Which are least successful?
3. Mark Twain is a great maker of phrases: "Man is the Animal that Blushes," for instance. Can you find some other examples?
4. The language is sometimes quite formal ("Note his history, as sketched above") and sometimes quite informal (the repetitions and variations of "he was at it" in paragraph 18). Explain why this mixture is effective or ineffective.

5. Does the writer rely on the block or alternating pattern (see pp. 148–152) to develop his ideas?
6. There are more "Vocabulary" entries for this selection than for many others. How do you account for this selection's still being fairly easy to read?

======================**WHAT ABOUT *YOUR* WRITING?**======================

According to Mary Poppins, "A spoonful of sugar makes the medicine go down." Think of humor as sugar. When you are dealing with intrinsically stodgy material or presenting a point of view toward which many readers might feel hostile, nothing can get your audience on your side faster than a few touches of humor. That's what Mark Twain knew throughout his career. For humor, readers will pardon a stretch of dullness, accept or at least bear with a point they strongly oppose, and generally let the writer get away with more than the writer would ever think of asking for.

There are dangers, of course. You don't want your readers to feel that your point isn't important, that beneath the humor you yourself don't take it seriously. You don't want to distract your reader from the significant intellectual content of your work. You don't want to come through as a crude smart aleck. With all these warnings, however, humor is a major resource for many good writers. Be cautious with it, but don't be shy.

THE PRISONER'S DILEMMA

STEPHEN CHAPMAN

Associate editor of *The New Republic* magazine, Stephen Chapman contrasts the legendary cruelty of Moslem forms of legal punishment to presumably humane American forms. "Legendary" and "presumably" seem accurate words because Chapman reaches some disturbing conclusions. As you read, note how the contrasts are always used to establish or support a point, never just to concoct a long list of differences.

Words to check:

punitive (epigraph)	flourish (3)
occidental (epigraph)	macabre (4)
fervor (paragraph 1)	decapitated (4)
stipulated (2)	regimen (6)
penological (2)	sociopaths (8)
malefactors (2)	impede (10)
squamish (2)	incarceration (12)
brazen (3)	recidivism (13)
superfluous (3)	

If the punitive laws of Islam were applied for only one year, all the devastating injustices would be uprooted. Misdeeds must be punished by the law of retaliation: cut off the hands of the thief; kill the murderers; flog the adulterous woman or man. Your concerns, your "humanitarian" scruples are more childish than reasonable. Under the terms of Koranic law, any judge fulfilling the seven requirements (that he have reached puberty, be a believer, know the Koranic laws perfectly, be just, and not be affected by amnesia, or be a bastard, or be of the female sex) is qualified to be a judge in any type of case. He can thus judge and dispose of twenty trials in a single day, whereas the Occidental justice might take years to argue them out.

—From *Sayings of the Ayatollah Khomeini* (New York: Bantam Books 1980).

1 One of the amusements of life in the modern West is the opportunity to observe the barbaric rituals of countries that are attached to the customs of the dark ages. Take Pakistan, for example, our newest ally and client state in Asia. Last October President Zia, in harmony with the Islamic fervor that is sweeping his part of the world, revived the traditional Moslem practice of flogging lawbreakers in public. In Pakistan, this qualified as mass entertainment, and no fewer than 10,000 law-abiding Pakistanis turned out to see justice done to 26 convicts. To Western sensibilities the spectacle seemed barbaric—both in the sense of cruel and in the sense of pre-civilized. In keeping with Islamic custom each of the unfortunates—who had been caught in prostitution raids the previous night and summarily convicted and sentenced—was stripped down to a pair of white shorts, which were painted with a red stripe across the buttocks (the target). Then he was shackled against an easel, with pads thoughtfully placed over the kidneys to prevent injury. The floggers were muscular, fierce-looking sorts—convicted murderers, as it happens—who paraded around the flogging platform in colorful loincloths. When the time for the ceremony began, one of the floggers took a running start and brought a five-foot stave down across the first victim's buttocks, eliciting screams from the convict and murmurs from the audience. Each of the 26 received from five to 15 lashes. One had to be carried from the stage unconscious.

2   Flogging is one of the punishments stipulated by Koranic law, which has made it a popular penological device in several Moslem countries, including Pakistan, Saudi Arabia, and, most recently, the ayatollah's Iran. Flogging, or *ta'zir,* is the general punishment prescribed for offenses that don't carry an explicit Koranic penalty. Some crimes carry automatic *hadd* punishments—stoning or scourging (a severe whipping) for illicit sex, scourging for drinking alcoholic beverages, amputation of the hands for theft. Other crimes—as varied as murder and abandoning Islam—carry the death penalty (usually carried out in public). Colorful practices like these have given the Islamic world an image in the West, as described by historian G. H. Jansen, "of blood dripping from the stumps of amputated hands and from the striped backs of malefactors, and piles of stones barely concealing the battered bodies of adulterous couples." Jansen, whose book *Militant Islam* is generally effusive in its praise of Islamic practices, grows squeamish when considering devices like flogging, amputation, and stoning. But they are given enthusiastic endorsement by the Koran itself.

3   Such traditions, we all must agree, are no sign of an advanced civilization. In the West, we have replaced these various punishments (including the death penalty in most cases) with a single device. Our custom is to confine criminals in prison for varying lengths of time. In Illinois, a reasonably typical state, grand theft carries a punishment of three to five years; armed robbery can get you from six to 30. The lowest form of felony theft is punishable by one to three years in prison. Most states impose longer sentences on habitual offenders. In Kentucky, for example, habitual offenders can be sentenced to life in prison. Other states are less brazen, preferring the more genteel sounding "indeterminate sentence," which allows parole boards to keep inmates locked up for as long as life. It was under an indeterminate sentence of one to 14 years that George Jackson served 12 years in California prisons for committing a $70 armed robbery. Under a Texas law imposing an automatic life sentence for a third felony conviction, a man was sent to jail for life last year because of three thefts adding up to less than $300 in property value. Texas also is famous for occasionally imposing extravagantly long sentences, often running into hundreds or thousands of years. This gives Texas a leg up on Maryland, which used to sentence some criminals to life plus a day—a distinctive if superfluous flourish.

4   The punishment *intended* by Western societies in sending their criminals to prison is the loss of freedom. But, as everyone knows, the actual punishment in most American prisons is of a wholly different order. The February 2 [1980] riot at New Mexico's state prison in Santa Fe, one of several bloody prison riots in the nine years since the Attica bloodbath, once

again dramatized the conditions of life in an American prison. Four hundred prisoners seized control of the prison before dawn. By sunset the next day 33 inmates had died at the hands of other convicts and another 40 people (including five guards) had been seriously hurt. Macabre stories came out of prisoners being hanged, murdered with blowtorches, decapitated, tortured, and mutilated in a variety of gruesome ways by drug-crazed rioters.

5   The Santa Fe penitentiary was typical of most maximum-security facilities, with prisoners subject to overcrowding, filthy conditions, and routine violence. It also housed first-time, non-violent offenders, like check forgers and drug dealers, with murderers serving life sentences. In a recent lawsuit, the American Civil Liberties Union called the prison "totally unfit for human habitation." But the ACLU says New Mexico's penitentiary is far from the nation's worst.

6   That American prisons are a disgrace is taken for granted by experts of every ideological stripe. Conservative James Q. Wilson has criticized our "[c]rowded, antiquated prisons that require men and women to live in fear of one another and to suffer not only deprivation of liberty but a brutalizing regimen." Leftist Jessica Mitford has called our prisons "the ultimate expression of injustice and inhumanity." In 1973 a national commission concluded that "the American correctional system today appears to offer minimum protection to the public and maximum harm to the offender." Federal courts have ruled that confinement in prisons in 16 different states violates the constitutional ban on "cruel and unusual punishment."

7   What are the advantages of being a convicted criminal in an advanced culture? First there is the overcrowding in prisons. One Tennessee prison, for example, has a capacity of 806, according to accepted space standards, but it houses 2300 inmates. One Louisiana facility has confined four and five prisoners in a single six-foot-by-six-foot cell. Then there is the disease caused by overcrowding, unsanitary conditions, and poor or inadequate medical care. A federal appeals court noted that the Tennessee prison had suffered frequent outbreaks of infectious diseases like hepatitis and tuberculosis. But the most distinctive element of American prison life is its constant violence. In his book *Criminal Violence, Criminal Justice,* Charles Silberman noted that in one Louisiana prison, there were 211 stabbings in only three years, 11 of them fatal. There were 15 slayings in a prison in Massachusetts between 1972 and 1975. According to a federal court, in Alabama's penitentiaries (as in many others), "robbery, rape, extortion, theft and assault are everyday occurrences."

8   At least in regard to cruelty, it's not at all clear that the system of punishment that has evolved in the West is less barbaric than the grotesque practices

of Islam. Skeptical? Ask yourself: would you rather be subjected to a few minutes of intense pain and considerable public humiliation, or be locked away for two or three years in a prison cell crowded with ill-tempered sociopaths? Would you rather lose a hand or spend 10 years or more in a typical state prison? I have taken my own survey on this matter. I have found no one who does not find the Islamic system hideous. And I have found no one who *given the choices* mentioned above, would not prefer its penalties to our own. . . .

9   Imprisonment is now the universal method of punishing criminals in the United States. It is thought to perform five functions, each of which has been given a label by criminologists. First, there is simple *retribution:* punishing the lawbreaker to serve society's sense of justice and to satisfy the victims' desire for revenge. Second, there is *specific deterrence:* discouraging the offender from misbehaving in the future. Third, *general deterrence:* using the offender as an example to discourage others from turning to crime. Fourth, *prevention:* at least during the time he is kept off the streets, the criminal cannot victimize other members of society. Finally, and most important, there is *rehabilitation:* reforming the criminal so that when he returns to society he will be inclined to obey the laws and able to make an honest living.

10   How satisfactorily do American prisons perform by these criteria? Well, of course, they do punish. But on the other scores they don't do so well. Their effect in discouraging future criminality by the prisoner or others is the subject of much debate, but the soaring rates of the last 20 years suggest that prisons are not a dramatically effective deterrent to criminal behavior. Prisons do isolate convicted criminals, but only to divert crime from ordinary citizens to prison guards and fellow inmates. Almost no one contends any more that prisons rehabilitate their inmates. If anything, they probably impede rehabilitation by forcing inmates into prolonged and almost exclusive association with other criminals. And prisons cost a lot of money. Housing a typical prisoner in a typical prison costs far more than a stint at a top university. This cost would be justified if prisons did the job they were intended for. But it is clear to all that prisons fail on the very grounds—humanity and hope of rehabilitation—that caused them to replace earlier, cheaper forms of punishment.

11   The universal acknowledgment that prisons do not rehabilitate criminals has produced two responses. The first is to retain the hope of rehabilitation but do away with imprisonment as much as possible and replace it with various forms of "alternative treatment," such as psychotherapy, supervised probation, and vocational training. Psychiatrist Karl Menninger, one of the principal critics of American penology, has suggested even

more unconventional approaches, such as "a new job opportunity or a vacation trip, a course of reducing exercises, a cosmetic surgical operation or a herniotomy, some night school courses, a wedding in the family (even one for the patient!), an inspiring sermon." This starry-eyed approach naturally has produced a backlash from critics on the right, who think that it's time to abandon the goal of rehabilitation. They argue that prisons perform an important service just by keeping criminals off the streets, and thus should be used with that purpose alone in mind.

12   So the debate continues to rage in all the same old ruts. No one, of course, would think of copying the medieval practices of Islamic nations and experimenting with punishments such as flogging and amputation. But let us consider them anyway. How do they compare with our American prison system in achieving the ostensible objectives of punishment? First, do they punish? Obviously they do, and in a uniquely painful and memorable way. Of course any sensible person, given the choice, would prefer suffering these punishments to years of incarceration in a typical American prison. But presumably no Western penologist would criticize Islamic punishments on the grounds that they are not barbaric enough. Do they deter crime? Yes, and probably more effectively than sending convicts off to prison. Now we read about a prison sentence in the newspaper, then think no more about the criminal's payment for his crimes until, perhaps, years later we read a small item reporting his release. By contrast, one can easily imagine the vivid impression it would leave to be wandering through a local shopping center and to stumble onto the scene of some poor wretch being lustily flogged. And the occasional sight of an habitual offender walking around with a bloody stump at the end of his arm no doubt also would serve as a forceful reminder that crime does not pay.

13   Do flogging and amputation discourage recidivism? No one knows whether the scars on his back would dissuade a criminal from risking another crime, but it is hard to imagine that corporal measures could stimulate a higher rate of recidivism than already exists. Islamic forms of punishment do not serve the favorite new right goal of simply isolating criminals from the rest of society, but they may achieve the same purpose of making further crimes impossible. In the movie *Bonnie and Clyde,* Warren Beatty successfully robs a bank with his arm in a sling, but this must be dismissed as artistic license. It must be extraordinarily difficult, at the very least, to perform much violent crime with only one hand.

14   Do these medieval forms of punishment rehabilitate the criminal? Plainly not. But long prison terms do not rehabilitate either. And it is just as plain

that typical Islamic punishments are no crueler to the convict than incarceration in the typical American state prison.

15   Of course there are other reasons besides its bizarre forms of punishment that the Islamic system of justice seems uncivilized to the Western mind. One is the absence of due process. Another is the long list of offenses—such as drinking, adultery, blasphemy, "profiteering," and so on—that can bring on conviction and punishment. A third is all the ritualistic mumbo-jumbo in pronouncements of Islamic law (like that talk about puberty and amnesia in the ayatollah's quotation at the beginning of this article). Even in these matters, however, a little cultural modesty is called for. The vast majority of American criminals are convicted and sentenced as a result of plea bargaining, in which due process plays almost no role. It has been only half a century since a wave of religious fundamentalism stirred this country to outlaw the consumption of alcoholic beverages. Most states also still have laws imposing austere constraints on sexual conduct. Only two weeks ago the *Washington Post* reported that the FBI had spent two and a half years and untold amounts of money to break up a nationwide pornography ring. Flogging the clients of prostitutes, as the Pakistanis did, does seem silly. But only a few months ago Mayor Koch of New York was proposing that clients caught in his own city have their names broadcast by radio stations. We are not so far advanced on such matters as we often like to think. Finally, my lawyer friends assure me that the rules of jurisdiction for American courts contain plenty of petty requirements and bizarre distinctions that would sound silly enough to foreign ears.

16   Perhaps it sounds barbaric to talk of flogging and amputation, and perhaps it is. But our system of punishment also is barbaric, and probably more so. Only cultural smugness about their system and willful ignorance about our own make it easy to regard the one as cruel and the other as civilized. We inflict our cruelties away from public view, while nations like Pakistan stage them in front of 10,000 onlookers. Their outrages are visible; ours are not. Most Americans can live their lives for years without having their peace of mind disturbed by the knowledge of what goes on in our prisons. To choose imprisonment over flogging and amputation is not to choose human kindness over cruelty, but merely to prefer that our cruelties be kept out of sight, and out of mind.

17   Public flogging and amputation may be more barbaric forms of punishment than imprisonment, even if they are not more cruel. Society may pay a higher price for them, even if the particular criminal does not. Revulsion against officially sanctioned violence and infliction of pain derives from

something deeply ingrained in the Western conscience, and clearly it is something admirable. Grotesque displays of the sort that occur in Islamic countries probably breed a greater tolerance for physical cruelty, for example, which prisons do not do precisely because they conceal their cruelties. In fact it is our admirable intolerance for calculated violence that makes it necessary for us to conceal what we have not been able to do away with. In a way this is a good thing, since it holds out the hope that we may eventually find a way to do away with it. But in another way it is a bad thing, since it permits us to congratulate ourselves on our civilized humanitarianism while violating its norms in this one area of our national life.

WHAT DID THE WRITER SAY AND WHAT DID YOU THINK?

1. What are the methods of punishment used in Moslem countries?
2. What is the one method used in "the West"? Why does the author feel the West is more cruel?
3. Does the author approve of Moslem methods?
4. Why is the author skeptical about prison reform?
5. Is the Western system equal or superior to the Moslem system in any respects, according to the author? Can anything be said in favor of Western methods? Does the author present only one side of the case?
6. What is the main reason that most Westerners think their system is less cruel?
7. Do the attacks on American prisons seem well substantiated, or are they merely unsupported outbursts?

HOW DID THE WRITER SAY IT?

1. Is the thesis of the whole essay ever stated directly? If so, where? If not, does it need to be?
2. Paragraphs 1–8 contrast the cruelty of the two systems. Paragraphs 9–17 contrast how well or poorly each system performs the five functions of imprisonment. Which comparison-contrast pattern is used in both sections? Which section more closely follows the instructions for comparison-contrast writing on pp. 107–108?
3. In paragraph 8, the author addresses his readers directly. "Ask yourself: would you rather be subjected to a few minutes of intense

pain and considerable public humiliation, or be locked away for two or three years in a prison cell crowded with ill-tempered sociopaths? Would you rather lose a hand or spend 10 years or more in a typical state prison?" Do you consider these sentences a clinching argument to establish the author's point or a cheap emotional appeal?

WHAT ABOUT *YOUR* WRITING?

Even people who boast about their ignorance of grammar think they know at least one rule: *never end a sentence with a preposition.* In paragraph 17 of Chapman's "The Prisoner's Dilemma," these people tremble with joy when they see the following sentence: "In fact it is our admirable intolerance for calculated violence that makes it necessary for us to conceal what we have not been able to do away with." Here's a professional writer who seems to know even less about grammar than they.

The truth is that for centuries good and great writers have been ending their sentences with prepositions. And the sentences have ended that way not through carelessness or lack of knowledge but through a sense of good style. Would anyone seriously propose that Chapman reword his sentence to read, "In fact it is our admirable intolerance for calculated violence that makes it necessary for us to conceal that with which we have not been able to do away"? Compared to the original, the revised sentence is stiff, wordy, awkward, and ugly.

For most practical purposes, the rule against ending a sentence with a preposition doesn't exist today. It's doubtful if it ever existed in any rigid way outside the heads of a few deranged schoolmasters and schoolmistresses. Extremely formal English, when given a choice, probably still leans toward avoiding the preposition at the end of a sentence when possible, but won't hesitate to use it if it improves the style. Less formal English generally does what comes naturally. Certainly, the issue is one of style, not of some imaginary, unbreakable rule of grammar.

As always, be careful of excess. The story is told of a father accustomed to read bedtime stories to his young son. One evening the child was sick in bed. The father took a book, brought it upstairs to the bedroom, and the child said, "What did you bring the book I didn't want to be read to out of up for?"

7

CAUSE
AND
EFFECT

T he school board of a suburban town near Denver has decided to ask the voters to approve a large increase in property tax assessments in order to construct a new high school. The board knows that, at best, its request will be unwelcome. It launches a vigorous campaign to make the voters more favorably inclined. Part of the campaign is a pamphlet setting forth the board's case. The pamphlet, of necessity, presents a study of cause-and-effect relationships.

The board first states the *causes* for its request. Student enrollment has more than doubled. Three years ago, the board had tried to cope with this problem by going to two sessions, but the classrooms are still too crowded for basic physical comfort as well as for optimum learning conditions. Moreover, the situation is not temporary; current enrollment in the junior high and elementary schools assures continued increases in the student population. Finally, the building is in poor physical condition: The roof leaks, the basement floods, the boiler is on its last legs. The board has investigated the possibility of remodeling and expanding the old building and has found that costs for that project would mean an average of only $35 a year less in taxes per family than if a completely new school were built.

Next, the board discusses the results, or *effects,* of voter approval. The town's leading eyesore will be replaced by a beautiful new structure in which everyone can take pride. New facilities for the most modern teaching devices will improve the quality of education. Experienced teachers will be more inclined to stay than to seek new employment. The strength of the town's educational system will be a selling point for new residents and consequently will increase property values.

The school board's pamphlet, in short, presents a thesis—the proposal for a new high school should be approved—and supports it with cause-and-effect writing.

It's worth noting here that cause-and-effect relationships can sometimes shift. In the first part of the pamphlet, for example, the proposal to build a new school is the effect that was caused by overcrowding and a decaying building. In the second part of the pamphlet, however, the approved proposal becomes the cause of such beneficial effects as beauty and improved education. A cause creates an effect, but that effect, in turn, can become the cause of another effect. No problems are likely to arise as long as the writer keeps any shifting relationships clearly in mind.

Many classroom papers are not lengthy enough to give equal weight to cause and effect and will emphasize one over the other. "Cause" papers might have theses like these:

The rioting at last week's rock concert was mostly the fault of the police.

The growth of interest in coin collecting is attributable to practical financial considerations.

Government policies penalize savers and reward borrowers.

Iago plots against Othello because of an accumulation of petty resentments.

The introduction of the cause paper will usually contain a brief description of the *effect*—the rioting that resulted from police actions, the decrease in bank deposits that resulted from government policies—and then the entire body of the paper will analyze the causes, giving a paragraph, perhaps, to each cause.

"Effect" papers might have theses like these:

Passage of a national health insurance program is going to result in heavy burdens on doctors.

Fear of germs made me a nervous wreck as a child.

The invention of the cotton gin helped perpetuate slavery in the South.

Rigid enforcement of holding penalties in professional football has made the sport less exciting than it used to be.

The introduction to an effect paper will naturally reverse the procedure of a cause paper. It will briefly describe or discuss the *cause*—the health insurance program, the cotton gin, and so on—and the rest of the paper will then be devoted to the effects.

As you plan your paper, try to remember a few logical requirements:

Do Not Oversimplify Causes.   Most subjects worth writing about have more than one cause. Sometimes particular combinations of causes have to be present at the same time and in certain proportions in order to bring about a particular result. Attributing a young man's delinquency solely to the poverty of his family oversimplifies what everyone knows about life. Poverty may have been a contributing cause, but there had to be others; plenty of poor children do not become delinquents, and plenty of rich ones do.

Beware especially of the *post hoc ergo propter hoc* fallacy: "after this, therefore because of this." After Herbert Hoover was elected president, America had a depression; therefore, America had a depression because Herbert Hoover was elected. An argument like this depends purely on an accident of time; the writer must point out, if possible, actual policies of the Hoover administration that brought about the depression. Otherwise, the argument has no more logical validity than "I lost my job after a black cat crossed my path; therefore, I lost my job because a black cat crossed my path."

Do Not Oversimplify Effects.   Uncontrolled enthusiasm is probably the biggest danger here. A writer may be able to present a strong case that an ill-conceived national health insurance program might have adverse effects on medical care; if the writer predicts that millions of people will die of neglect in waiting lines in the doctor's office, however, the writer's case—and common sense—is sure to be viewed skeptically. The school board's pamphlet said that a new high school would be an additional selling point to attract new residents; if it had said that property values would triple within five years, it would have oversimplified the effects in an irresponsible and hysterical fashion.

Distinguish When Necessary Between Direct and Indirect Causes and Effects.   Don't treat all causes and effects equally. Some are more remote than others, and the distinctions need to be made clear.

Bad design and incompetent management were direct causes of the nuclear disaster at Chernobyl in 1986. The centuries-old desire for cheap sources of energy was an indirect cause. Though indirect causes and effects can sometimes be important, you need to set limits on how many of them you can deal with, or nearly every cause-and-effect essay will turn into a history of the world.

Distinguish When Necessary Between Major and Minor Causes and Effects. The Confederacy's firing on Fort Sumter was a direct cause of the Civil War, but not nearly as important as the issues of secession and slavery. Although acknowledging minor causes and effects, a paper should naturally spend most of its time on major ones.

Do Not Omit Links in a Chain of Causes and Effects. As previously noted, you may not always be faced with a set of separate causes for a particular effect or separate effects from a particular cause. One cause leads to another, the second to a third, and so on—and only then is the given effect brought about. Unless you carefully discuss each part of the sequence, your reader may get lost. One effect of television, for example, may be a growing number of discipline problems in elementary and high school classrooms, but before you can persuade your reader of that point, you will have to examine many intermediate effects.

Play Fair. Give some attention, where appropriate, to causes and effects that opponents of your thesis may point to. You may justifiably want to pin the rioting at the rock concert on the police, but your case will be strengthened, not weakened, if you concede that the promoters' selling of more tickets than there were seats and the attempt of a few fans to rush the stage and tear the clothes off the performers' backs also contributed to the disaster. You don't need to make a lavish production of these arguments on the other side; just show that you're aware of them and have given them serious consideration.

WRITING SUGGESTIONS FOR CAUSE-AND-EFFECT PAPERS

Any of the listed subjects offers good opportunities for a cause-and-effect, cause-only, or effect-only paper. Explore each cause and effect thoroughly; don't just write a list.

1. A personal, unreasonable fear (your own or someone else's)
2. A personal, unreasonable irritation (your own or someone else's)
3. A personal habit or mannerism (your own or someone else's)
4. Outlawing of prayers in public schools
5. Violence on children's television programs
6. A personal experience with racial or religious discrimination
7. Your first romantic attachment
8. The quality of food at the school cafeteria

9. The popularity or decline in popularity of a hairstyle or clothing style
10. High school graduates who still can't read
11. Your like or dislike of a particular book or writer, movie, painter, musician, television program
12. Children's lack of respect for parents
13. Acceptance of "the pill"
14. A minor invention (Scotch tape, electric toothbrushes, pay toilets, parking meters)
15. Your interest or lack of interest in a sport
16. Your passionate like or dislike of a food
17. Your decision to continue your education
18. Being overweight or underweight
19. Swearing
20. Gossip

A Few Short Words

Matthew Monroe (student)

Thesis: My height seems to bring out the worst in everyone.

    I.   Stupid jokes
       A. When accepting an award
       B. From my girlfriend's dad

   II. Rudeness
       A. When trying to buy a suit
       B. When shopping for cars
       C. From total strangers

 III. Being overlooked
       A. In bars
       B. For sports
       C. By women

Conclusion: Although people assume I don't mind the abuse I take because of my height, it really does make me angry.

I am short. How short? Suffice it to say that for a man of almost twenty-two years of age, I am very short indeed. Now, I am comfortable with my height. I've lived with it for years, and it just doesn't bother me anymore. It is the effect that my height has on other people that I just can't stand. My height seems to bring out the worst in everyone.

People seem to see my height as an excellent excuse to try to be funny. Stupid jokes follow me wherever I go. When I had to accept an award for perfect high-school attendance, some jerk at the back of the room waited until I was about to say a gracious thank you, and then he hollered, "Stand up, pal. We can't see you!" There was, of course, much laughter, just as there was when my girlfriend's dad told her to "Throw the boy back. He's too small to keep!"

The jokes, though, are easier to handle than outright rudeness. There was the time I was trying to buy a suit and was told that not even the "very best" cut could disguise my height. There was the car salesman who refused to show me anything but sub-compacts, insisting that anything else would be far too big for such a little fellow. And then, I cannot forget the random strangers who feel compelled to walk up to me and say "Wow! You're really short." Thanks guys, I hadn't noticed.

The worst part, though, is being overlooked because of my height. I'm the last to get served at any bar, because the bartender can't see me. I'm never chosen for any pick-up sports teams, even though being short doesn't mean I can't run as fast or throw as straight as any other guy. Women look right past me and right into the eyes of the six-foot-tall idiot at the other end of the room. Sometimes they pat me on the head as they pass by.

People assume that my height makes me nothing more than a target for their dumb wisecracks, their insensitive rudenesses, or their complete disregard. They assume that because I can laugh it off, I just don't care. One day I will surprise them by taking a stand, making a statement, walking right up to them, and punching them in the kneecaps.

THE DECISIVE ARREST

MARTIN LUTHER KING, JR.

Perhaps best remembered for his "I Have a Dream" speech delivered during the civil rights movement of the 1960s, Martin Luther King, Jr., had gained international fame when he organized the black citizens of Montgomery, Alabama, to boycott the city's segregated bus system in the mid-1950s. Realizing the power of language, both spoken and written, King used his talents as a minister to convince many that nonviolent resistance to segregation would bring about change. In this brief account of Rosa Parks' refusal to obey the bus driver's order, King recounts the event that gave impetus to the bus boycott which in turn would ultimately lead to the striking down of sanctioned segregation in public facilities.

Words to check:

plausible (paragraph 2)   affirmation (3)
intrepid (3)

1   On December 1, 1955, an attractive Negro seamstress, Mrs. Rosa Parks, boarded the Cleveland Avenue Bus in downtown Montgomery. She was returning home after her regular day's work in the Montgomery Fair—a leading department store. Tired from long hours on her feet, Mrs. Parks sat down in the first seat behind the section reserved for whites. Not long after she took her seat, the bus operator ordered her, along with three other Negro passengers, to move back in order to accommodate boarding white passengers. By this time every seat in the bus was taken. This meant that if Mrs. Parks followed the driver's command she would have to stand while a white male passenger, who had just boarded the bus, would sit. The other three Negro passengers immediately complied with the driver's request. But Mrs. Parks quietly refused. The result was her arrest.

2   There was to be much speculation about why Mrs. Parks did not obey the driver. Many people in the white community argued that she had been "planted" by the NAACP in order to lay the groundwork for a test case, and at first glance that explanation seemed plausible, since she was a former secretary of the local branch of the NAACP. So persistent and persuasive was this argument that it convinced many reporters from all over the country. Later on, when I was having press conferences three times a week—in order to accommodate the reporters and journalists who came to Montgomery from all over the world—the invariable first question was: "Did the NAACP start the bus boycott?"

3   But the accusation was totally unwarranted, as the testimony of both Mrs. Parks and the officials of the NAACP revealed. Actually, no one can understand the action of Mrs. Parks unless he realizes that eventually the cup of endurance runs over, and the human personality cries out, "I can take it no longer." Mrs. Parks's refusal to move back was her intrepid affirmation that she had had enough. It was an individual expression of a timeless longing for human dignity and freedom. She was not "planted" there by the NAACP, or any other organization; she was planted there by her personal sense of dignity and self-respect. She was anchored to that seat by the accumulated indignities of days gone by and the boundless aspirations of generations yet unborn. She was a victim of both the forces of history and the forces of destiny. She had been tracked down by the *Zeitgeist*—the spirit of the time.

WHAT DID THE WRITER SAY AND WHAT DID YOU THINK?

1. What is King's thesis? Does he state it outright?
2. Why does the author mention the speculation about Mrs. Parks's motives? Why does he agree that the accusations seemed plausible?
3. What does King believe were Mrs. Parks's immediate reasons for not giving up her bus seat? What does he cite as her deeper reasons?
4. Does King convince you that this nonviolent act sparked a national movement? If so, how?
5. Is King critical of the press? Why or why not?

HOW DID THE WRITER SAY IT?

1. Why is King's factual account important at the beginning of the essay? What pattern does he use in this first paragraph?
2. Look at the placement of the words "ordered," "command," "complied," and "request" in the first paragraph. How is their placement significant? Do they diminish the factual tone?
3. Is the essay concerned equally with cause and effect? Or does it deal with one more than the other? If so, which aspect seems more important to King?
4. In the last paragraph, King repeats "she was" four times in succession. Why does the author use such repetition?

==================**WHAT ABOUT *YOUR* WRITING?**==================

An allusion is a reference, usually brief and often indirect, to a character, event, activity, work of art, and so on, distinct from what is being discussed. In paragraph 3 of "The Decisive Arrest," Martin Luther King, Jr. alludes to the Bible with the phrase "the cup of endurance runs over." The phrase is meant to remind readers of "my cup runneth over" from the Twenty-third Psalm, perhaps also suggesting the stark contrast between the contentment expressed in the original phrase and the frustration and anger felt by Mrs. Parks. Well-managed allusions, employed sparingly—don't use them for mere showing off—can add depth to a writer's style and thought. They can reveal unsuspected resemblances, relate unfamiliar material to material the reader knows, make abstract subjects seem more specific, and help establish confidence in a writer's range of knowledge.

You don't need to be an expert in any particular field to add an occasional allusion to your writing; anyone with ordinary education and some experience of life has a rich fund on which to draw.

Television: My father reminds me of Dan Rather. Whenever I see him, he's talking.

History: The teacher gave unannounced quizzes throughout the term. Every week was another Pearl Harbor.

Movies: The stranger had Robert Redford eyes, a Clark Gable moustache, and a Woody Allen physique.

Famous quotes: It's true that nothing is more powerful than an idea whose time has come, but encounter groups are an idea whose time has gone.

Sports: The administration has given up. Its game plan can be summed up in one word: Punt.

Literature: The lawyers indicated at first that we would be entitled to a beautiful tax deduction. Then they told us about Catch-22.

Advertisements: The senator can't help being embarrassed. He hasn't exactly broken the law, but he has surely been discovered to have a bad case of ring around the collar.

THE BEST YEARS OF MY LIFE

BETTY ROLLIN

Betty Rollin has been editor for *Vogue* and *Look* magazines and a news correspondent for NBC and ABC. Her best-selling book *First, You Cry* (1976) describes her operation for breast cancer. Among her other books are *Am I Getting Paid for This?* (1982), and *Last Wish* (1985). "The Best Years of My Life" analyzes the effects of her operation—and survival.

Words to check:

intrinsically (paragraph 1)	orthopedist (8)
chemotherapy (2)	parsimonious (9)
harrowing (2)	hedonism (10)
hypochondriac (7)	masochism (11)
gynecologist (8)	voracious (11)

1 I am about to celebrate an anniversary. Not that there will be a party with funny hats. Nor do I expect any greetings in the mail. Hallmark, with its infinite variety of occasions about which to fashion a 50-cent card, has skipped this one. This, you see, is my cancer anniversary. Five years ago tomorrow, at Beth Israel Hospital in New York City, a malignant tumor was removed from my left breast and, along with the tumor, my left breast. To be alive five years later means something in cancer circles. There is nothing intrinsically magical about the figure five, but the numbers show that if you have survived that many years after cancer has been diagnosed, you have an 80 percent shot at living out a normal life span.

2 Still, you probably think Hallmark is right not to sell a card, and that it's weird to "celebrate" such a terrible thing as cancer. It's even weirder than you imagine. Because not only do I feel good about (probably) having escaped a recurrence of cancer, I also feel good about having gotten cancer in the first place. Here is the paradox: although cancer was the worst thing that ever happened to me, it was also the best. Cancer (the kind I had, with no spread and no need of chemotherapy, with its often harrowing side effects) enriched my life, made me wiser, made me happier. Another paradox: although I would do everything possible to avoid getting cancer again, I am glad I had it.

3 There is a theory about people who have had a life-and-death scare that goes something like this: for about six months after surviving the scare, you feel shaken and grateful. Armed with a keen sense of what was almost The

End, you begin to live your life differently. You pause during the race to notice the foliage, you pay more attention to the people you love—maybe you even move to Vermont. You have gained, as they say, a "new perspective." But then, according to this theory, when the six months are over, the "new perspective" fades, you sell the house in Vermont and go back to the same craziness that was your life before the car crash or whatever it was. What has happened is that you've stopped feeling afraid. The crash is in the past. The it-can't-happen-to-me feelings that were dashed by the accident re-emerge, after six months, as it-can't-happen-to-me-*again.*

4   It's different for people whose crash is cancer. You can stay off the freeways, but you can't do much about preventing whatever went wrong in your own body from going wrong again. Unless your head is buried deep in the sand, you know damn well it *can* happen again. Even though, in my case, the doctors say it isn't likely, the possibility of recurrence is very real to me. Passing the five-year mark is reassuring, but I know I will be a little bit afraid for the rest of my life. But—ready for another paradox?—certain poisons are medicinal in small doses. To be a little bit afraid of dying can do wonders for your life. It has done wonders for mine. That's because, unlike the way most people feel, my sense of death is not an intellectual concept. It's a lively presence in my gut. It affects me daily—for the better.

5   First, when you're even slightly afraid of death, you're less afraid of other things—e.g., bosses, spouses, plumbers, rape, bankruptcy, failure, not being liked, the flu, aging. Next to the Grim Reaper, how ferocious can even the most ferocious boss be? How dire the direst household calamity? In my own professional life, I have lost not only some big fears, but most of the small ones. I used to be nervous in front of television cameras. That kind of nervousness was a fear of not being thought attractive, smart and winning. It still pleases me greatly if someone besides my husband and mother thinks I'm attractive, smart and winning; but I am no longer afraid that someone won't. Cancer made me less worried about what people think of me, both professionally and socially. I am less concerned about where my career is going. I don't know where it's going. I don't think about that. I think about where I am and what I'm doing and whether I like it. The result is that these days I continually seem to be doing what I like. And probably I'm more successful than when I aimed to please.

6   My book *First, You Cry,* which has given me more pleasure than anything else in my professional life, is a good example of this. As a career move, leaving television for six months to write a book about a cancer operation seemed less than sensible. But as soon as I got cancer, I stopped being "sensible." I wanted to write the book. And, just in case I croaked, I wanted

to write it the way that was right for me, not necessarily for the market. So I turned down the publisher who wanted it to be a "how-to" book. I like to think I would have done that, cancer or not, but had it not been for cancer, I probably wouldn't have written a book at all, because I would have been too afraid to drop out of television even for six months. And if I had written a book, I doubt that I would have been so open about my life and honest about my less-than-heroic feelings. But, as I wrote, I remember thinking, "I might die, so what does it matter what anyone thinks of me?" A lot of people write honestly and openly without having had a disease, but I don't think I would have. I hadn't done it before.

7   A touch of cancer turns you into a hypochondriac. You get a sore throat and you think you've got cancer of the throat; you get a corn from a pair of shoes that are too tight and you're sure it's a malignant tumor. But—here's the bright side—cancer hypochondria is so compelling it never occurs to you that you could get anything *else*. And, when you do, you're so glad it's not cancer that you feel like celebrating. "Goody, it's the flu!" I heard myself say to myself a couple of weeks ago.

8   Some physicians are more sensitive than others to cancer anxiety. My gynecologist prattled on once about some menstrual irregularity without noticing that, as he spoke, I had turned to stone. "Is it cancer?" I finally whispered. He looked dumbfounded and said, "Of course not!" As if to say, "How could you think such a thing?" But an orthopedist I saw about a knee problem took an X-ray and, before saying a word about what it was (a torn cartilage), told me what it wasn't. I limped home joyously.

9   I never went to Vermont because I can't stand that much fresh air; but in my own fashion, I sop up pleasure where and when I can, sometimes at the risk of professional advancement and sometimes at the risk of bankruptcy. An exaggeration, perhaps, but there's no question about it: since cancer, I spend more money than I used to. (True, I have more to spend, but that's mostly because of the book, which is also thanks to cancer.) I had always been parsimonious—some would say cheap—and I'm not anymore. The thinking is, "Just in case I do get a recurrence, won't I feel like a fool for having flown coach to Seattle?" (I like to think I'm more generous with others as well. It seems to me that, since having cancer, I give better presents.)

10   Cancer kills guilt. You not only take a vacation now because next year you might be dead, but you take a *better* vacation because, even if you don't die soon, after what you've been through, you feel you deserve it. In my own case, I wouldn't have expected that feeling to survive six months because, once those months passed, I realized that, compared to some people, I had

not been through much at all. But my hedonism continues to flourish. Maybe it was just a question of changing a habit.

11   My girlish masochism didn't resurface, either. Most women I know go through at least a phase of needing punishment from men. Not physical punishment, just all the rest: indifference, harshness, coldness, rudeness or some neat combination. In the past, my own appetite for this sort of treatment was voracious. Conversely, if I happened to connect with a man who was nice to me, I felt like that song: "This can't be love because I feel so well." The difference was that, in the song, it really *was* love, and with me, it really *wasn't.* Only when I was miserable did I know I really cared.

12   The minute I got cancer, my taste in men improved. It's not that my first husband was a beast. I'm fond of him, but even he would admit he was very hard on me. Maybe I asked for it. Well, once you've been deftly kicked in the pants by God (or whoever distributes cancer), you stop wanting kicks from mortals. Everyone who knows the man I married a year ago thinks I'm lucky—even my mother!—and I do, too. But I know it wasn't only luck. It was that cancer made me want someone wonderful. I wasn't ready for him before. I was so struck by this apparent change in me that I checked it out with a psychoanalyst, who assured me that I was not imagining things—that the damage to my body had, indeed, done wonders for my head.

13   Happiness is probably something that shouldn't be talked about too much, but I can't help it. Anyway, I find the more I carry on about it, the better it gets. A big part of happiness is noticing it. It's trite to say, but if you've never been ill, you don't notice—or enjoy—not being ill. I even notice my husband's good health. (He doesn't, but how could he?)

14   I haven't mentioned losing that breast, have I? That's because, in spite of the fuss I made about it five years ago, that loss now seems almost not worth mentioning. Five years ago, I felt sorry for myself that I could no longer keep a strapless dress up. Today I feel that losing a breast saved my life, and wasn't I lucky. And when I think of all the other good things that have come from that loss, I just look at that flat place on my body and think: small price.

15   Most of my friends who are past 40 shudder on their birthdays. Not me. They feel a year closer to death, I suppose. I feel a year further from it.

16   O.K., what if I get a recurrence? I'm not so jolly all the time that I haven't given this some serious thought. If it happens, I'm sure I won't be a good sport about it—especially if my life is cut short. But even if it is, I will look back at the years since the surgery and know I got the best from them. And I will be forced to admit that the disease that is ending my life is the very thing that made it so good.

WHAT DID THE WRITER SAY AND WHAT DID YOU THINK?

1. What is Rollin's thesis?
2. Does the essay strike you as convincing and realistic or as too overwhelmingly cheerful?
3. Does the author deal with any unpleasant effects? What are they?
4. Do you think the author wants the essay to come through as purely personal comments or as a piece with a message that people in general can apply to their own lives?
5. Explain in your own words the change in Rollin's "taste in men."
6. How much attention does Rollin pay to the often traumatic physical and emotional effects of losing a breast (rather than surviving an operation for cancer)? What is her current attitude toward the loss?
7. Explain these lines: "Most of my friends who are past 40 shudder on their birthdays. Not me. They feel a year closer to death, I suppose. I feel a year further from it."

HOW DID THE WRITER SAY IT?

1. Point out some instances of the author's use of humor. Is the humor appropriate for the subject?
2. The writing is frequently informal, even slangy—"you know damn well," "just in case I croaked," and so on. Is this tone appropriate for the subject?
3. In paragraph 2, the author mentions the "paradox" that cancer was the worst and best thing that ever happened to her. Are there other paradoxes in the reading selection, either direct or implied?

══════════WHAT ABOUT *YOUR* WRITING?══════════

In paragraph 3, the author writes, "You pause during the race to notice the foliage, you pay more attention to the people you love. . . ." Two sentences later, she writes, ". . . the 'new perspective' fades, you sell the house in Vermont . . ."

Betty Rollin is an experienced, professional writer who has written a moving and inspirational essay, but the chances are at least fair that your instructor would have used some red ink on those sentences. (The chances are even better that your instructor would have complained about the many sentence fragments, such as the second sentence in paragraph 1, but that's another matter. See pp. 229–230.) The red ink would have underlined or circled the commas in both sentences, and then above those commas or out in the margin would be the letters CS, meaning *comma splice.*

The comma splice is one of the most frequent errors in punctuation. From the point of view of many instructors, it's also more serious than most punctuation errors because it suggests that the writer not only doesn't know about commas but also doesn't know what a sentence is. In your own writing, you need to avoid comma splices and know how to get rid of them if they do pop up. You need to know, too, about those special occasions when, like Betty Rollin, you may be able to use a comma splice deliberately—and get away with it.

A comma splice results when the writer forgets this simple rule: *a comma all by itself cannot join independent clauses.* (An independent clause is a group of words with a subject and verb that can stand alone as a separate sentence.)

Let's look first at an old-fashioned *fused-sentence,* sometimes called a run-on sentence:

> I took an aspirin and went straight to bed I had a headache.

Few writers are likely to make this gross an error. The sentence contains two independent clauses—*I took an aspirin and went straight to bed* and *I had a headache* —with no punctuation of any kind between them.

The comma splice occurs when the writer sees that something is wrong with the fused sentence, knows precisely where it's wrong, and tries to fix the sentence like this:

> I took an aspirin and went straight to bed, I had a headache.

Remember the rule: *a comma all by itself cannot join independent clauses.* The writer has created a comma splice, a kind of sophisticated fused sentence. It's a slight improvement, probably, but it's still wrong.

A comma splice can be eliminated in a variety of ways:

1. Replace the commas with a period.

    I took an aspirin and went straight to bed. I had a headache.

2. Replace the commas with a semicolon.

    I took an aspirin and went straight to bed; I had a headache.

3. Add one of the following coordinating conjunctions *after* the comma: *and, but, or, nor, for, yet, so.* Which word you choose, obviously, will depend on the logical relationship between clauses.

    I took an aspirin and went straight to bed, for I had a headache.

4. Change one of the independent clauses to a dependent clause:

> Because I had a headache, I took an aspirin and went straight to bed.
> I took an aspirin and went straight to bed because I had a headache.

All four of these techniques result in correctly punctuated sentences. Which one you choose often depends on subtle issues of style, and sometimes any of the four can work well. Nevertheless, it's not always a pure matter of taste. If you've just written a string of short sentences, for example, you'd want to break the monotony with a longer sentence—and thus avoid replacing the comma with a period. Conversely, with a string of long sentences, the period would probably be your first choice.

Now what about those sentences by Betty Rollin? Why was an experienced writer guilty of comma splices? Why did this discussion begin by saying that the chances of your instructor's objecting to the comma splices were only "fair"? The answer is that rules almost always have exceptions. When the clauses are short and express activities going on at the same time or an unbroken sequence of activities, comma splices can sometimes be acceptable.

> I came, I saw, I conquered.

> Add the eggs, beat the mixture, pour it in the pan.

> The wedding was an emotional explosion. We laughed, we cried, we danced, we hugged, we kissed.

> . . . the "new perspective" fades, you sell the house in Vermont . . .

If you're tempted deliberately to use a comma splice, make certain that the writing assignment does not call for a highly formal tone, as in a scholarly research paper. If in doubt, check with your instructor.

WHY WE CRAVE HORROR MOVIES

STEPHEN KING

It's a reasonable guess that if asked to "name a writer" most average citizens would name Stephen King. With total sales comfortably above 20 million, King's horror tales seem to have achieved a popularity unrestricted by education or social class. Among his books are *Carrie* (1974), *Salem's Lot* (1975), *The Shining* (1977), *The Dead Zone* (1979), *Firestarter* (1980), *Christine* (1983), *Pet Sematary*

(1983), and *The Tommyknockers* (1988). Many of these titles, as well as others, have been made into films, and King can write with considerable authority on the subject of horror movies.

Words to check:

grimaces (paragraph 1)	status quo (9)
depleted (3)	sanctions (10)
innately (4)	remonstrance (10)
voyeur (6)	anarchistic (11)
penchant (7)	

1   I think that we're all mentally ill; those of us outside the asylums only hide it a little better—and maybe not all that much better, after all. We've all known people who talk to themselves, people who sometimes squinch their faces into horrible grimaces when they believe no one is watching, people who have some hysterical fear—of snakes, the dark, the tight place, the long drop . . . and, of course, those final worms and grubs that are waiting so patiently underground.

2   When we pay our four or five bucks and seat ourselves at tenth-row center in a theater showing a horror movie, we are daring the nightmare.

3   Why? Some of the reasons are simple and obvious. To show that we can, that we are not afraid, that we can ride this roller coaster. Which is not to say that a really good horror movie may not surprise a scream out of us at some point, the way we may scream when the roller coaster twists through a complete 360 or plows through a lake at the bottom of the drop. And horror movies, like roller coasters, have always been the special province of the young; by the time one turns 40 or 50, one's appetite for double twists or 360-degree loops may be considerably depleted.

4   We also go to re-establish our feelings of essential normality; the horror movie is innately conservative, even reactionary. Freda Jackson as the horrible melting woman in *Die, Monster, Die!* confirms for us that no matter how far we may be removed from the beauty of a Robert Redford or a Diana Ross, we are still light-years from true ugliness.

5   And we go to have fun.

6   Ah, but this is where the ground starts to slope away, isn't it? Because this is a very peculiar sort of fun, indeed. The fun comes from seeing others menaced—sometimes killed. One critic has suggested that if pro football has become the voyeur's version of combat, then the horror film has become the modern version of the public lynching.

7   It is true that the mythic, "fairy-tale" horror film intends to take away the shades of gray. . . . It urges us to put away our more civilized and adult penchant for analysis and to become children again, seeing things in pure blacks and whites. It may be that horror movies provide psychic relief on this level because this invitation to lapse into simplicity, irrationality and even outright madness is extended so rarely. We are told we may allow our emotions a free rein . . . or no rein at all.

8   If we are all insane, then sanity becomes a matter of degree. If your insanity leads you to carve up women like Jack the Ripper or the Cleveland Torso Murderer, we clap you away in the funny farm (but neither of those two amateur-night surgeons was ever caught, heh-heh-heh); if, on the other hand, your insanity leads you only to talk to yourself when you're under stress or to pick your nose on your morning bus, then you are left alone to go about your business . . . though it is doubtful that you will ever be invited to the best parties.

9   The potential lyncher is in almost all of us (excluding saints, past and present; but then, most saints have been crazy in their own ways), and every now and then, he has to be let loose to scream and roll around in the grass. Our emotions and our fears form their own body, and we recognize that it demands its own exercise to maintain proper muscle tone. Certain of these emotional muscles are accepted—even exalted—in civilized society; they are, of course, the emotions that tend to maintain the status quo of civilization itself. Love, friendship, loyalty, kindness—these are all the emotions that we applaud, emotions that have been immortalized in the couplets of Hallmark cards and in the verses (I don't dare call it poetry) of Leonard Nimoy.

10   When we exhibit these emotions, society showers us with positive reinforcement; we learn this even before we get out of diapers. When, as children, we hug our rotten little puke of a sister and give her a kiss, all the aunts and uncles smile and twit and cry, "Isn't he the sweetest little thing?" Such coveted treats as chocolate-covered graham crackers often follow. But if we deliberately slam the rotten little puke of a sister's fingers in the door, sanctions follow—angry remonstrance from parents, aunts and uncles; instead of a chocolate-covered graham cracker, a spanking.

11   But anticivilization emotions don't go away, and they demand periodic exercise. We have such "sick" jokes as, "What's the difference between a truckload of bowling balls and a truckload of dead babies?" (You can't unload a truckload of bowling balls with a pitchfork . . . a joke, by the way, that I heard originally from a ten-year-old). Such a joke may surprise a laugh or a grin out of us even as we recoil, a possibility that confirms the thesis: If we

share a brotherhood of man, then we also share an insanity of man. None of which is intended as a defense of either the sick joke or insanity but merely as an explanation of why the best horror films, like the best fairy tales, manage to be reactionary, anarchistic, and revolutionary all at the same time.

12   The mythic horror movie, like the sick joke, has a dirty job to do. It deliberately appeals to all that is worst in us. It is morbidity unchained, our most base instincts let free, our nastiest fantasies realized . . . and it all happens, fittingly enough, in the dark. For those reasons, good liberals often shy away from horror films. For myself, I like to see the most aggressive of them—*Dawn of the Dead,* for instance—as lifting a trap door in the civilized forebrain and throwing a basket of raw meat to the hungry alligators swimming around in that subterranean river beneath.

13   Why bother? Because it keeps them from getting out, man. It keeps them down there and me up here. It was Lennon and McCartney who said that all you need is love, and I would agree with that.

14   As long as you keep the gators fed.

WHAT DID THE WRITER SAY AND WHAT DID YOU THINK? _____

1. What is the thesis?
2. What are the main reasons why people like horror movies?
3. In what ways other than horror movies do we exercise our "anti-civilization emotions?"
4. What is the purpose of mentioning the "sick joke" in paragraph 11?
5. Explain the last sentence.

HOW DID THE WRITER SAY IT? _____

1. In paragraph 1, why is "I think we're all mentally ill" better than "I think people are all mentally ill?"
2. In paragraph 10, why is "rotten little puke of a sister" better than "irritating little sister?"
3. The author claims that horror movies urge us to "become children again." Where does the writing make use of some of the language of childhood?
4. Explain the meaning of "heh-heh-heh" in paragraph 8.

WHAT ABOUT *YOUR* WRITING?

In paragraph 9, Stephen King writes, "The potential lyncher is in almost all of us . . . and every now and then, he has to be let loose to scream and roll around in the grass." Most American publishers would strongly urge the author to rewrite this sentence—and some publishers would insist. The "potential lyncher" could just as easily be a woman as a man, after all. In fact, the sex of the person is totally irrelevant to the meaning of the sentence. Isn't the use of *he* both illogical and unfair (even though few people actually want to be a lyncher)? In a technical sense, the wording in King's sentence is grammatical, of course, but isn't there a way of being correct without the risk of offending some readers?

Many feminists have charged that our language echoes the sexual discrimination of society as a whole. The ease with which jokes, sometimes good ones, can be manufactured at the expense of the feminist movement probably tends to make it too easy for some to shrug off legitimate complaints. One may feel entitled to laugh at the insanely enlightened captain of a sinking ship who yells "Person the lifeboats" instead of "Man the lifeboats." One should be more hesitant, however, about laughing at the female employee of the post office who has spent an exhausting day trudging through the snow and who resents being known as a "mailman" instead of a "mail carrier." In any event, feminists have singled out for special attack the use of *he, his, him,* and *himself* when sex is unknown, mixed, or immaterial.

Whatever your personal preferences may be, most publishers of books, magazines, and newspapers have responded positively to the complaints. The *he, his, him, himself* usage has all but disappeared from print, and the trend is virtually certain to continue. A sentence like *A driver needs to know how his car works* is already beginning to sound as outdated as words like *icebox* and *Victrola*.

The best and easiest way to solve the *he* problem without damaging your style is to rephrase into plural forms whenever possible:

Original	Rephrased
A good student turns in his assignments on time.	Good students turn in their assignments on time.
Nobody wants his friends to take him for granted.	People do not want their friends to take them for granted.
Everyone at the banquet rose from his seat to give the senator an ovation.	All the guests at the banquet rose from their seats to give the senator an ovation.

(*Note: Nobody* and *everyone,* in the original sentences, always take a singular verb and pronoun in standard written English. Use of *they, them, their* in those sentences would be flatly incorrect.)

The word *one* can also be helpful at times, though it often creates an excessively formal tone. The plural approach is generally more satisfactory:

Original	Rephrased
A person must concentrate on his own happiness first.	One must concentrate on one's own happiness first.
Anybody can break his bad habits if he only tries.	One can break one's bad habits if one only tries.

If you find yourself, for some reason, locked into a singular form, repetition or substantial revisions may be necessary. In King's complete sentence, for example, he mentions *saints* as well as the *lyncher.* Changing *lyncher* to *lynchers* would create confusion because the nonsexist *they* could then refer to two different groups of people. When the plural form won't work, look for other possibilities.

Original	Rephrased
The potential lyncher is in all of us (excluding saints, past and present; but then, most saints have been crazy in their own ways), and every now and then, he has to be let loose to scream and roll around in the grass.	The potential lyncher is in all of us (excluding saints, past and present; but then, most saints have been crazy in their own ways), and every now and then, the lyncher has to be let loose to scream and roll around in the grass.
The reader will need to use all his attention to understand the plot.	The reader will need to be extremely attentive to understand the plot.
The best policy for someone who has been arrested is to keep his mouth shut.	The best policy for someone who has been arrested is to say as little as possible.

Now for two warnings. First, do what you can to avoid habitual reliance on the phrases *he or she, his or hers, him or her, himself or herself.* These expressions belong more to legal contracts than to ordinary writing, and when they are used repeatedly, the result is often absurd.

Poor	Better
A writer always should remember that he or she is writing for his or her audience, not just for himself or herself.	Writers always should remember that they are writing for their audience, not just for themselves.

Second, avoid artificial constructions like *s/he* or *he/she*. Many readers, and most English teachers, will view them as strained efforts to show off the writer's devotion to equal rights. The devotion may deserve praise, but straining and showing off have almost never resulted in good writing.

THINKING LIKE A MOUNTAIN

ALDO LEOPOLD

Best known for his book *A Sand County Almanac* (1949), Aldo Leopold (1886–1948) wrote extensively on nature and the environment. He is often credited with being among the first to apply scientific knowledge rather than emotional rhetoric to conservation and ecology.

Words to check:

rimrock (paragraph 1)	melee (4)
gleanings (2)	extirpate (7)
decipher (3)	anaemic (7)
implicit (3)	desuetude (7)
tyro (3)	defoliated (7)
fording (4)	dictum (10)

1   A deep chesty bawl echoes from rimrock to rimrock, rolls down the mountain, and fades into the far blackness of the night. It is an outburst of wild defiant sorrow, and of contempt for all the adversities of the world.

2   Every living thing (and perhaps many a dead one as well) pays heed to that call. To the deer it is a reminder of the way of all flesh, to the pine a forecast of midnight scuffles and of blood upon the snow, to the coyote a promise of gleanings to come, to the cowman a threat of red ink at the bank, to the hunter a challenge of fang against bullet. Yet behind these obvious and immediate hopes and fears there lies a deeper meaning, known only to the mountain itself. Only the mountain has lived long enough to listen objectively to the howl of a wolf.

3   Those unable to decipher the hidden meaning know nevertheless that it is there, for it is felt in all wolf country, and distinguishes that country from all other land. It tingles in the spine of all who hear wolves by night, or who scan their tracks by day. Even without sight or sound of wolf, it is implicit in a hundred small events: the midnight whinny of a pack horse, the rattle of rolling rocks, the bound of a fleeing deer, the way shadows lie under the spruces. Only the ineducable tyro can fail to sense the presence or absence of wolves, or the fact that mountains have a secret opinion about them.

4   My own conviction on this score dates from the day I saw a wolf die. We were eating lunch on a high rimrock, at the foot of which a turbulent river elbowed its way. We saw what we thought was a doe fording the torrent, her breast awash in white water. When she climbed the bank toward us and shook out her tail, we realized our error: it was a wolf. A half-dozen others, evidently grown pups, sprang from the willows and all joined in a welcoming mêlée of wagging tails and playful maulings. What was literally a pile of wolves writhed and tumbled in the center of an open flat at the foot of our rimrock.

5   In those days we had never heard of passing up a chance to kill a wolf. In a second we were pumping lead into the pack, but with more excitement than accuracy: how to aim a steep downhill shot is always confusing. When our rifles were empty, the old wolf was down, and a pup was dragging a leg into impassable slide-rocks.

6   We reached the old wolf in time to watch a fierce green fire dying in her eyes. I realized then, and have known ever since, that there was something new to me in those eyes—something known only to her and to the mountain. I was young then, and full of trigger-itch; I thought that because fewer wolves meant more deer, that no wolves would mean hunters' paradise. But after seeing the green fire die, I sensed that neither the wolf nor the mountain agreed with such a view.

7   Since then I have lived to see state after state extirpate its wolves. I have watched the face of many a newly wolfless mountain, and seen the south-facing slopes wrinkle with a maze of new deer trails. I have seen every edible bush and seedling browsed, first to anaemic desuetude, and then to death. I have seen every edible tree defoliated to the height of a saddlehorn. Such a mountain looks as if someone had given God a new pruning shears, and forbidden Him all other exercise. In the end the starved bones of the hoped-for deer herd, dead of its own too-much, bleach with the bones of the dead sage, or molder under the high-lined junipers.

8   I now suspect that just as a deer herd lives in mortal fear of its wolves, so does a mountain live in mortal fear of its deer. And perhaps with better cause, for while a buck pulled down by wolves can be replaced in two or

three years, a range pulled down by too many deer may fail of replacement in as many decades.

9   So also with cows. The cowman who cleans his range of wolves does not realize that he is taking over the wolf's job of trimming the herd to fit the range. He has not learned to think like a mountain. Hence we have dust-bowls, and rivers washing the future into the sea.

10   We all strive for safety, prosperity, comfort, long life, and dullness. The deer strives with his supple legs, the cowman with trap and poison, the statesman with pen, the most of us with machines, votes, and dollars, but it all comes to the same thing: peace in our time. A measure of success in this is all well enough, and perhaps is a requisite to objective thinking, but too much safety seems to yield only danger in the long run. Perhaps this is behind Thoreau's dictum: In wildness is the salvation of the world. Perhaps this is the hidden meaning in the howl of the wolf, long known among mountains, but seldom perceived among men.

WHAT DID THE WRITER SAY AND WHAT DID YOU THINK?

1. What is the thesis?
2. Why are wolves so important to the "life" of a mountain?
3. What does it mean to "think like a mountain?"
4. How have Leopold's feelings about wolves changed over the years?
5. What does the howl of a wolf signify to a deer? to a pine? to a coyote? to a cowman?
6. Why is the mountain afraid of deer?
7. Why does Leopold consider wildness a salvation?

HOW DID THE WRITER SAY IT?

1. Does Leopold use any jargon (see p. 293)? If so, where?
2. What image does Leopold use to describe an overgrazed mountain? Explain the effectiveness of this image?
3. What is the intended audience for this essay? Are the style and vocabulary appropriate?
4. What is the purpose of the hunting story in paragraphs 4-6?

========WHAT ABOUT *YOUR* WRITING?========

Leopold makes frequent use of words that belong far more to formal English than to the everyday English more familiar to most people. He writes *tyro* instead of *beginner, extirpate* instead of *wipe out, desuetude* instead of *lack of use.* Isn't this language too fancy? Is fancy writing good English?

The best reply to those questions is that they need to be rethought. It's like asking if a tuxedo is good dress. It's good dress for formal dances, but it's bad dress for mowing the lawn. Shorts and a T-shirt are good dress for mowing the lawn, but bad dress for a formal dance. There's no one kind of good dress. A good dresser is someone who knows what kind of clothes to wear for different occasions.

There's no one kind of good English, either. It varies. It's what's appropriate to the subject, situation, and audience. As these elements change, the nature of what's appropriate will change. Tuxedo English is appropriate for ceremonial occasions, serious studies of specialized subjects, and so on. Lincoln's Gettysburg Address is written in formal English. If it had been written in a chatty, conversational style with folksy anecdotes about Lincoln's childhood, it would have been written in bad English and bad taste. On the other hand, shorts-and-T-shirt English is good English for much conversation and the dialogue of certain characters in works of fiction. A quarterback in a huddle says, "Play 32. Left tackle. Let's get the bums"—or something like that. It would be bad English for him to say, "Let us, my teammates, utilize Play 32 to assault the left tackle position of our adversaries."

Most Freshman English papers should probably be written at the sportcoat-and-necktie level. A tuxedo is absurd. Even a business suit might sometimes be a bit stiff for the subject, situation, and audience. But shorts and a T-shirt are also out of place. Grammar still counts. Organization still counts. There aren't as many rules to worry about as in tuxedo English, but there are still plenty of rules.

In "Thinking Like a Mountain," Leopold is probably writing what could be called business-suit English. The subject is a serious one on life and death issues, and the author feels it needs to be treated with gravity and dignity. He doesn't write everyday English because he's not dealing with an everyday subject. Good English changes all the time—and it doesn't have much to do with avoiding words like *ain't* or *desuetude.*

MY WOOD

E. M. FORSTER

Although British novelist and literary critic Edward Morgan Forster (1879–1970)
was born and formally educated in England, he traveled and lived abroad for a
number of years. His most famous novel, *A Passage to India* (1924), was the result
of his serving as private secretary to the Maharajah of Dewas State Senior in India
after World War I. He also lived in Greece and Italy for a time. Among his other
novels are *Where Angels Fear to Tread* (1905), *The Longest Journey* (1907), *A Room
with a View* (1908), *Howards End* (1910), and *Maurice* (posthumous). The essay
"My Wood" from *Abinger Harvest* (1936) is an account of the effects which Forster
believes are the unsettling companions of ownership.

Words to check:

parable (paragraph 2)	carnal (5)
asceticism (2)	meagre (7)
antithesis (2)	traverses (7)
depreciating (4)	bracken (7)
amiss (4)	gorges (7)
pretentious (5)	avaricious (7)
exquisite (5)	quadruple (7)

1   A few years ago I wrote a book which dealt in part with the difficulties of the
English in India. Feeling that they would have had no difficulties in India
themselves, the Americans read the book freely. The more they read it the
better it made them feel, and a cheque to the author was the result. I bought
a wood with the cheque. It is not a large wood—it contains scarcely any
trees, and it is intersected, blast it, by a public footpath. Still, it is the first
property that I have owned, so it is right that other people should participate
in my shame, and should ask themselves, in accents that will vary in horror,
this very important question: What is the effect of property upon the character? Don't let's touch economics; the effect of private ownership upon the
community as a whole is another question—a more important question, perhaps, but another one. Let's keep to psychology. If you own things, what's
their effect on you? What's the effect on me of my wood?

2   In the first place, it makes me feel heavy. Property does have this effect.
Property produces men of weight, and it was a man of weight who failed
to get into the Kingdom of Heaven. He was not wicked, that unfortunate
millionaire in the parable, he was only stout; he stuck out in front, not to

mention behind, and as he wedged himself this way and that in the crystalline entrance and bruised his well-fed flanks, he saw beneath him a comparatively slim camel passing through the eye of a needle and being woven into the robe of God.[1] The Gospels all through couple stoutness and slowness. They point out what is perfectly obvious, yet seldom realized: that if you have a lot of things you cannot move about a lot, that furniture requires dusting, dusters require servants, servants require insurance stamps, and the whole tangle of them makes you think twice before you accept an invitation to dinner or go for a bathe in the Jordan. Sometimes the Gospels proceed further and say with Tolstoy[2] that property is sinful; they approach the difficult ground of asceticism here, where I cannot follow them. But as to the immediate effects of property on people, they just show straightforward logic. It produces men of weight. Men of weight cannot, by definition, move like the lightning from the East unto the West, and the ascent of a fourteen-stone[3] bishop into a pulpit is thus the exact antithesis of the coming of the Son of Man.[4] My wood makes me feel heavy.

3   In the second place, it makes me feel it ought to be larger.

4   The other day I heard a twig snap in it. I was annoyed at first, for I thought that someone was blackberrying, and depreciating the value of the undergrowth. On coming nearer, I saw it was not a man who had trodden on the twig and snapped it, but a bird, and I felt pleased. My bird. The bird was not equally pleased. Ignoring the relation between us, it took fright as soon as it saw the shape of my face, and flew straight over the boundary hedge into a field, the property of Mrs. Henessy, where it sat down with a loud squawk. It had become Mrs. Henessy's bird. Something seemed grossly amiss here, something that would not have occurred had the wood been larger. I could not afford to buy Mrs. Henessy out, I dared not murder her, and limitations of this sort beset me on every side. Ahab[5] did not want that vineyard—he only needed it to round off his property, preparatory to plotting a new curve—and all the land around my wood has become necessary to me in order to round off the wood. A boundary protects. But—poor

---

[1] "It is easier for a camel to go through the eye of a needle than for a rich man to enter the kingdom of God." Matthew 19:24, Mark 10:25, Luke 18:25.

[2] Leo Tolstoy (1828–1910), Russian writer and philosopher.

[3] A stone is a British term for fourteen pounds. A fourteen-stone bishop weighs 196 pounds.

[4] A traditional term for Jesus.

[5] An ironic reference to a king of ancient Israel. Ahab coveted the vineyard of Naboth the Jezreelite. When Naboth refused to sell, Ahab's wife Jezebel accused him of "cursing God and King," and Naboth was stoned to death. Ahab was denounced by the prophet Elijah as a murderer.

little thing—the boundary ought in its turn to be protected. Noises on the edge of it. Children throw stones. A little more, and then a little more, until we reach the sea. Happy Canute![6] Happier Alexander![7] And after all, why should even the world be the limit of possession? A rocket containing a Union Jack,[8] will, it is hoped, be shortly fired at the moon. Mars. Sirius.[9] Beyond which . . . But these immensities ended by saddening me. I could not suppose that my wood was the destined nucleus of universal dominion—it is so very small and contains no mineral wealth beyond the blackberries. Nor was I comforted when Mrs. Henessy's bird took alarm for the second time and flew clean away from us all, under the belief that it belonged to itself.

5   In the third place, property makes its owner feel that he ought to do something to it. Yet he isn't sure what. A restlessness comes over him, a vague sense that he has a personality to express—the same sense which, without any vagueness, leads the artist to an act of creation. Sometimes I think I will cut down such trees as remain in the wood, at other times I want to fill up the gaps between them with new trees. Both impulses are pretentious and empty. They are not honest movements towards money-making or beauty. They spring from a foolish desire to express myself and from an inability to enjoy what I have got. Creation, property, enjoyment form a sinister trinity in the human mind. Creation and enjoyment are both very very good, yet they are often unattainable without a material basis, and at such moments property pushes itself in as a substitute, saying, "Accept me instead—I'm good enough for all three." It is not enough. It is, as Shakespeare said of lust, "The expense of spirit in a waste of shame": it is "Before, a joy proposed; behind, a dream." Yet we don't know how to shun it. It is forced on us by our economic system as the alternative to starvation. It is also forced on us by an internal defect in the soul, by the feeling that in property may lie the germs of self-development and of exquisite or heroic deeds. Our life on earth is, and ought to be, material and carnal. But we have not yet learned to manage our materialism and carnality properly; they are still entangled with the desire for ownership, where (in the words of Dante) "Possession is one with loss."

6   And this brings us to our fourth and final point: the blackberries.

---

[6] King Canute, a Danish king of England (1016-1035), is said by legend to have realized the limits of his powers when he commanded the tide to stop rising, and the tide refused to obey.

[7] Alexander the Great (356–323 B.C.) is said to have wept because he had no more worlds to conquer.

[8] Traditional term for the flag of the United Kingdom.

[9] Sirius is the brightest star in the heavens, 8.6 light years from Earth.

7   Blackberries are not plentiful in this meagre grove, but they are easily seen from the public footpath which traverses it, and all too easily gathered. Foxgloves, too—people will pull up the foxgloves, and ladies of an educational tendency even grub for toadstools to show them on the Monday in class. Other ladies, less educated, roll down the bracken in the arms of their gentlemen friends. There is paper, there are tins. Pray, does my wood belong to me or doesn't it? And, if it does, should I not own it best by allowing no one else to walk there? There is a wood near Lyme Regis, also cursed by a public footpath, where the owner has not hesitated on this point. He has built high stone walls each side of the path, and has spanned it by bridges, so that the public circulate like termites while he gorges on the blackberries unseen. He really does own his wood, this able chap. Dives in Hell did pretty well, but the gulf dividing him from Lazarus could be traversed by vision, and nothing traverses it here.[10] And perhaps I shall come to this in time. I shall wall in and fence out until I really taste the sweets of property. Enormously stout, endlessly avaricious, pseudo-creative, intensely selfish, I shall weave upon my forehead the quadruple crown of possession until those nasty Bolshies[11] come and take it off again and thrust me aside into the outer darkness.

WHAT DID THE WRITER SAY AND WHAT DID YOU THINK? _____

1. Is Forster's thesis evident? What is it?
2. Why is the author's view of ownership the reverse of what might be expected?
3. Who does Forster believe would criticize him for owning property?
4. For whom do you suppose this essay was originally intended?
5. Does the philosophy of this essay coincide with modern America's beliefs? Why or why not?
6. How would people who own vast properties react to Forster's essay? Would they feel empathy?
7. Why do you feel that Forster carefully distinguishes property from money? Is there any difference in their effects on the owner?

[10] The reference is to Luke 16:19–26. A rich man, traditionally known as Dives, rejects the beggar Lazarus. After their deaths, the rich man, tormented in hell, can see Lazarus in heaven.
[11] Slang for Bolsheviks, the revolutionary group which formed the Communist Party in Russia.

HOW DID THE WRITER SAY IT? ——————————————

1. Is Forster's essay mainly one of cause or effect? How many effects does he cite? How many causes?
2. Why does Forster choose to use two one-sentence paragraphs (3 and 5)? What purpose do these two sentences fulfill?
3. Is it a problem that Forster does not include a separate concluding paragraph after conveying his fourth point? Why or why not?

============WHAT ABOUT *YOUR* WRITING?============

Don't underestimate the *topic sentence.* Teachers and textbooks sometimes terrorize students into the mistaken belief that topic sentences are synonymous with moral virtue, but topic sentences still demand your attention.

A topic sentence, usually appearing at or near the beginning or end of a paragraph, identifies the subject of the paragraph and frequently indicates the writer's attitude toward the subject. In a well-organized paper, each topic sentence usually expresses a major supporting point for the thesis; then the sentences in the rest of each paragraph directly support that paragraph's own topic sentence. It's often possible to write out the thesis statement and each topic sentence and end with an excellent summary of a whole essay.

E.M. Forster in "My Wood" begins with a one-paragraph introduction that presents the thesis that property ownership does not always produce positive effects for the owner. In the next paragraph, he begins with the topic sentence, "In the first place, it makes me feel heavy." Now notice this sequence of topic sentences in remaining paragraphs:

In the second place, it makes me feel it ought to be larger.

In the third place, property makes its owner feel he ought to do something to it.

And this brings us to our fourth and final point: the blackberries.

The topic sentences give structure to the essay, and the structure makes it easy for the reader to follow the author's thoughts.

Don't assume from these quoted passages that all well-organized papers must number each of their points. Don't assume that all subjects can be given the tight organization that Forster is able to employ. Don't even assume that every paragraph in every paper needs an explicit topic sentence. Sometimes transitional paragraphs, linking separate sections of a paper, are needed to restate the subject just dealt with and to announce the next subject. They are rarely more than one or two sentences long and have no topic sentence:

The writer, then, has involved her characters in an interesting dilemma. How does she get them out of it?

Having now removed the drumsticks and wings, you are ready for the next step: carving.

Many paragraphs in narration and description may also do without explicit topic sentences. A descriptive paragraph dealing solely with a person's clothing may often have what can be thought of as a topic idea and manage quite well without a topic sentence. A narrative passage about a murderer concealing evidence or a child throwing a temper tantrum may also be sustained by an unstated topic idea. The paragraph you are now reading, in fact, tries to get by without an explicit topic sentence such as "There's nothing sacred about topic sentences."

With all these warnings, the teachers and textbooks are far more right than wrong. Topic sentences are a major aid to organization and clarity. They help your reader, and they help you.

8

DIVISION AND CLASSIFICATION

S ome topics are difficult or impossible to attack head on. Such topics are often best approached through analysis: studying a complex subject by breaking it down into smaller units. Analysis itself calls for analysis and can be broken down into division and classification.

DIVISION

What are the moving parts of a rotary engine? What are the major characteristics of realism in literature? What are the three major divisions of the federal government? The United States of America is divided into fifty states. Can you name them all? Your own state is divided into counties or parishes. How many of them can you name?

In *division* (also known as *partition*) a subject commonly thought of as a single unit is reduced to its separate parts. Potential renters of an apartment rarely begin by thinking of the apartment as a whole. They mentally divide it into living room, bedroom, kitchen, and bathroom. If they think it worthwhile, they may go on to subdivisions of each room: walls, ceiling, floor, for example. At any rate, they study each division separately before reaching any useful conclusion about the entire apartment. Soldiers use division to study a rifle; chemists use division to find out the ingredients of a compound; doctors use division in a physical checkup to examine a patient— heart, lungs, blood, and so forth.

Division is a natural, logical, and necessary form of thought. For writing purposes, however, it often tends to be more cut-and-dried than classification, and most English teachers generally prefer classification assignments. Besides, any students who have written a process paper (see Chapter 5) have already used a form of division to break the process into its separate steps. For these reasons, the rest of this chapter concentrates on classification.

CLASSIFICATION

Are you an introvert or an extrovert? Are you lower class, middle class, or upper class? Are you a Democrat, Republican, or Independent? Are you a Protestant, Catholic, Jew, Moslem, Hindu, Buddhist, Sikh, atheist, agnostic, or "other"? Are you heterosexual or homosexual? Are you left-handed, right-handed, or ambidextrous? Are you a nondrinker, light drinker, normal drinker, heavy drinker, or alcoholic?

No answers are necessary. The questions aren't intended to snoop. They're intended to demonstrate the universality of classification.

In *classification* we analyze a subject like apartments, not *an* apartment; engines, not an engine. We analyze the subject by arranging it into groups or categories rather than separate parts. We divide an apartment into rooms, but we classify apartments into high rises, garden apartments, tenements, and so on. We classify when we make out a shopping list to deal with the thousands of articles in a supermarket: dairy, meats, produce, paper goods, and other obvious groupings. A business manager classifies: complaints I can ignore, complaints I have to do something about. A college catalog classifies: required courses, elective courses.

Without classification certain kinds of systematic thought would be impossible. Biologists, for example, classify in order to make basic sense of the world, in order to be able to function at all. They classify living things into plants and animals. They classify animals into Vertebrates and Invertebrates. They classify Vertebrates into Mammals, Birds, Reptiles, Amphibians, and Fish. Each class has its distinct characteristics, so when biologists meet some wriggly little item they haven't seen before, they have some way of at least beginning to cope with it. As another example, political leaders in presidential elections undoubtedly classify the states. They classify because no other way exists to handle reality. Which states are Sure for Us? Which states are Sure for Them? Which states are Toss-ups? Classification here is not a parlor game or intellectual exercise. It's the only way of determining where the time and money should go.

Classification can sometimes be a game, however, and it can lead to excellent humorous papers. Members of a bad football team could be classified as Hopeless Bums, Hopeless Mediocrities, and Hopeless Physical Wrecks. Household chores could be classified as Chores I Can Put Off for a Week, Chores I Can Put Off for a Month, and Chores I Can Put Off Forever. A student once classified teachers as Fascist Pigs, Middle-of-the-Road Sheep, and Mad Dog Radicals.

The pattern of a classification—or division—paper is straightforward and pretty much self-evident. Each class or division generally represents a major section of the paper. Each is defined and described, with as many examples as are needed for clarity. Each is carefully differentiated from the others when any possibility of confusion occurs.

In writing a classification paper, keep these elementary principles of logic in mind:

Use Only One Principle of Classification.   Different classifications can apply at different times to the same subject, depending on one's interests and insights. The essential requirement is that only one basis of classification be used at a time. Cars, for instance, can be classified by size. They can also be classified by manufacturer, price, body style, country of origin, and so on. Choose the principle of classification suitable to your purpose. Something is obviously cockeyed in this arrangement of cars: subcompact, compact, intermediate, Fords, full-size.

EXERCISE

What are the errors in the following classification outlines?

Schools	**Students**
I. Elementary schools	I. Bright
II. Junior high schools	II. Average
III. Parochial schools	III. Hardworking
IV. High schools	IV. Dull
V. Colleges and universities	

Teachers	**Crimes**
I. Hard graders	I. Violent
II. Friendly	II. Non-violent
III. Easy graders	III. Fraud

Sections of America	**Politicians**
I. East	I. Good
II. South	II. Bad
III. Midwest	III. Mediocre
IV. Slums	IV. Honest
V. Far West	

Be Consistent. Once you have determined a principle of classification, stick with it throughout the paper. Mixing principles invariably creates illogical overlapping of classes.

Make the Classifications as Complete as Possible. All individual units within your subject should be able to fit into one of the classes you have devised. Classifying politicians as only good or bad doesn't take care of the many who are neither all one nor all the other; you need another category. When you face the prospect of an endless number of classes, it's generally better to revise the subject a bit than to add a catch-all class like "Miscellaneous" or "Others." A paper classifying religions, for example, could go on forever, whereas a paper classifying "Major Religions in America" would have a much simpler task.

EXERCISE

Point out incompleteness in the following classification outlines.

Academic Degrees	**Career Opportunities**
I. B.A.	I. Business
II. B.S.	II. Government
III. M.A.	
IV. Ph.D.	

Television Programs	**Where to Live in America**
I. Comedies	I. Cities
II. Dramas	II. Suburbs
III. Sports	
IV. Quiz shows	

Acknowledge Any Complications.   Classification is logical and essential, but it's also arbitrary and artificial. It pins labels on materials that weren't born with them. It may be helpful at times to classify people as introverts or extroverts, but a good paper points out that introverts can sometimes be outgoing among close friends, and extroverts can sometimes be shy in unfamiliar or threatening circumstances. Similarly, labels like liberal and conservative can be valuable, but a good paper will mention that few people are entirely liberal or conservative about everything.

Follow the Persuasive Principle.   Finally, what of the persuasive principle? A classification paper classifies. What does it have to persuade anyone about?

In a fussy, technical sense, every classification paper has a thesis whether the writer wants one or not. The writer asserts that there are three classes of teachers or four classes of mental illness or five classes of surgeons. By the end of the paper, sure enough, there are the three, four, or five classes, logically consistent and complete.

And there, sure enough, if that's all the writer does, is a distortion of the persuasive principle.

A good classification paper can utilize the persuasive principle in far more effective ways. To the logic and order of classification it can add the power and bite of a forceful point of view. In some papers, the naming of classes in itself can express the writer's attitude. An introductory paragraph stating that the three kinds of teachers are fascist pigs, middle-of-the-road sheep, and mad dog radicals probably doesn't need an explicit thesis statement that all three classes are obnoxious. A paper with less dramatic labels can declare a thesis by expressing a strong preference for one class over the others. It can express scorn for all classes. It can ridicule traditional classifications. Almost all the subjects for classification brought up in this chapter invite a thesis:

Each different kind of car has serious drawbacks.

Good politicians in this country are vastly outnumbered by the bad and mediocre.

Every major religion in America has a similar concept of God.

The distinctions among normal drinkers, heavy drinkers, and alcoholics are dangerously vague.

Only one kind of television program makes any appeal to the viewer's intelligence.

It's not hard to see the extra interest such approaches can give a paper. Don't just classify, then. Convince.

WRITING SUGGESTIONS FOR CLASSIFICATION THEMES

Use classification to analyze one of the following subjects. Narrow down any of the subjects as necessary, and remember the importance of working a thesis into your paper. With slight changes, some topics may also lend themselves to analysis by division.

1. Television detectives
2. Snobbishness
3. Drug users
4. People at a concert or sporting event
5. Methods of making excuses
6. Cashiers in supermarkets
7. Clothing
8. Parents
9. Love
10. Hate
11. Laziness
12. News programs or commentators
13. Freshman English students
14. Managers or coaches of athletic teams
15. Ambition
16. Summer jobs
17. Pessimists or optimists
18. Attitudes toward Christmas
19. Attitudes toward money
20. Attitudes toward sex

Three Kinds of Clean

Christine J. Hall (student)

Thesis: My friends fall neatly into three categories of
cleanliness, only one of which makes much sense
to me.

    I.   Messy friends
       A. Messy household
       B. Messy animals and children
   II.   Clean friends
       A. Organized messes
       B. Freedom combined with neatness
 III. Fanatical friends
       A. Houses almost sterile
       B. Essentials of life all invisible
       C. Stifled atmosphere

Conclusion: Those who go to either extreme about cleanliness
make me uncomfortable.

Lately, I have been running a less than extensive and scientific study on my friends and how clean their houses are. Though my friends live in all parts of the state, have a wide variety of jobs, and an even wider variety of children and house pets, their houses fall neatly into three categories of cleanness. Some of them are messy; some are clean; and some are fanatical.

My messy friends live in houses and apartments that look like the last days of a going-out-of-business sale. Everything is piled up and jumbled together. Clean clothes are indistinguishable from dirty laundry. The new groceries are tossed on the table with leftovers from the pizza they had two nights ago. Bits and pieces of everyone's favorite hobbies drift through the house. Quilt squares, clay, model airplane parts and paint are underfoot, overhead, and in the way. Dogs, cats, and kids tend to wander through the mess, eating and playing with anything they can reach. This kind of life disgusts a lot of people, but my messy friends thrive on it. Neatness, they say, stifles them.

My clean friends live in saner, calmer places. The occasional mess still exists, true, but such messes are usually tucked away in basements and closets, where no one has to look at them. My clean friends keep things . . . clean. Their dirty laundry is in the laundry room, and their clean clothes are in drawers or folded and stacked at the end of the bed. Groceries are put away, and even leftover pizza gets stuck in the fridge. The things they do for pleasure—video games, embroidery, lawn darts, or whatever— are out and visible, but not in anyone's way. Their children play anywhere and everywhere, but learn to clean up when they finish. Their animals are lively, but go outside to be wild. My clean friends love the way they live. They feel relaxed, yet civilized. The only thing they can't stand is a visit from a fanatical friend.

My fanatical friends live in houses that are so clean they are almost sterile. They live for the motto, "A place for everything, and everything in its place." There is no mess anywhere. Their closets, basements, and garages are as neat as their living rooms. I don't know if they give their clothes permission to get dirty, but I have certainly never seen any evidence of anything so untidy as a washing machine or box of detergent. I am not even sure if my fanatical friends eat because there is absolutely no sign of food anywhere. I suspect that their only hobbies are untangling phone cords and scrubbing bathroom grout. They only have tropical fish for pets, and their children are sent out of the house before they can fingerpaint and play with clay. Having them at home is too messy. My fanatical friends, of course, don't think they're fanatical. They think the rest of the world is a bunch of slobs.

It's not my part to make judgments on my friends and their houses. Each group—messy, clean, or fanatical—keeps their houses the way they please, and that's just fine. But I do worry about people who care so little about their home that they can't see what it looks like, and about people who care so much that they can't see anything else.

HOW FIT ARE YOU?

KENNETH H. COOPER

Kenneth Cooper's book *Aerobics,* based on his experience as a doctor in the U.S. Air Force, presents a physical fitness program designed to increase the oxygen capacity of the body through exercises like swimming, jogging, walking, and cycling. The selection is an excerpt from the second chapter of the book.

Words to check:

physiological (paragraph 2)	calisthenics (13)
candidly (3)	skeletal (19)
isometrics (5)	cardiovascular (21)
treadmill (12)	

1   I was visiting a colleague who was testing volunteers for a special project that would require men in the best possible condition. I passed three of the volunteers in the hall. Two had normal builds, but the third was definitely muscular.

2   "Which of the three do you think will get our recommendation?" my friend asked, tossing their medical records across the desk. I skimmed over the physiological data until I came to the slot where it asked, "Regular exercise?"

3   One wrote, candidly, "None."

4   The second, "Nothing regular. Just ride my bike to the base and back every day. About three miles one way."

5   The third, "Isometrics and weight lifting, one hour a day, five days a week." The muscular one!

6   I glanced back over each of the records. All pilots, all in their early 30s, none with any history of illness.

7   "Well?" asked my friend.

8   "I'd bet on the cyclist."

9   "Not the weight lifter?"

10   "Not if that's all he does."

11   My friend smiled. "I think you're right."

12   Next day he proved it. The three came back for their treadmill tests and the nonexerciser and the weight lifter were completely fatigued within the first five minutes. The cyclist was still going strong 10 minutes later, running uphill at a 6½ mph clip. He was recommended for the project. The other two weren't.

13   This story, when I use it in my lectures, always surprises people. The nonexerciser they can believe. The cyclist, maybe. But the weight lifter, or anyone who does strictly isometrics or calisthenics, they all *look* in such good condition!

14   In my business, looks are deceitful. Some exceptionally physically fit men tested in our laboratory were middle-aged types with slight builds, including an occasional one with a paunch. Some of the most unfit we've ever seen were husky young men with cardiac conditions.

15   If this shatters any illusions about slim waistlines and large biceps being the key to good health, I'm sorry. They're not a deterrent, but they're no guarantee either. They're mostly a byproduct. The real key is elsewhere.

16   Take those three volunteers. By ordinary standards, all three should have been accepted. None of them had any physical defects, or ever had any. Why the discrimination?

17   For special projects, the military services can afford to be discriminate. They can afford to classify the physically fit into their three classic categories and choose only the most fit.

18   The nonexerciser represents passive fitness. There's nothing wrong with him—not yet anyway—but there's nothing really right with him either. If he's lucky, he can coast like that for years. But, without any activity, his body is essentially deteriorating.

19   The weight lifter, or those who emphasize isometrics or calisthenics, represent muscular fitness. These types, who have the right motives but the wrong approach, are struck with the myth that muscular strength or agility means physical fitness. This is one of the great misconceptions in the field of exercise. The muscles that show—the skeletal muscles—are just one system in the body, and by no means the most important. If your exercise program is directed only at the skeletal muscles, you'll never achieve real physical fitness.

20   The cyclist, whether he knew it or not, had found one of the most basic means to overall fitness. . . . By riding three miles to work, six miles round trip, he was earning more than enough points to answer the question, "How much exercise?"* and he proved it on the treadmill.

21   The cyclist represents the third, and best, kind of fitness, overall fitness. We call it endurance fitness, or working capacity, the ability to do prolonged work without undue fatigue. It assumes the absence of any ailment, and it has little to do with pure muscular strength or agility. It has very much to do with the body's *overall* health, the health of the heart, the lungs, the entire cardiovascular system and the other organs, *as well as* the muscles.

* Cooper had devised a point system for measuring physical fitness.

WHAT DID THE WRITER SAY
AND WHAT DID YOU THINK? _____

1. What group does Cooper classify?
2. Is there a thesis? If so, what is it?
3. What is the main advantage of cycling over weight lifting and calisthenics?
4. Does the writer maintain that anything is wrong with weight lifting and calisthenics in themselves?

HOW DID THE WRITER SAY IT? _____

1. What purposes are served by starting with a story rather than with the system of classification?
2. Does the writer merely describe each class, or does he also provide convenient labels for each?
3. Does the writer recognize the possibility that the second and third classes can overlap?

══════════════WHAT ABOUT *YOUR* WRITING?══════════════

"The cyclist, maybe." Isn't that a sentence fragment? "Why the discrimination?" Isn't that another sentence fragment? Aren't sentence fragments illegal? The answers to these questions are *yes, yes,* and *sort of.*

Look at it this way: there's a sensible speed limit on the road. One night you're driving well over the limit. A police officer who is worth anything would stop you to give you a ticket. This night an officer stops you and finds that you're speeding in order to get a pregnant woman to the hospital on time or a badly beaten man to the emergency ward. If the officer is worth anything now, you get a siren escort that enables you to break the law more safely and efficiently.

Your instructor, in some respects, is the police officer. By and large, sentence fragments are not standard written English, and your instructor rightly gives you a ticket for them. Every once in a while, a situation turns up when a fragment can be justified. You want a special dramatic effect, a sudden note of breeziness or informality, perhaps, that a grammatically complete sentence could not achieve as well. In that case, your instructor usually tries to be cooperative.

You don't speed to the emergency ward often, however, and sentence fragments, too, should be saved for special occasions. The burden of proof is on you: The officer wants to see the pregnant woman or beaten man, and the instructor wants to be convinced that the sentence fragment was justified by the demands of your paper. Finally, just as the officer wants assurance that you knew you were speeding and were in constant control, the instructor wants assurance that your sentence fragment was a deliberate stylistic device, not a simple grammatical error.

MOTHER-IN-LAW

CHARLOTTE LATVALA

Charlotte Latvala, a free-lance writer who lives near Pittsburgh, has fun in this essay analyzing the many different kinds of bad mothers-in-law and longing for the one good kind.

Words to check:

nirvana (paragraph 3)	harpies (16)
adversary (5)	vipers (16)
guises (5)	impromptu (20)
fallopian tubes (10)	maxims (32)
uterus (10)	decadence (34)
precocious (15)	liposuction (37)

1   You're in heaven. You've found a man who adores you, who makes you laugh and keeps you sane. For the first time in your life, you're thinking about a long-term commitment; in fact, you're discussing *the* long-term commitment, the June bride, till-death-do-us-part one.

2   Everything's going well; you've worked out a plan for careers, children, where you'll live, etc. Your bliss knows no bounds; your world is a sunny, positive place where birds chirp from dawn to dusk and all the movies have happy endings.

3   Sooner or later, however, you must leave nirvana for a few moments and face the one very real obstacle that women throughout the centuries have faced: You must meet his mother.

4   Never underestimate a mother's influence on her son. (If you're feeling brave, watch "The Manchurian Candidate" right before your meeting.) She

was the first and most important woman in his life, and their complex relationship, good or bad, has spanned decades. She's seen him through the chicken
pox, the prom and his first major heartache. You are cutting in on a dance
that's been going on for years.

5   A potential mother-in-law can be a lot of things. She can be your adversary,
your ally, or your critic. Once in a while she might become your friend. She is
never your own mother. Here are a few of the different guises she may take.

The Naysayer

6   This woman looks at the world through dark-gray glasses; she is negativity
personified. She has frequent imagined illnesses and pains no one can ease.
One of her favorite lines is "No one cares about me," closely followed by "He
never comes to see me anymore."

7   The Naysayer sees the world as a bleak and dreary place, full of suffering
and torment. She is convinced that human nature is rotten, and that young
people today are selfish and immoral. Nothing, though, looks darker to her
than her son's future with you.

8   You really don't have many options here; she will assign evil motives to
your most innocent actions. No matter how hard you try to please her, she
will find a way to get her digs in. "I really had no idea that Frank was dating
such a talented girl. I don't know whether I'd spend so much money on
painting lessons, though."

9   Grit your teeth and smile. You can probably pick up tips from your future
husband.

The Baby-Crazed Fanatic

10   This woman's excitement at meeting you has nothing to do with you as an
individual. She looks at you and sees fallopian tubes and a uterus. You are the
answer to her prayers, the woman who will provide her with a soft little bundle of joy to croon sweet nothings to.

11   Within minutes of meeting you, she has informed you that most of her
friends are grandparents already. "Do you come from a large family?" she
asks eagerly, and coos with delight when you tell her that your younger sister
already has three children.

12   You hate to burst her bubble; you hate to tell her that you really want to
get your career off to a solid start before you even consider children. You
honestly don't think you should be discussing the subject with her in the
first place. But, before you can say anything, she puts her arm around your
shoulder and says, "Well, I'm sure it won't be long before you have one, too."

"No One's Good Enough For My Son"

13   Similar to The Naysayer, but more upbeat. At least on one subject.

14   God made one perfect man, and it is her son. He has never done anything wrong in his life. He is handsome, talented and generous. His manners are beyond reproach, and he is so intelligent he scares her.

15   She has a tendency to rattle on and on about his accomplishments throughout the years, from the precocious age at which she removed his training wheels to the ease with which he graduated from college with honors.

16   This wonderful man, however, has dated only harpies and vipers, of which you are the latest. At the slightest prompting, she will tell you much more than you want to know about the terrible women who have tried to trap her little boy into matrimonial hell. Don't bother trying to impress her with your sweet nature or good intentions. This woman would think Mother Teresa was a conniving shrew.

The Woman Of The World

17   This mother-in-law has been everywhere, and she wants to make sure you know it. She's fond of saying things like, "And as you know, Paris is so lovely in the spring! You *have* been to Paris, haven't you, dear?" while you squirm on the couch and try to think of an impressive way to say that you've only been out of the Tri-State area four times in your life.

18   To her, you are a provincial little drip, and you will probably hinder her son's progress in life by making him settle down in some wretched suburb and take vacations to the Poconos.

19   There is only one way to deal with this woman. Lie. For every trip abroad, for every exotic excursion that she brags about, make up one of your own.

The Accomplished Mother-In-Law

20   It's impossible to compete with a woman who has more talents than Madonna has bras. She's a heart surgeon who also has a Ph.D. in romance poetry. She's a nationally ranked chess champion. In her spare time, she plays the violin in a string quartet, teaches blind children to ride horses and whips up impromptu four-star meals in her gourmet kitchen.

21   Just listening to her exhausts you. Your fiance warned you about her (he said, "Oh, Mother keeps herself busy"), but you never dreamed any single human being could cram so much into a lifetime.

22   On top of it all, she's polite and charming. And when she asks you, "And what do *you* do, dear?" you would rather curl up and die than admit you're a word processor who rents a lot of movies and takes three-hour naps on Sunday afternoon.

The Experienced Mother-In-Law

23   This mother has been through it before. You are not the first woman to sit in her house and joyously proclaim that you really and truly love her son and will do everything in your power to make him happy forever and ever.

24   Divorce has a strange effect on people, and it tends to make mothers either extremely suspicious or nostalgic, depending on her opinion of Wife No. 1.

25   If she hated Wife No. 1, you're in luck, because you are the sensible decision that her son made when he was old enough for it.

26   If she was fond of Wife No. 1, you're in trouble. You will be forever compared, unfairly, to a woman who's not there to speak for herself. Little comments and asides ("Well, a lot of women these days can't cook. Of course, Freddy never could get Patrice out of the kitchen; she was always in there whipping up his favorites . . .") will forever remind you of who you're not.

The Pal

27   On the surface, this woman looks like a treat. She takes you warmly by the arm and insists that you call her Gladys. How sweet, you think. How friendly.

28   One day she wants to meet you for lunch. Next, she wants to go shopping for lingerie with you. Soon, she wants to double-date with you and her son. Her boyfriend has a tan and wears jogging shoes everywhere.

29   Before long, you start to feel as if you've inherited a younger sister. Things get bad when you get phone calls from her and she wants to talk about her sex life, or when she introduces you to the members of her jogging club as "my new best friend."

30   You will find yourself longing for the distance that your friends have from their mothers-in-law. You will find yourself plotting evil deeds that will make her despise you.

31   You find yourself saying "yes" when she asks you if you want to play tennis next weekend.

The Know-It-All

32   This woman knows more maxims than Aesop, and she won't keep any opinion to herself.

33   "All that will change when you get married," she says smugly when the two of you announce you're going out to dinner and a movie. "You won't have the money to fritter away."

34   When you get married and still fritter money away on going out, she predicts the end is near. "You won't be able to do that when you have kids."

35   You could try to shock her into silence by announcing that you aren't intending to have children, that you plan to go on throwing money away foolishly, living a life of decadence at expensive restaurants and nightclubs. However, she'll probably just nod and mumble about a fool and his money.

The Hot Tamale

36   Like The Pal, this woman sees you as a contemporary. Unlike The Pal, she sees you as competition.

37   This mother-in-law refuses to age, gracefully or not. She'll do whatever it takes to maintain her face and body; liposuction, face lifts and tummy tucks are as routine to her as a visit to the post office. She wears mini-skirts and too much mascara. Her CD rack is filled with the B-52's and Paula Abdul, not Glenn Miller.

38   She coyly asks you if you want to borrow her Victoria's Secret catalog, then says that you probably won't find anything in it that's "your style."

39   She treats her son like a bit of an old fogey, and you find yourself feeling rather prudish around her. You may as well get used to this role reversal, unless you want to begin a long uphill battle to outdo a woman who's been practicing her young and silly act longer than you've been alive.

The Mother-In-Law Who Isn't

40   Maybe you're *not* getting married. Maybe you've decided, for whatever complicated reasons people decide these things today, that you're going to live together as man and wife without the benefit of official documents, bouquet-throwing and name-changing.

41   Do you still have a mother-in-law?

42   Well, yes. That is, she has the job without the title. Call her what you like (my lover's mother, my live-in-law, the mother of my significant other), she's still your mother-in-law, subject to all the complications that arise in legal unions.

43   You just can't call her Mom.

The Saint

44   For every hundred difficult mothers-in-law, there is one perfect one. She is as precious as she is rare.

45   She never insists that you call her "Mom-mom" or "Binky."

46   She never introduces you to her friends as "the one who finally snagged Junior."

47   She is friendly and warm without being overbearing; she doesn't plant slobbery kisses on your cheek when she hasn't seen you for a week.

48   You are comfortable talking to her about world events, shared friends and literature; neither of you feels the need to discuss your sex life or her friend's divorces.

49   She recognizes that however much she loves her son, he is a human being, complete with faults and virtues.

50   She accepts the fact that you have a career and interests of your own; she encourages and supports them.

51   She doesn't call you "that woman" when speaking to the other relatives.

52   She keeps her opinions on child-rearing to herself.

53   If you find yourself related by marriage to such a woman, cherish the connection as if she were royalty. She is.

54   So, there you have it. You may have spotted someone you know. You may be shaking your head wisely. But, before you get too carried away with yourself, remember one thing.

55   Someday, you might have a son. Someday, that son may fall in love with a woman he believes is *the one*. And someday, you may be stuck with a daughter-in-law you can't stand.

WHAT DID THE WRITER SAY AND WHAT DID YOU THINK?

1. Is there a thesis? If so, is it stated or implied?
2. Do any of the classifications overlap or repeat themselves?
3. Does the author show any sympathy for mothers-in-law? If so, where?
4. First published in a newspaper, this article provoked a number of angry letters. What would you guess the complaints were about?

HOW DID THE WRITER SAY IT?

1. Why is the introduction so much longer than usual?
2. How much of the humor is merely good-natured joking, and how much covers genuine irritation or resentment?
3. How does the description of "The Saint" help serve as a summary of the essay?
4. What stylistic features indicate this essay was first written for a newspaper?

===============WHAT ABOUT *YOUR* WRITING?===============

Charlotte Latvala's discussion of "The Hot Tamale" mother-in-law makes topical references to a "CD rack filled with the B-52s and Paula Abdul as well as to a Victoria's Secret catalog. A topical reference is one pertaining to current events, personalities, problems, culture, and so on. Topicality presents some obvious opportunities for any writer—together with some not-so-obvious dangers.

Topical references, by their very nature, are specific references, and specific writing adds to the prospects for reader interest. Moreover, any writer may want to strike readers as being well informed and up-to-date. Topical references, too, may be more readily understood than more obscure references and allusions (see p. 195). Your reference to a current television show or movie, a politician, a sports figure, a trial can enliven your essay and impress your audience.

While topicality, then, can certainly help your writing from time to time, remember that it has its dangers. It can give a bogus contemporary feel that distracts a reader's attention from the real subject. It can date the essay and the ideas—sometimes overnight. Tastes in music change; businesses fold; television shows are cancelled; politicians retire or get defeated; athletes become newscasters. Today's pleased recognition becomes tomorrow's puzzled stare. Today's fad becomes tomorrow's footnote. Don't be afraid of topical references, but do be careful.

THE PLOT AGAINST PEOPLE

RUSSELL BAKER

Aside from his humorous *New York Times* columns, Russell Baker also has written many books, among the most recent of which are *The Good Times* (1989), and *There's a Country in My Cellar* (1990). Educated at Johns Hopkins University, Baker started his newspaper career with the *Baltimore Sun* in 1947 and then moved to the *New York Times* in 1954. He received journalism's Pulitzer Prize in 1979. "The Plot Against People," a humorous classification of methods which inanimate objects use to defeat mankind, first appeared in 1968 in the *New York Times.*

Words to check:

inanimate (paragraph 1)   conciliatory (12)
cunning (3)   attained (15)
plausible (7)   aspire (15)
inherent (10)

1   Inanimate objects are classified scientifically into three major categories—those that don't work, those that break down and those that get lost.

2   The goal of all inanimate objects is to resist man and ultimately to defeat him, and the three major classifications are based on the method each object uses to achieve its purpose. As a general rule, any object capable of breaking down at the moment when it is most needed will do so. The automobile is typical of the category.

3   With the cunning typical of its breed, the automobile never breaks down while entering a filling station with a large staff of idle mechanics. It waits until it reaches a downtown intersection in the middle of the rush hour, or until it is fully loaded with family and luggage on the Ohio turnpike.

4   Thus it creates maximum misery, inconvenience, frustration and irritability among its human cargo, thereby reducing its owner's life span.

5   Washing machines, garbage disposals, lawn mowers, light bulbs, automatic laundry dryers, water pipes, furnaces, electrical fuses, television tubes, hose nozzles, tape recorders, slide projectors—all are in league with the automobile to take their turn at breaking down whenever life threatens to flow smoothly for their human enemies.

6   Many inanimate objects, of course, find it extremely difficult to break down. Pliers, for example, and gloves and keys are almost totally incapable of breaking down. Therefore, they have had to evolve a different technique for resisting man.

7   They got lost. Science has still not solved the mystery of how they do it, and no man has ever caught one of them in the act of getting lost. The most plausible theory is that they have developed a secret method of locomotion which they are able to conceal the instant a human eye falls upon them.

8   It is not uncommon for a pair of pliers to climb all the way from the cellar to the attic in its single-minded determination to raise its owner's blood pressure. Keys have been known to burrow three feet under mattresses. Women's purses, despite their great weight, frequently travel through six or seven rooms to find hiding space under a couch.

9   Scientists have been struck by the fact that things that break down virtually never get lost, while things that get lost hardly ever break down.

10   A furnace, for example, will invariably break down at the depth of the first winter cold wave, but it will never get lost. A woman's purse, which

after all does have some inherent capacity for breaking down, hardly ever does; it almost invariably chooses to get lost.

11   Some persons believe this constitutes evidence that inanimate objects are not entirely hostile to man, and that a negotiated peace is possible. After all, they point out, a furnace could infuriate a man even more thoroughly by getting lost than by breaking down, just as a glove could upset him far more by breaking down than by getting lost.

12   Not everyone agrees, however, that this indicates a conciliatory attitude among inanimate objects. Many say it merely proves that furnaces, gloves and pliers are incredibly stupid.

13   The third class of objects—those that don't work—is the most curious of all. These include such objects as barometers, car clocks, cigarette lighters, flashlights and toy-train locomotives. It is inaccurate, of course, to say that they never work. They work once, usually for the first few hours after being brought home, and then quit. Thereafter, they never work again.

14   In fact, it is widely assumed that they are built for the purpose of not working. Some people have reached advanced ages without ever seeing some of these objects—barometers, for example—in working order.

15   Science is utterly baffled by the entire category. There are many theories about it. The most interesting holds that the things that don't work have attained the highest state possible for an inanimate object, the state to which things that break down and things that get lost can still only aspire.

16   They have truly defeated man by conditioning him never to expect anything of them, and in return they have given man the only peace he receives from inanimate society. He does not expect his barometer to work, his electric locomotive to run, his cigarette lighter to light or his flashlight to illuminate, and when they don't it does not raise his blood pressure.

17   He cannot attain that peace with furnaces and keys, and cars and women's purses as long as he demands that they work for their keep.

WHAT DID THE WRITER SAY AND WHAT DID YOU THINK? _____

1. What is Baker's thesis?
2. What are the three methods used by inanimate objects to defeat people? How are they a part of Baker's thesis?
3. When are objects most likely to break down? Use one of Baker's examples to explain your answer.
4. Why does Baker feel that "those that don't work" have attained the highest state possible for an inanimate object"?

5. What relationship do "those that break down" and "those that get lost" share?
6. Why do you suppose that Baker uses the word "plot" in the title?

HOW DID THE WRITER SAY IT? _____

1. Although Baker introduces his classification as "those that don't work," "those that break down," and "those that get lost," he saves "those that don't work" for last in his discussion. Why? Do you think his change in order is a distraction? Explain.
2. Aside from the primary classification pattern, can you find secondary rhetorical modes used here? If so, what are they?
3. What is the essay's tone? Do you agree that Baker's subject calls for such a tone? Why or why not?
4. What is Baker's single principle of classification?
5. What is the purpose of paragraph 6?
6. Why does Baker give the inanimate objects human traits? List at least two examples.

==============WHAT ABOUT *YOUR* WRITING?==============

An earlier "What About *Your* Writing?" entry discussed problems of sexist language with the pronoun *he*. Russell Baker shows us that eliminating sexist language goes beyond pronouns. The days when *man* and *mankind* were just other words for the human race or humanity are long gone, for example, and many modern readers will cringe when they read in Baker's second paragraph, "The goal of all inanimate objects is to resist man."

Sexist language, often used without any conscious sexist intent, can intrude in many other areas:

Occupational stereotypes:

Barbara Torres is an outstanding female policeman.

When Jill left the filing department, we had to hire a new girl.

Behavioral stereotypes:

All she needs is a good cry.

A competent shopper organizes all her coupons.

Condescending or insulting language:

I support equal opportunities for the fair sex.

What became of all the babes who used to try out for cheerleading?

FRIENDS, GOOD FRIENDS—
AND SUCH GOOD FRIENDS

JUDITH VIORST

Judith Viorst is a contributing editor and columnist for *Redbook* magazine. She has also written children's fiction and nonfiction books, including *Alexander and the Terrible, Horrible, No Good, Very Bad Day* (1982). Her adult books include *If I Were in Charge of the World and Other Worries* (1981), *Love and Guilt and the Meaning of Life* (1984), *Necessary Losses* (1986), *The Good-bye Book* (1988), and *Forever Fifty* (1989). "Friends, Good Friends—and Such Good Friends," which classifies friends in more than the traditional ways, first appeared in 1982 in *Redbook* magazine.

Words to check:

charades (paragraph 2)	endodontist (14)
ardor (2)	sibling (16)
nonchalant (3)	calibrated (29)
sufficient (8)	

1   Women are friends, I once would have said, when they totally love and support and trust each other, and bare to each other the secrets of their souls, and run—no questions asked—to help each other, and tell harsh truths to each other (no, you can't wear that dress unless you lose ten pounds first) when harsh truths must be told.

2   Women are friends, I once would have said, when they share the same affection for Ingmar Bergman,[1] plus train rides, cats, warm rain, charades, Camus,[2] and hate with equal ardor Newark and Brussels sprouts and Lawrence Welk[3] and camping.

3   In other words, I once would have said that a friend is a friend all the way, but now I believe that's a narrow point of view. For the friendships I have and the friendships I see are conducted at many levels of intensity, serve many different functions, meet different needs and range from those as all-the-way as the friendship of the soul sisters mentioned above to that of the most nonchalant and casual playmates.

---

[1] Swedish film director.
[2] French writer and philosopher (1913–1960).
[3] American conductor of popular music (1903–1992).

4   Consider these varieties of friendship:

5   1. Convenience friends. These are the women with whom, if our paths weren't crossing all the time, we'd have no particular reason to be friends: a next-door neighbor, a woman in our car pool, the mother of one of our children's closest friends or maybe some mommy with whom we serve juice and cookies each week at the Glenwood Co-op Nursery.

6   Convenience friends are convenient indeed. They'll lend us their cups and silverware for a party. They'll drive our kids to soccer when we're sick. They'll take us to pick up our car when we need a lift to the garage. They'll even take our cats when we go on vacation. As we will for them.

7   But we don't, with convenience friends, ever come too close or tell too much; we maintain our public face and emotional distance. "Which means," says Elaine, "that I'll talk about being overweight but not about being depressed. Which means I'll admit being mad but not blind with rage. Which means I might say that we're pinched this month but never that I'm worried sick over money."

8   But which doesn't mean that there isn't sufficient value to be found in these friendships of mutual aid, in convenience friends.

9   2. Special-interest friends. These friendships aren't intimate, and they needn't involve kids or silverware or cats. Their value lies in some interest jointly shared. And so we may have an office friend or a yoga friend or a tennis friend or a friend from the Women's Democratic Club.

10   "I've got one woman friend," says Joyce, "who likes, as I do, to take psychology courses. Which makes it nice for me—and nice for her. It's fun to go with someone you know and its fun to discuss what you've learned, driving back from the classes." And for the most part, she says, that's all they discuss.

11   "I'd say that what we're doing is *doing* together, not being together," Suzanne says of her Tuesday-doubles friends. "It's mainly a tennis relationship, but we play together well. And I guess we all need to have a couple of playmates."

12   I agree.

13   *My* playmate is a shopping friend, a woman of marvelous taste, a woman who knows exactly *where* to buy *what*, and furthermore is a woman who always knows beyond a doubt what one ought to be buying. I don't have the time to keep up with what's new in eyeshadow, hemlines and shoes and whether the smock look is in or finished already. But since (oh shame!) I care a lot about eyeshadow, hemlines and shoes, and since I don't *want* to wear smocks if the smock look is finished, I'm very glad to have a shopping friend.

14   3. Historical friends. We all have a friend who knew us when . . . maybe way back in Miss Meltzer's second grade, when our family lived in

that three-room flat in Brooklyn, when our dad was out of work for seven months, when our brother Allie got in that fight where they had to call the police, when our sister married the endodontist from Yonkers and when, the morning after we lost our virginity, she was the first, the only friend we told.

15   The years have gone by and we've gone separate ways and we've little in common now, but we're still an intimate part of each other's past. And so whenever we go to Detroit we always go to visit this friend of our girlhood. Who knows how we looked before our teeth were straightened. Who knows how we talked before our voice got unBrooklyned. Who knows what we ate before we learned about artichokes. And who, by her presence, puts us in touch with an earlier part of ourself, a part of ourself it's important never to lose.

16   "What this friend means to me and what I mean to her," says Grace, "is having a sister without sibling rivalry. We know the texture of each other's lives. She remembers my grandmother's cabbage soup. I remember the way her uncle played the piano. There's simply no other friend who remembers those things."

17   4. Crossroads friends. Like historical friends, our crossroads friends are important for *what was*—for the friendship we shared at a crucial, now past, time of life. A time, perhaps, when we roomed in college together; or worked as eager young singles in the Big City together; or went together, as my friend Elizabeth and I did through pregnancy, birth and that scary first year of new motherhood.

18   Crossroads friends forge powerful links, links strong enough to endure with not much more contact than once-a-year letters at Christmas. And out of respect for those crossroads years, for those dramas and dreams we once shared, we will always be friends.

19   5. Cross-generational friends. Historical friends and crossroads friends seem to maintain a special kind of intimacy—dormant but always ready to be revived—and though we may rarely meet, whenever we do connect, it's personal and intense. Another kind of intimacy exists in the friendships that form across generations in what one woman calls her daughter-mother and her mother-daughter relationships.

20   Evelyn's friend is her mother's age—"but I share so much more than I ever could with my mother"—a woman she talks to of music, of books and of life. "What I get from her is the benefit of her experience. What she gets—and enjoys—from me is a youthful perspective. It's a pleasure for both of us."

21   I have in my own life a precious friend, a woman of 65 who has lived very hard, who is wise, who listens well; who has been where I am and can help

me understand it; and who represents not only an ultimate ideal mother to me but also the person I'd like to be when I grow up.

22   In our daughter role we tend to do more than our share of self-revelation; in our mother role we tend to receive what's revealed. It's another kind of pleasure—playing wise mother to a questing younger person. It's another very lovely kind of friendship.

23   6. Part-of-a-couple friends. Some of the women we call our friends we never see alone—we see them as part of a couple at couples' parties. And though we share interests in many things and respect each other's views, we aren't moved to deepen the relationship. Whatever the reason, a lack of time or—and this is more likely—a lack of chemistry, our friendship remains in the context of a group. But the fact that our feeling on seeing each other is always, "I'm *so* glad she's here" and the fact that we spend half the evening talking together says that this too, in its own way, counts as a friendship.

24   (Other part-of-a-couple friends are the friends that came with the marriage, and some of these are friends we could live without. But sometimes, alas, she married our husband's best friend; and sometimes, alas, she *is* our husband's best friend. And so we find ourself dealing with her, somewhat against our will, in a spirit of what I'll call *reluctant* friendship.)

25   7. Men who are friends. I wanted to write just of women friends, but the women I've talked to won't let me—they say I must mention man-woman friendships too. For these friendships can be just as close and as dear as those that we form with women. Listen to Lucy's description of one such friendship:

26   "We've found we have things to talk about that are different from what he talks about with my husband and different from what I talk about with his wife. So sometimes we call on the phone or meet for lunch. There are similar intellectual interests—we always pass on to each other the books that we love—but there's also something tender and caring too."

27   In a couple of crises, Lucy says, "he offered himself, for talking and for helping. And when someone died in his family he wanted me there. The sexual, flirty part of our friendship is very small, but *some*—just enough to make it fun and different." She thinks—and I agree—that the sexual part, though small is always *some,* is always there when a man and a woman are friends.

28   It's only in the past few years that I've made friends with men, in the sense of a friendship that's *mine,* not just part of two couples. And achieving with them the ease and the trust I've found with women friends has value indeed. Under the dryer at home last week, putting on mascara and rouge, I comfortably sat and talked with a fellow named Peter. Peter, I finally

decided, could handle the shock of me minus mascara under the dryer. Because we care for each other. Because we're friends.

29   8. There are medium friends, and pretty good friends, and very good friends, indeed, and these friendships are defined by their level of intimacy. And what we'll reveal at each of these levels of intimacy is calibrated with care. We might tell a medium friend, for example, that yesterday we had a fight with our husband. And we might tell a pretty good friend that this fight with our husband made us so mad that we slept on the couch. And we might tell a very good friend that the reason we got so mad in that fight that we slept on the couch had something to do with that girl who works in his office. But it's only to our very best friends that we're willing to tell all, to tell what's going on with that girl in his office.

30   The best of friends, I still believe, totally love and support and trust each other, and bare to each other the secrets of their souls, and run—no questions asked—to help each other, and tell harsh truths to each other when they must be told.

31   But we needn't agree about everything (only 12-year-old girl friends agree about *everything*) to tolerate each other's point of view. To accept without judgment. To give and to take without ever keeping score. And to *be* there, as I am for them and as they are for me, to comfort our sorrows, to celebrate our joys.

WHAT DID THE WRITER SAY AND WHAT DID YOU THINK?

1. What is Viorst's thesis?
2. How does Viorst's new definition of women friends differ from her original definition?
3. How many different kinds of friends does Viorst classify? Can you think of additional types? If so, name them.
4. Why does Viorst include men friends although her thesis does not indicate that she do so? Is her explanation adequate? Why or why not?
5. Why do you think Viorst separates "historical friends" and "crossroads friends" into distinct categories? How are they alike? Different?
6. Why do you think Viorst saves "best" friends for last? Do you think that she implies that they also have traits of some of the other types? Explain your answer.
7. Why does the author say that best friends "needn't agree about everything"?

HOW DID THE WRITER SAY IT? _____

1. What is Viorst's single principle of classification?
2. What purpose do the first three paragraphs serve?
3. Aside from the primary classification system, what other rhetorical modes does the author use?
4. Although most students are admonished to avoid sentence fragments, Viorst uses three of them in the final paragraph. Are they effective? Why or why not? (See What About Your Writing, pp. 229-230.)

════════════WHAT ABOUT *YOUR* WRITING?════════

"Woman are friends, I once would have said, when they share the same affection for personalities, travel, pets, climates, games, authors, and hate with equal ardor certain cities, foods, musicians, and leisure activities." That's what many authors would have settled for. The writing would have been passable, and few readers would have complained.

Now look at what Judith Viorst wrote in paragraph 2: "Women are friends, I once would have said, when they share the same affection for Ingmar Bergman, plus train rides, cats, warm rain, charades, Camus, and hate with equal ardor Newark and Brussels sprouts and Lawrence Welk and camping." The words here are far more specific and the writing far better than passable.

Elsewhere (see p. 54) we have discussed the importance of specific details to support a thesis. Here we are dealing with specific words, not adding more details or more words, but choosing one word in preference to another, choosing a word that tells us more and interests us more.

In your own writing, don't automatically accept the first word that comes to mind. Too often, the word is likely to be abstract, only a vague approximation of what you want to express. *Use specific words.* The benefits of specific words are particularly apparent when choosing verbs, for verbs in themselves are action words, and the more specific the verb, the more probable that a sense of action will be communicated.

Don't settle for "He looked at her" when you really mean *stared* or *gawked* or *leered* or *ogled* or *squinted* or *studied* or *glanced.* Don't settle for "He hit him" when you really mean *slapped* or *punched* or *smacked* or *belted* or *jabbed* or *socked* or *poked* or *clubbed.* Don't settle for "She laughed" when you really mean *giggled* or *guffawed* or *tittered* or *roared* or *chuckled.* Using specific words, especially specific verbs, is guaranteed to make your writing more lively and interesting. Certainly, you'll be thinking the way most good writers do.

THREE KINDS OF DISCIPLINE

JOHN HOLT

John Holt (1923-1985) was one of the important voices in modern American education. His work is much admired, even by many of those who disagree with his conclusions, for his ability to identify with children and sometimes to seem to enter their minds. Too sophisticated a writer and thinker to be associated consistently with any particular party line in education, Holt is viewed as one of the influences behind experiments with open classrooms in the 1960s and early 1970s. His books include *How Children Fail* (1964), *How Children Learn* (1967), *The Underachieving School* (1969), *What Do I Do Monday?* (1970), *Escape from Childhood* (1974), and *Never Too Late* (1978). This selection is an excerpt from Holt's influential *Freedom and Beyond* (1972).

Words to check:

impartial (paragraph 1)	autocratic (4)
wheedled (1)	suppleness (4)
impotent (3)	novice (4)

1   A child, in growing up, may meet and learn from three different kinds of disciplines. The first and most important is what we might call the Discipline of Nature or of Reality. When he is trying to do something real, if he does the wrong thing or doesn't do the right one, he doesn't get the result he wants. If he doesn't pile one block right on top of another, or tries to build on a slanting surface, his tower falls down. If he hits the wrong key, he hears the wrong note. If he doesn't hit the nail squarely on the head, it bends, and he has to pull it out and start with another. If he doesn't measure properly what he is trying to build, it won't open, close, fit, stand up, fly, float, whistle, or do whatever he wants it to do. If he closes his eyes when he swings, he doesn't hit the ball. A child meets this kind of discipline every time he tries to *do* something, which is why it is so important in school to give children more chances to do things, instead of just reading or listening to someone talk (or pretending to). This discipline is a great teacher. The learner never has to wait long for his answer; it usually comes quickly, often instantly. Also it is clear, and very often points toward the needed correction; from what happened he can not only see that what he did was wrong, but also why, and what he needs to do instead. Finally, and most important, the giver of the answer, call it Nature, is impersonal, impartial, and indifferent. She does not give opinions, or make judgments; she cannot be wheedled, bullied, or

fooled; she does not get angry or disappointed; she does not praise or blame; she does not remember past failures or hold grudges; with her one always gets a fresh start, this time is the one that counts.

2   The next discipline we might call the Discipline of Culture, of Society, of What People Really Do. Man is a social, a cultural animal. Children sense around them this culture, this network of agreements, customs, habits, and rules binding the adults together. They want to understand it and be a part of it. They watch very carefully what people around them are doing and want to do the same. They want to do right, unless they become convinced they can't do right. Thus children rarely misbehave seriously in church, but sit as quietly as they can. The example of all those grownups is contagious. Some mysterious ritual is going on, and children, who like rituals, want to be part of it. In the same way, the little children that I see at concerts or operas, though they may fidget a little, or perhaps take a nap now and then, rarely make any disturbance. With all those grownups sitting there, neither moving nor talking, it is the most natural thing in the world to imitate them. Children who live among adults who are habitually courteous to each other, and to them, will soon learn to be courteous. Children who live surrounded by people who speak a certain way will speak that way, however much we may try to tell them that speaking that way is bad or wrong.

3   The third discipline is the one most people mean when they speak of discipline—the Discipline of Superior Force, of sergeant to private, of "You do what I tell you or I'll make you wish you had." There is bound to be some of this in a child's life. Living as we do, surrounded by things that can hurt children, or that children can hurt, we cannot avoid it. We can't afford to let a small child find out from experience the danger of playing in a busy street, or of fooling with the pots on the top of a stove, or of eating up the pills in the medicine cabinet. So, along with other precautions, we say to him, "Don't play in the street, or touch things on the stove, or go into the medicine cabinet, or I'll punish you." Between him and the danger too great for him to imagine we put a lesser danger, but one he can imagine and maybe therefore wants to avoid. He can have no idea of what it would be like to be hit by a car, but he can imagine being shouted at, or spanked, or sent to his room. He avoids these substitutes for the greater danger until he can understand it and avoid it for its own sake. But we ought to use this discipline only when it is necessary to protect the life, health, safety, or well-being of people or other living creatures, or to prevent destruction of things that people care about. We ought not to assume too long, as we usually do, that a child cannot understand the real nature of the danger from which we want to protect him. The sooner he avoids the danger, not to escape our punishment, but as a matter of

good sense, the better. He can learn that faster than we think. In Mexico, for example, where people drive their cars with a good deal of spirit, I saw many children no older than five or four walking unattached on the streets. They understood about cars, they knew what to do. A child whose life is full of the threat and fear of punishment is locked into babyhood. There is no way for him to grow up, to learn to take responsibility for his life and acts. Most important of all, we should not assume that having to yield to the threat of our superior force is good for the child's character. It is never good for *anyone's* character. To bow to superior force makes us feel impotent and cowardly for not having had the strength or courage to resist. Worse, it makes us resentful and vengeful. We can hardly wait to make someone pay for our humiliation, yield to us as we were once made to yield. No, if we cannot always avoid using the Discipline of Superior Force, we should at least use it as seldom as we can.

4   There are places where all three disciplines overlap. Any very demanding human activity combines in it the disciplines of Superior Force, of Culture, and of Nature. The novice will be told, "Do it this way, never mind asking why, just do it that way, that is the way we always do it." But it probably *is* just the way they always do it, and usually for the very good reason that it is a way that has been found to work. Think, for example, of ballet training. The student in a class is told to do this exercise, or that; to stand so; to do this or that with his head, arms, shoulders, abdomen, hips, legs, feet. He is constantly corrected. There is no argument. But behind these seemingly autocratic demands by the teacher lie many decades of custom and tradition, and behind that, the necessities of dancing itself. You cannot make the moves of classical ballet unless over many years you have acquired, and renewed every day, the needed strength and suppleness in scores of muscles and joints. Nor can you do the difficult motions, making them look easy, unless you have learned hundreds of easier ones first. Dance teachers may not always agree on all the details of teaching these strengths and skills. But no novice could learn them all by himself. You could not go for a night or two to watch the ballet and then, without any other knowledge at all, teach yourself how to do it. In the same way, you would be unlikely to learn any complicated and difficult human activity without drawing heavily on the experience of those who know it better. But the point is that the authority of these experts or teachers stems from, grows out of their greater competence and experience, the fact that what they do *works,* not the fact that they happen to be the teacher and as such have the power to kick a student out of the class. And the further point is that children are always and everywhere attracted to that competence, and ready and eager to submit themselves to a discipline that grows out of it. We hear constantly that children will never do anything

unless compelled to by bribes or threats. But in their private lives, or in extracurricular activities in school, in sports, music, drama, art, running a newspaper, and so on, they often submit themselves willingly and wholeheartedly to very intense disciplines, simply because they want to learn to do a given thing well. Our Little-Napoleon football coaches, of whom we have too many and hear far too much, blind us to the fact that millions of children work hard every year getting better at sports and games without coaches barking and yelling at them.

WHAT DID THE WRITER SAY AND WHAT DID YOU THINK?

1. The author neatly defines and gives examples of three kinds of discipline. Where does he follow this book's advice to acknowledge the not-so-neat complications (see p. 223)? What is the complication?
2. What is the single principle of classification?
3. Is there a thesis? If so, is it ever stated?
4. Which kind of discipline does the author like most and which kind does he like least?
5. What are the dangers of "Discipline of Superior Force"? Why is it sometimes necessary?
6. Does the author paint too cheerful a picture of the "Discipline of Nature"? What happens with the child who bends the nail, gives up, and never learns how to use a hammer? How would the author reply to these questions?
7. A parent tells a child wearing a thin T-shirt to put on a coat before the child steps outside into bitter cold weather. The child refuses. What would the author's advice be?
8. Do you think the essay as a whole diminishes or increases the importance of a teacher? Explain.

HOW DID THE WRITER SAY IT?

1. Many English instructors would probably criticize Holt for his comma splices—a frequent punctuation error of many student writers (see pp. 200–202). Find at least two of the author's comma splices.
2. The description of Nature at the end of paragraph 1 presents an unstated contrast to someone or something else: "She does not give

opinions or make judgments; she cannot be wheedled, bullied, or fooled; she does not get angry or disappointed; she does not praise or blame; she does not remember past failures or hold grudges; with her one always gets a fresh start, this time is the one that counts." What is Nature being contrasted to?

3. The author has least to say about the "Discipline of Society." Would more examples have been a good idea?

4. Do the concluding observations on football coaches strike you as an effective ending or the sudden raising of a trivial side issue?

================WHAT ABOUT *YOUR* WRITING?================

Critics make much, as they always have, about the sounds and "music" of poetry, but generally not enough is made of the sounds of prose. All readers have an inner ear that hears what they are reading, no matter how silent outwardly the act of reading may be. And the sounds can be good or bad, pleasant or unpleasant.

Apart from the rhymes and meter of poetry, the most common musical device is probably *alliteration:* the repetition of identical sounds at the beginning of words. (Once limited to consonant sounds only, alliteration in general usage now refers to vowel sounds as well.) Holt uses alliteration effectively when he writes in paragraph 1 that Nature is "impersonal, impartial, and indifferent." The repetition of sounds is pleasing, even downright catchy, in itself. Moreover, the repetition of sounds helps to reinforce thought: the three alliterative words are all related by being qualities of nature, and the identical sounds drive home that relationship.

A few moments' consideration can turn up a host of titles and famous phrases that show the appeal of alliteration:

"Little Boy Blue"	*The Great Gatsby*
East of Eden	calm, cool, and collected
in fine fettle	*The Brady Bunch*
Sighted sub, sank same	*All Things Bright and Beautiful*
The Pride and the Passion	"Love Me or Leave Me"
Boston Bruins	dry as dust
Philadelphia Phillies	through thick and thin
wit and wisdom	*The Doctor's Dilemma*

On a humble level, Chapter 1 of this book used alliteration to describe the importance to good writing of a thesis and support of a thesis: "The Persuasive Principle." The phrase seemed more vivid and easier to remember than "The Persuasive Idea" or "The Persuasive Slant."

Like most other good things, alliteration can be abused. Beware of pouring on too many identical sounds all at once. Remember, too, that alliteration is a special stylistic touch; if your reader expects it in every sentence, it loses its impact and distracts attention from your thought. Shakespeare parodied simple-minded overindulgence in alliteration in *A Midsummer Night's Dream* as some amateur playwrights came up with these lines for "he stabbed himself":

> Whereat, with blade, with bloody blameful blade,
> He bravely broach'd his boiling bloody breast.

9

DEFINITION

*O*ne of the most frequent impediments to clear communication is the failure to define terms. Some conversations and writings aren't just impeded by that failure; they're made incomprehensible. In isolation, a catch phrase like *power to the people,* for example, can mean anything from revolution to better electric service. Far more often, failure to define or to agree on a definition can lead to hours—and years—of futile controversy, complete with name-calling and shaking fists. Think of UN debates on *aggression.* Think of the storms in American history over terms like *free speech, due process, states' rights,* and *quotas.*

A definition essay often includes a "dictionary definition" but goes far beyond it and is best thought of as providing an *extended definition.* It discusses the meaning of words and phrases to which even the best dictionaries can't do full justice.

Dictionary definitions work in two ways, both of them short, and one of them extremely formal. First, a dictionary can define by giving a direct synonym: *liberty* means *freedom; couch* means *sofa; plate* means *dish; cry* means *weep.* Second, a dictionary can, and for many terms must, use the techniques of a formal definition: A term is placed in the class it belongs to and then is differentiated from all the other members of the same class.

Term	Class	Differentiation
convertible	a car	with a top that can be raised and lowered
widow	a woman	whose husband has died
martini	a cocktail	made with gin or vodka and dry vermouth

Dictionary definitions, to repeat, are often incorporated into an extended definition, but no definition paper will discuss a term for which a dictionary definition alone would be sufficient. Some definition papers, in fact, may have as their central point the inadequacy or impossibility of good dictionary definitions for the term under consideration. (The skilled writer, however, will almost always avoid starting off with such tired phrases as "According to the dictionary" or "Webster says that.")

What terms are promising candidates for definition papers? Here are some suggestions:

Abstract concepts: love, morality, patriotism, apathy, equality

Controversial terms: the sexual revolution, the generation gap, women's liberation, police brutality, racism

Common phrases and ideas: a good movie, the ideal vacation, the perfect job

Clearly, a definition paper usually turns out to be an expression of opinion, a "What Such-and-Such Means to Me" paper. A good movie for one person will have to stimulate the mind; for another person it will have to give the mind a rest. The expression of an attitude toward the term is what gives life to a definition paper and makes it more interesting to read than a dictionary. In other words, a definition paper benefits from a thesis:

An ideal vacation can mean snoozing in the backyard just as much as seeing new sights.

The generation gap is one of humanity's best hopes for progress.

Love is a severe mental illness curable only by time.

Definition papers follow no set pattern. Most turn out to be combinations of patterns that are studied separately in other chapters of this book. Which pattern or combination of patterns is used depends on which works best, and which works best depends on what's being defined and what the writer has to say about it.

A Definition Paper Can Compare and Contrast. A term can be made clearer and more interesting by distinguishing it from similar terms: a paper on socialism might distinguish it from communism; a paper on love might distinguish it from infatuation. Discussing opposites sometimes works well, too: a definition paper on a *liberal* might take the same set of circumstances and contrast a liberal's behavior to a conservative's. These negative techniques—showing what a term is not—often lead to successful papers.

A Definition Paper Can Classify.   It may be both convenient and insightful to break some terms into separate classifications. Morality, for example, could be considered in two parts: passive morality—not doing evil; and active morality—doing good.

A Definition Paper Can Give Examples.   A paper defining a good movie would naturally discuss specific examples of good movies that fit the definition. Without the examples the paper would probably be abstract and dull.

A Definition Paper Can Trace a Process.   A writer engaged in defining *schizophrenia* might make the illness more understandable with a step-by-step analysis of its progress from the first signs of mental aberration to its full development.

A Definition Paper Can Study Cause-and-Effect Relationships.   An advocate of women's liberation, in defining the term, could make the definition fuller and more persuasive by devoting some attention to the decades of polite and impolite discrimination that helped cause the birth, or rebirth, of the women's liberation movement.

A Definition Paper Can Use Narration.   Narration is the telling of a story. A paper on *competition* could show the good and the bad sides of the term in action by telling the story of the author's friendly and unfriendly rivalry with a fellow student during high school days.

WRITING SUGGESTIONS
FOR DEFINITION ESSAYS _____

Any of the terms below lend themselves to extended definitions. Remember that definition papers are not tied down to any one writing pattern. Use whatever approach works best. (See p. 254 for other subjects.)

1. Soul food
2. A ham actor
3. Good sportsmanship
4. Conflict of interest
5. A good teacher
6. Fad
7. Atheism
8. An intellectual
9. Courtesy
10. Worship
11. A good marriage
12. Child abuse
13. Conscience
14. The ideal college
15. A good salesperson
16. Friendship

17. Courage
18. Jealousy
19. Obscenity
20. Humanity's best friend
21. Humanity's worst enemy

22. Fear
23. Road hypnosis
24. Frustration
25. Writer's block

Growing Up

Anonymous (student)

Thesis: Being tested for HIV taught me how to be a grown-up.

    I.   Grown-ups and fear
       A. Still get scared
       B. Face the fear

   II. Grown-ups and responsibility
       A. Temptation to ignore it
       B. Responsibility to others

 III. Grown-ups and reality
       A. Temptation to deny it
       B. Need to accept real world

Conclusion: Although being a grown-up is difficult, we can each work to become one.

    Many, many years ago, I thought that a grown-up was someone who could drive a car. But when I finally was old enough to drive, I found out that I wasn't a grown-up yet. Then, I figured that a grown-up was a person who could vote. But when I cast my first vote, I realized that I still wasn't a grown-up. A little later, I decided that a grown-up was someone who went to college. But college wasn't what helped me to become a grown-up either.

It wasn't until I decided to get tested for HIV that I learned what really made someone a grown-up. I like to think, too, that as I learned what defined a grown-up, I also became one.

I had stopped by the free clinic where a friend of mine works, and while I was waiting for her, one of the other volunteers asked me if I wanted to be tested. My immediate reaction was, "Who, me?" As I thought about it for a while, though, I realized that the only reason not to be tested would be fear—fear of testing positive, fear of facing the facts. I took a deep breath, and I got tested. Grown-ups get scared, but they don't let fear keep them from doing what they need to do.

My test results, the clinic said, wouldn't come back for ten days. Those were ten very long days. I spent a lot of time thinking about what I would do if my results were positive. Who would I tell? Could I tell anyone? Was it really my problem if I had infected anyone? Would I have to change my life, or could I just pretend it wasn't true? I wrestled with those questions and many more for days, deciding that, however awful it might be, I would have to tell my "exes" if my test was positive, and that my life would have to change drastically. I owed that to anyone I had ever loved. Besides, however unpleasant it may be, a grown-up has a sense of responsibility to other people.

The day my results came back, I thought that I might try to avoid the whole problem by just not showing up to get my results. That way, I'd be no better or worse off than I had been before the test. I could just forget about it. I could go on as I had been going. When the time came, though, I knew that I had to go find out, that I couldn't ignore reality any longer. A grown-up has to learn to accept the real world.

The medical results of my test aren't important to anyone but myself and my "exes," but the mental results are important to anyone who has ever wondered what a grown-up is. I have discovered that grown-ups face fear, have a sense of responsibility, and learn to handle realities, even the grimmest ones. That's a lot to aim for, and no one can do all that all the time. Everyone, though, can do it sometimes. Whatever your age, once you find out what it means to be a grown-up, you can always work to be one.

THE WORKAHOLIC

ELLEN GOODMAN

Ellen Goodman's published books include *At Large* (1981), *Keeping in Touch* (1985), and *Making Sense* (1989). "The Workaholic" comes from Goodman's syndicated newspaper column. To define a workaholic, Goodman uses the narrative pattern—she tells a story. Are the characters presented as particular individuals, or are they meant to stand for general types?

Words to check:

obituary (paragraph 2)   deceased (15)
coronary thrombosis (2)   discreetly (18)

1   He worked himself to death finally and precisely at 3 A.M. Sunday morning.

2   The obituary didn't say that, of course. It said that he died of a coronary thrombosis—I think that was it—but every one of his friends and acquaintances knew it instantly. He was a perfect Type A, a workaholic, a classic, they said to each other and shook their heads—and thought for five or ten minutes about the way they lived.

3   This man who worked himself to death finally and precisely at 3 A.M. Sunday morning—on his day off—was 51 years old and he was a vice-president. He was, however, one of the six vice-presidents, and one of three who might conceivably—if the president died or retired soon enough—have moved to the top spot. Phil knew that.

4   He worked six days a week, five of them until 8 or 9 at night, during a time when his own company had begun the four-day week for everyone but the executives. He worked like the Important People. He had no outside "extracurricular interests," unless, of course, you think about a monthly golf game that way. To Phil, it was work. He always ate egg-salad sandwiches at his desk. He was, of course, overweight, by 20 or 25 pounds. He thought it was okay though, because he didn't smoke.

5   On Saturdays, Phil wore a sports jacket to the office instead of a suit, because it was the weekend.

6   He had a lot of people working for him, maybe 60, and most of them liked him most of the time. Three of them will be seriously considered for his job. The obituary didn't mention that.

7   But it did list his "survivors" quite accurately. He is survived by his wife, Helen, 48, a good woman of no particular marketable skills, who worked in an office before marrying and mothering.

8   She had, according to her daughter, given up trying to compete with his work years ago, when the children were small. A company friend said, "I know how much you will miss him." And she answered, "I already have."

9   "Missing him all these years," she must have given up part of herself which had cared too much for the man. She would be "well taken care of."

10   His eldest of the "dearly beloved" children is a hard-working executive in a manufacturing firm down South. In the day and a half before the funeral, he went around the neighborhood researching his father, asking the neighbors what he was like. They were embarrassed.

11   His second child was a girl, who is 24 and newly married. She lives near her mother and they are close, but whenever she was alone with her father, in a car driving somewhere, they had nothing to say to each other.

12   The youngest is 20, a boy, a high-school graduate who has spent the last couple of years, like a lot of his friends, doing enough odd jobs to stay in grass and food. He was the one who tried to grab at his father, and tried to mean enough to him to keep the man at home.

13   He was his father's favorite. Over the last two years, Phil stayed up nights worrying about the boy.

14   The boy once said, "My father and I only board here."

15   At the funeral, the 60-year-old company president told the 48-year-old widow that the 51-year-old deceased had meant much to the company and would be missed and would be hard to replace. The widow didn't look him in the eye. She was afraid he would read her bitterness and, after all, she would need him to straighten out the finances—the stock options and all that.

16   Phil was overweight and nervous and worked too hard. If he wasn't at the office, he was worried about it. Phil was a Type A, a heart-attack natural. You could have picked him out in a minute from a lineup.

17   So when he finally worked himself to death, at precisely 3 A.M. Sunday morning, no one was really surprised.

18   By 5 P.M. the afternoon of the funeral, the company president had begun, discreetly of course, with care and taste, to make inquiries about his replacement. One of three men. He asked around: "Who's been working the hardest?"

WHAT DID THE WRITER SAY AND WHAT DID YOU THINK?

1. Is the thesis directly stated? If not, should it be?
2. Besides driving one to an early grave, what is wrong with being a workaholic? Wasn't Phil doing what he wanted, after all?
3. Why are Phil's habits of dress worth mentioning (paragraph 5)?
4. Does the author express any sympathy for Phil? If not, is the reader expected to feel sympathy, even though unexpressed?
5. Weren't many or most of the people who have achieved greatness actually workaholics? Mozart, Dickens, Edison, and Pasteur are just a few names that come to mind. Einstein once observed, "Well-being and happiness are such trivial goals in life that I can imagine them being entertained only by pigs." Is the alternative to being a workaholic of some kind being a nobody?

HOW DID THE WRITER SAY IT?

1. Quotation marks are sometimes misused for cheap sarcasm or strained cuteness. Are the quotation marks justified around *extracurricular interests* (paragraph 4), *survivors* (paragraph 7), *missing him all these years* (paragraph 9), *well taken care of* (paragraph 9), and *dearly beloved* (paragraph 10)?
2. Is there an actual conclusion, or does the article simply end when the story ends?
3. The writer generally tries to give the impression of letting the facts speak for themselves. Where does she editorialize directly?
4. Are the characters given enough individuality to be interesting in themselves, or are they interesting only because of what they represent?

═══════════WHAT ABOUT *YOUR* WRITING?═══════

Ellen Goodman uses what can best be called *ironic quotation marks* in paragraph 4 when she writes, "He had no outside 'extracurricular interests.'" She uses them again in paragraph 7: "But it did list his 'survivors' quite accurately." The quotation marks indicate that in some way the writer is distancing herself from the word: She disapproves of it or is amused by it or feels generally that it is inappropriate.

Be cautious with ironic quotation marks. Some instructors may advise you to avoid them entirely. Too often writers use them as a kind of cheap visual aid instead of letting the careful choice and arrangement of words do the job more effectively. Goodman is at least putting the quotation marks around words that we can imagine other people actually saying. When writers put the quotation marks around their own words, the results are almost always crude sarcasm:

My high school "teacher" was a disgrace to the system.

Eleanor's good "friend" betrayed her.

Our family's "vacation" last summer was a catastrophe.

Closely related to this writing problem is the use of quotation marks around slang or other informal words and phrases.

The policeman continued to "hassle" us.

The fraternity party caused many people to get "looped."

I don't dislike "veggies" nearly as much as I used to.

First, effective slang should sound natural, and if it does, there's no need to call special attention to it with quotation marks. Second, and more important, the writer frequently comes through as an offensive snob: "I'm far too cultivated to employ language like this myself, but look how cute I can be."

By and large, quotation marks are best reserved for their more common functions:

Words and phrases pointed to as such

If I ever find out what the word "love" means, I won't tell you—I'll write a book.

He keeps confusing "there" and "their."

Note: Italics often substitute for quotation marks here.

Dialogue and short quotations

"Sit down and relax," she said.

Which Dickens novel begins with "It was the best of times, it was the worst of times"?

Titles of short works—stories, poems, magazine articles, songs, and so on

"The Workaholic" was written by Ellen Goodman.

I love that old record of Judy Garland singing "Over the Rainbow."

WHAT DOES IT MEAN TO BE CREATIVE?

S.I. HAYAKAWA

Best known as a scholar of general semantics, the study of word meanings and their influence, Samuel Ichiye Hayakawa (1906-1992) wrote several books on the subject, including *Language in Thought and Action.* Aside from his teaching career, Hayakawa was San Francisco State College President and a United States Senator. The following essay, which appears in his book *Through the Communication Barrier: On Speaking, Listening, and Understanding* (1979), defines the creative person.

Words to check:

ridicule (paragraph 6)   imponderable (8)
hunches (8)   inclination (9)
hooligan (8)

1   What distinguishes the creative person? By creative person I don't mean only the great painter or poet or musician. I also want to include the creative housewife, teacher, warehouseman, sales manager—anyone who is able to break through habitual routines and invent new solutions to old problems, solutions that strike people with their appropriateness as well as originality, so that they say, "Why didn't I think of that?"

2   A creative person, first, is not limited in his thinking to "what everyone knows." "Everyone knows" that trees are green. The creative artist is able to see that in certain lights some trees look blue or purple or yellow. The creative person looks at the world with his or her own eyes, not with the eyes of others. The creative individual also knows his or her own feelings better than the average person. Most people don't know the answer to the question, "How are you? How do you feel?" The reason they don't know is that they are so busy feeling what they are supposed to feel, thinking what they are supposed to think, that they never get down to examining their own deepest feelings.

3   "How did you like the play?" "Oh, it was a fine play. It was well reviewed in *The New Yorker.*"

4   With authority figures like drama critics and book reviewers and teachers and professors telling us what to think and how to feel, many of us are busy playing roles, fulfilling other people's expectations. As Republicans, we think what other Republicans think. As Catholics, we think what other Catholics

think. And so on. Not many of us ask ourselves, "How do I feel? What do I think?"—and wait for answers.

5   Another characteristic of the creative person is that he is able to entertain and play with ideas that the average person may regard as silly, mistaken, or downright dangerous. All new ideas sound foolish at first, because they are new. (In the early days of the railroad, it was argued that speeds of twenty-five mph or over were impractical because people's brains would burst.) A person who is afraid of being laughed at or disapproved of for having "foolish" or "unsound" ideas will have the satisfaction of having everyone agree with him, but he will never be creative, because creativity means being willing to take a chance—to go out on a limb.

6   The person who would be creative must be able to endure loneliness— even ridicule. If he has a great and original idea that others are not yet ready to accept, there will be long periods of loneliness. There will be times when his friends and relatives think he is crazy, and he'll begin to wonder if they are right. A genuinely creative person, believing in his creation, is able to endure this loneliness—for years if necessary.

7   Another trait of the creative person is idle curiosity. Such a person asks questions, reads books, conducts investigations into matters apparently unrelated to job or profession—just for the fun of knowing. It is from these apparently unrelated sources that brilliant ideas often emerge to enrich one's own field of work.

8   Finally, the creative person plays hunches. "Pure intellect," says Dr. Hans Selye, the great medical researcher at the University of Montreal, "is largely a quality of the middle-class mind. The lowliest hooligan and the greatest creator in the fields of science are activated mainly by imponderable instincts and emotions, especially faith. Curiously, even scientific research, the most intellectual creative effort of which man is capable, is no exception in this respect."

9   Alfred Korzybski also understood well the role of undefinable emotions in the creative life. He wrote, "Creative scientists know very well from observation of themselves that all creative work starts as a feeling, inclination, suspicion, intuition, hunch, or some other nonverbal affective state, which only at a later date, after a sort of nursing, takes the shape of verbal expression worked out later in a rationalized, coherent . . . theory."

10   Creativity is the act of bringing something new into the world, whether a symphony, a novel, an improved layout for a supermarket, a new and unexpected casserole dish. It is based first on communication with oneself, then testing that communication with experience and the realities one has to contend with. The result is the highest, most exciting kind of learning.

WHAT DID THE WRITER SAY AND WHAT DID YOU THINK?

1. What is Hayakawa's thesis?
2. Why does he say that creative people are not only painters, poets, or musicians but also housewives, teachers, warehousemen, or sales managers?
3. What are the four traits, according to Hayakawa, that creative people possess?
4. What is the major negative side effect that creative people often suffer? Why?
5. Why does Hayakawa spend most of his essay on traits of creative people rather than the concept of creativity itself?
6. How do Dr. Hans Selye and Alfred Korzybske, in paragraphs 8 and 9, support Hayakawa's ideas?
7. Why does the author wait until the conclusion to cite his own definition of creativity?

HOW DID THE WRITER SAY IT?

1. What word in Hayakawa's opening sentence indicates that contrast will be essential to defining "creative"?
2. For whom do you believe this essay is intended? How can you tell?
3. How long is the introduction? The conclusion?
4. In the essay's body, how does Hayakawa signal that he is moving to the next trait? Cite two examples that show this transition.

WHAT ABOUT *YOUR* WRITING?

The introduction of "What Does It Mean to Be Creative?" begins with a question: "What distinguishes the creative person?" There are dozens of ways to start a paper, and beginning with a question or series of questions and then providing answers in the remainder of your paper can sometimes be extremely effective. The question-and-answer technique can create in your reader a sense of personal participation in the quest for an answer. It can contribute to a feeling of suspense. Certainly, this technique is one of the most commonly used. It can be applied to any of the patterns discussed in the various chapters of this book.

Narrative

Is college registration like this for everyone? Is frustration a prerequisite for enrolling? Although I was among herds of other bewildered freshmen, I felt my misery greater than all of theirs put together. That day ranks right up there with the horror of my first operation.

Description

Have you ever looked at a cat's whiskers up close or felt their texture? Whiskers are more than just coarse feline facial hair. They help cats live.

Examples

Is the corruption we see in public officials simply the accepted way of getting things done today? I think it is—and a few examples will show why.

Process

Have you ever seen those commercials with ladies in elegant gowns putting down a new floor in the rec room? Have you ever felt you'd like to do the same? Don't. It's a long, complicated process.

Comparison And Contrast

What would happen if through some time machine we could get Muhammad Ali in the same ring with Jack Dempsey? Who would win? Would it be the quickest hands and feet of all time or the strongest punch?

Cause and Effect

Can anything be done about the terrifying growth of child abuse in this country? Maybe. Maybe not. But we'll certainly never make any progress unless we first understand what causes parents to beat and otherwise abuse their own children.

Division and Classification

Will fast foods wreck our health? "Not so," say some of the vendors who are putting more "good for you" items on their menus. Basically, there are four healthy varieties—still fast, but now nutritious.

Taking the mental and emotional leap of getting the first words down on paper can be a problem for any writer, no matter how experienced. The question-and-answer approach is one device that can help.

CYSTIC FIBROSIS

FRANK DEFORD

Frank Deford, vice-president of the Cystic Fibrosis Foundation, is the author of the powerful book from which this selection is taken, *Alex: The Life of a Child* (1983), an account of his daughter who died of cystic fibrosis at the age of eight. Deford is the author of many other books and a writer for *Sports Illustrated.*

Words to check:

cysts (paragraph 1)	ravaged (3)
pathology (1)	illusory (4)
disparate (1)	prophylactic (4)
pancreas (1)	chronic (7)
pulmonary (3)	ambivalent (7)
spectrum (3)	enzyme (11)

1   Cystic fibrosis is, notwithstanding its name, a disease primarily of the lungs. It has nothing to do with cysts. It was not identified as a distinct clinical entity until the midthirties, and not until some years later was the full pathology comprehended. Inexplicably, the disease attacks not only the lungs but other disparate parts of the body: the pancreas, the major digestive organ; and, in males, the testes. So it undermines breathing, eating, reproduction— all of life itself.

2   The common agent in all cases is mucus. The cystic fibrosis victim's body manufactures too much mucus, or the mucus is too thick, or both. So baffling is the disease that nobody knows for sure which basic factor is the issue. Whatever, the mucus obstructs the airflow in the lungs and clogs the pancreas and the testes. Adding to the perplexity is the fact that no two patients have the same history, except in the sense that CF is always progressive, always terminal.

3   The luckiest patients are those born without lung involvement. Others have such mild cases that they go undetected for years; quite possibly there are even some CF patients who never know they have the disease, but die relatively young of some misunderstood pulmonary involvement. At the other end of the spectrum, some infants are essentially born dead, their tiny bodies so ravaged by the disease that they cannot even begin to draw breath.

4   As events proved, Alex was toward the worse end of the spectrum. While she died at eight, half of the children now born in the United States with

cystic fibrosis who are diagnosed and treated live to the age of eighteen. Be grateful for small favors. Back in the midfifties, when the Cystic Fibrosis Foundation was started, a child with CF could not even expect to live to kindergarten. Regrettably, early steady advances stopped just about the time Alex was born. Until the early seventies almost every passing year saw another year of life expectancy added for a CF kid, but these advances were somewhat illusory. They were largely prophylactic, stemming almost entirely from better maintenance and more powerful antibiotics. The longer life span in no way indicated an approaching cure, nor even a control (as, for example, insulin keeps diabetes under control). In a sense, it isn't accurate to say that we kept Alex alive—we merely postponed her dying.

5   Alex's day would start with an inhalation treatment that took several minutes. This was a powerful decongestant mist that she drew in from an inhaler to loosen the mucus that had settled in her lungs. Then, for a half hour or more, we would give her postural drainage treatment to accomplish the same ends physically. It is quite primitive, really, but all we had, the most effective weapon against the disease. Alex had to endure eleven different positions, each corresponding to a section of the lung, and Carol or I would pound away at her, thumping her chest, her back, her sides, palms cupped to better "catch" the mucus. Then, after each position, we would press hard about the lungs with our fingers, rolling them as we pushed on her in ways that were often more uncomfortable than the pounding.

6   Some positions Alex could do sitting up, others lying flat on our laps. But a full four of the eleven she had to endure nearly upside down, the blood rushing to her head, as I banged away on her little chest, pounding her, rattling her, trying somehow to shake loose that vile mucus that was trying to take her life away. One of her first full sentences was, "No, not the down ones now, Daddy."

7   Psychologists have found that almost any child with a chronic disease assumes that the illness is a punishment. Soon, the treatment itself blurs with the disease and becomes more punishment. Sick children have highly ambivalent feelings about their doctors, on the one hand hating them for the pain and suffering they inflict, on the other admiring them, wanting to grow up and be doctors. Wendy Braun and Aimee Spengler, Alex's best friends, told me after Alex died that whenever the three of them played doctors and nurses, Alex participated with enthusiasm, but when she played the doctor, it was always cancer she was seeking to cure. She could not bring herself to be a cystic fibrosis doctor. As much as she adored and trusted her specialist, Tom Dolan, she must have associated too much pain with him ever to want to *be* him.

8   In cystic fibrosis a child must transfer this attitude toward the parents, as well, for we were intimately and daily involved in the medical process. Imagine, if you will, that every day of your child's life you forced medicines upon her, although they never seemed to do any good; you required her to participate in uncomfortable regimens, which you supervised; and then, for thirty minutes or more, twice a day, you turned her upside down and pounded on her. And this never seemed to help either. I have been told that parents let their self-conscious resentment of the illness surface during the treatments, and I must face the fact that this was sometimes surely true of me too. In some moments I must have thought that I was also being punished.

9   And say what you will, explain to me intellectually all you want about how much the postural drainage helped Alex—still, when every day I had to thump my little girl, pound away on her body, sometimes when she was pleading with me, crying out in pain to stop, something came over me, changed me. I guess, over eight years, I did therapy two thousand times, and Carol many more, probably three thousand, having to manage both times each day when I was traveling. I never understood how she managed. But still, me: Two thousand times I had to beat my sick child, make her hurt and cry and plead—"No, not the down ones, Daddy"—and in the end, for what?

10   After the therapy was finished, we had to start on the medicines. I recall how exciting it was during one period—Alex was two and a half—when she *only* had to take one antibiotic. How glorious that was, just one antibiotic every day. Usually it was two, and Dr. Dolan had to keep changing them, as Alex's body built up immunities.

11   She had to take many other medications, too, including, relentlessly, an enzyme preparation named Viokase. The bulk of Viokase is animal enzyme, which Alex needed because her pancreas couldn't produce sufficient enzymes of its own. Relative to the medicines that dealt primarily with her lung problems, Viokase was pretty effective. The minority of CF patients who don't have lung involvement initially can get by with the pancreas problem as long as they diligently take their enzyme substitutes. Alex had to take Viokase every time she ate anything. Of course, considering her lung condition, this seemed like small potatoes. Carol and I didn't even think about it much.

12   For most of her life, before she learned to swallow pills, Alex took the Viokase as a powder, mixed into apple sauce, which was an inexpensive carrying agent that could transport the drug into the system without its

breaking down. And so, before every meal she ever ate, Alex had a plate of apple sauce with the enzyme powder mixed in. It was foul-tasting stuff, a bitter ordeal to endure at every meal. "Oh, my appasaws," she would moan, "my appasaws," always pronouncing it as if it were a cousin to chain saws or buzz saws.

13   "Come on Alex, eat your Viokase," I would say, and rather impatiently, too. After all, she had already been through an inhalation treatment, a half hour of physical therapy, several liquid medications—so what was the big deal with the apple sauce. *Come on, let's go.* Alex had had a great appetite when she was younger, but a few years later she'd just pick at her food. It occurred to me then that if all your life eating was a project, and you couldn't eat a lot of the delicious things everybody else enjoyed, eventually eating would bore you. Imagine having to start off with apple sauce every time you ate anything—and not getting much sympathy for it, either.

14   Later, doctors and nurses or other people would say, "Alex seems to have lost her appetite," and I would nod gravely, being pretty sure by then that it was psychological. Eating, like everything else for Alex, had become strictly a matter of staying alive.

15   When she was very young, before she began to comprehend how pointless it all was, Alex was wonderfully accepting of all that was demanded of her. At first, like any baby, she wasn't in any position to quibble; she just seemed to go along, assuming that inhalation, apple sauce, and all that were things all babies endured. When she played with her dolls, she would give them therapy, putting off the down ones if the dolls behaved. After a time Alex began to notice that her brother was not required to endure what she did every day, but that didn't bother her too much either. Since she was the only baby girl around, she simply assumed that therapy was something that all babies and/or girls must go through.

16   Only slowly did the recognition come that she was singled out for these things. Then she began to grope for the implications. One spring day when she was four, Alex came into my office and said she had a question. Just one was all she would bother me with. All right, I asked, what was it. And Alex said, "I won't have to do therapy when I'm a lady, will I?"

17   It was a leading question; she knew exactly where she was taking me.

18   As directly as I could I said, "No, Alex"—not because I would lie outright about it, but because I knew the score by then. I knew that she would not grow up to be a lady unless a cure was found.

WHAT DID THE WRITER SAY AND WHAT DID YOU THINK?

1. What is the thesis? Is it stated directly?
2. What specific details are emphasized to increase our understanding of Alex's suffering?
3. What part of Alex's therapy caused her father the most pain?
4. What was Alex's attitude towards her doctor?
5. Why does the author feel Alex lost her appetite?

HOW DID THE WRITER SAY IT

1. Although writing for a general audience, the author does not define all the medical terms he uses in the essay. Why not?
2. Why is so much more attention given to the treatment of the disease than to the symptoms, the causes, hopes for the future, and so on?
3. Where does the author sound most like a scientific observer? Where does he sound most like an angry parent?

═══════════════WHAT ABOUT *YOUR* WRITING?═══════════════

Paragraph 3 begins this way: "The luckiest patients are those born without lung involvement. Others have such mild cases that they go undetected for years; quite possibly there are even some CF patients who never know they have the disease, but die relatively young of some misunderstood pulmonary involvement." Why "pulmonary involvement?" Why not just repeat "lung involvement?" It's possible that Frank Deford fell victim to *elegant variation.*

Too many writers worry about repeating a word in the same sentence or in sentences close to each other. This worry sometimes leads them into using synonyms—often "elegant" ones—that can be more distracting than any repetition.

As mother brought the turkey to the table, I thought of how often that fowl had added to the joys of Thanksgiving.

In planning your wedding, remember that nuptial ceremonies are largely a matter of individual choice.

A previous "What About *Your* Writing?" section, while warning against monotony, has discussed how repetition can often be an effective stylistic device (see p. 74). But even when the issue is direct communication of meaning rather than a distinguished style, straightforward repetition is preferable to elegant variation.

> As mother brought the turkey to the table, I thought of how often turkey has added to the joys of Thanksgiving.

> In planning your wedding, remember that weddings are largely a matter of individual choice.

The quest for elegant variation is what sometimes leads people to misuse the thesaurus. Fearful of repetition, they consult the thesaurus for a synonym, assuming that all words in the same group have the same meaning. They don't. *Handsome* and *pretty,* for example, are likely to be in the same group; they belong within a certain related family of meanings, but they don't mean the same, and they are not interchangeable. The thesaurus is generally most helpful when writers already know the word they want but can't quite recall it. Used improperly, the thesaurus leads writers to create sentences like *Defenestration has had serious pecuniary ramifications for schools* instead of *Broken windows have added to schools' financial problems.*

Aside from commonsense concern about monotony, the only serious danger in repetition is when the same word in the same sentence or in sentences close to each other *changes in meaning.* (This warning includes different forms of the same word: *convention-conventional,* for example.) Do, at all costs, avoid confusing repetition like

The heart of our medical research project is heart failure.

The one bright spot in his report card was his brightness in math.

I can't bear the thought of the polar bear's becoming extinct.

The plain truth is that Deborah is very plain-looking.

The two little shavers love to watch their daddy shave.

AMERICANIZATION IS TOUGH ON "MACHO"

ROSE DEL CASTILLO GUILBAULT

Born in Mexico, the author is a San Francisco television executive and a syndicated writer for Pacific News Service. "Americanization Is Tough on 'Macho'" first appeared in her weekly column for the magazine of the *San Francisco Chronicle*. As you read, notice how Guilbault uses the techniques of comparison and contrast to develop her definitions.

Words to check:

patriarch (paragraph 5)   stoically (10)
quintessential (7)   upbraided (10)
ambiguities (10)   transgressions (15)
recalcitrant (10)

1   What is *macho?* That depends which side of the border you come from.

2   Although it's not unusual for words and expressions to lose their subtlety in translation, the negative connotations of *macho* in this country are troublesome to Hispanics.

3   Take the newspaper descriptions of alleged mass murderer Ramon Salcido. That an insensitive, insanely jealous, hard-drinking, violent Latin male is referred to as *macho* makes Hispanics cringe.

4   *"Es muy macho,"* the women in my family nod approvingly, describing a man they respect. But in the United States, when women say, "He's so macho," it's with disdain.

5   The Hispanic *macho* is manly, responsible, hardworking, a man in charge, a patriarch. A man who expresses strength through silence. What the Yiddish language would call a *mensch*.

6   The American *macho* is a chauvinist, a brute, uncouth, selfish, loud, abrasive, capable of inflicting pain, and sexually promiscuous.

7   Quintessential *macho* models in this country are Sylvester Stallone, Arnold Schwarzenegger and Charles Bronson. In their movies, they exude toughness, independence, masculinity. But a closer look reveals their machismo is really violence masquerading as courage, sullenness disguised as silence and irresponsibility camouflaged as independence.

8   If the Hispanic idea of *macho* were translated to American screen roles, they might be Jimmy Stewart, Sean Connery and Laurence Olivier.

9   In Spanish, *macho* ennobles Latin males. In English it devalues them. This pattern seems consistent with the conflicts ethnic minority males

experience in this country. Typically the cultural traits other societies value don't translate as desirable characteristics in America.

10   I watched my own father struggle with these cultural ambiguities. He worked on a farm for twenty years. He laid down miles of irrigation pipe, carefully plowed long, neat rows in fields, hacked away at recalcitrant weeds and drove tractors through whirlpools of dust. He stoically worked twenty-hour days during harvest season, accepting the long hours as part of agricultural work. When the boss complained or upbraided him for minor mistakes, he kept quiet, even when it was obvious the boss had erred.

11   He handled the most menial tasks with pride. At home he was a good provider, helped out my mother's family in Mexico without complaint, and was indulgent with me. Arguments between my mother and him generally had to do with money, or with his stubborn reluctance to share his troubles. He tried to work them out in his own silence. He didn't want to trouble my mother—a course that backfired, because the imagined is always worse than the reality.

12   Americans regarded my father as decidedly un-*macho*. His character was interpreted as nonassertive, his loyalty, non-ambition, and his quietness, ignorance. I once overhead the boss's son blame him for plowing crooked rows in a field. My father merely smiled at the lie, knowing the boy had done it, but didn't refute it, confident his good work was well known. But the boss instead ridiculed him for being "stupid" and letting a kid get away with a lie. Seeing my embarrassment, my father dismissed the incident, saying "They're the dumb ones. Imagine, me fighting with a kid."

13   I tried not to look at him with American eyes because sometimes the reflection hurt.

14   Listening to my aunts' clucks of approval, my vision focused on the qualities America overlooked. "He's such a hard worker. So serious, so responsible." My aunts would secretly compliment my mother. The unspoken comparison was that he was not like some of their husbands, who drank and womanized. My uncles represented the darker side of *macho*.

15   In a patriarchal society, few challenge their roles. If men drink, it's because it's the manly thing to do. If they gamble, it's because it's how men relax. And if they fool around, well, it's because a man simply can't hold back so much man! My aunts didn't exactly meekly sit back, but they put up with these transgressions because Mexican society dictated this was their lot in life.

16   In the United States, I believe it was the feminist movement of the early '70s that changed *macho*'s meaning. Perhaps my generation of Latin women was in part responsible. I recall Chicanas complaining about the chauvinistic nature of Latin men and the notion they wanted their women barefoot,

pregnant and in the kitchen. The generalization that Latin men embodied chauvinistic traits led to this interesting twist of semantics. Suddenly a word that represented something positive in one culture became a negative prototype in another.

17   The problem with the use of *macho* today is that it's become an accepted stereotype of the Latin male. And like all stereotypes, it distorts truth.

18   The impact of language in our society is undeniable. And the misuse of *macho* hints at a deeper cultural misunderstanding that extends beyond mere word definitions.

WHAT DID THE WRITER SAY AND WHAT DID YOU THINK?

1. What is the thesis?
2. What is a typically "American" definition of macho? How does it differ from the Hispanic definition?
3. Does the author completely reject the American definition of macho?
4. How did Guilbault's father's interpretation of "macho" cause him trouble?
5. Why does Guilbault blame the feminist movement for changing the meaning of "macho"?

HOW DID THE WRITER SAY IT?

1. In what respects other than mere length does the author's definition of *macho* differ from a dictionary definition?
2. What is the purpose of the reference to film stars in paragraphs 7 and 8?
3. What writing pattern or patterns (see the previous chapters of this book) are used to build this definition essay?
4. What purpose is served by describing the father's farm labor?

═══════════WHAT ABOUT *YOUR* WRITING?═══════════

One of the superstitions about writing beloved by fussbudgets is that criticism must be constructive. "Don't tear down without building up." "If you don't have something nice to say, don't say anything at all." As writing superstitions go, it's way up there with the ones about never ending a sentence with a preposition (see p. 185) and never beginning a sentence with *and* (see pp. 160–161).

Constructive criticism has its place, of course, and it's an important place. Pointing out a stupidity or evil, for example, and then telling people how to eliminate it is fine—if you know how. But nothing is wrong with just pointing out the evil, either, especially when nobody else has done it or done it well.

Rose del Castillo Guilbault offers no proposal for making users of English more aware of the original meaning of the word *macho.* Chances are that she doubts whether other people have any practical proposals. So what? She hates what has happened to a once noble word; she thinks she has an insight; and she wants to hold forth. Hold forth she does, and she creates an interesting essay. Anything from pet gripes to pet rages can be rich sources of material for your own writing, too. And don't feel threatened by goody-goody calls for constructive criticism.

TELEVISION ADDICTION

MARIE WINN

Born in Czechoslovakia, Marie Winn emigrated to the United States as a child. She has written a number of books about children, the best known of which are probably *The Plug-In Drug* (1977)—from which this reading selection is taken—*Children Without Childhood* (1983) and *Unplugging the Plug-In Drug* (1987).

Words to check:

sated (paragraph 4)	ruefully (10)
inchoately (7)	satiation (12)
enervated (9)	

1   The word "addiction" is often used loosely and wryly in conversation. People will refer to themselves as "mystery book addicts" or "cookie addicts." E. B. White writes of his annual surge of interest in gardening: "We are hooked and are making an attempt to kick the habit." Yet nobody really believes that reading mysteries or ordering seeds by catalogue is serious enough to be compared with addictions to heroin or alcohol. The word "addiction" is here used jokingly to denote a tendency to overindulge in some pleasurable activity.

2   People often refer to being "hooked on TV." Does this, too, fall into the lighthearted category of cookie eating, and other pleasures that people pursue with unusual intensity, or is there a kind of television viewing that falls into the more serious category of destructive addiction?

3   When we think about addiction to drugs or alcohol, we frequently focus on negative aspects, ignoring the pleasures that accompany drinking or drug-taking. And yet the essence of any serious addiction is a pursuit of pleasure, a search for a "high" that normal life does not supply. It is only the inability to function without the addictive substance that is dismaying, the dependence of the organism upon a certain experience and an increasing inability to function normally without it. Thus a person will take two or three drinks at the end of the day not merely for the pleasure drinking provides, but also because he "doesn't feel normal" without them.

4   An addict does not merely pursue a pleasurable experience and need to experience it in order to function normally. He needs to *repeat* it again and again. Something about that particular experience makes life without it less than complete. Other potentially pleasurable experiences are no longer possible, for under the spell of the addictive experience, his life is peculiarly distorted. The addict craves an experience and yet he is never really satisfied. The organism may be temporarily sated, but soon it begins to crave again.

5   Finally a serious addiction is distinguished from a harmless pursuit of pleasure by its distinctly destructive elements. A heroin addict, for instance, leads a damaged life: his increasing need for heroin in increasing doses prevents him from working, from maintaining relationships, from developing in human ways. Similarly an alcoholic's life is narrowed and dehumanized by his dependence on alcohol.

6   Let us consider television viewing in the light of the conditions that define serious addictions.

7   Not unlike drugs or alcohol, the television experience allows the participant to blot out the real world and enter into a pleasurable and passive mental state. The worries and anxieties of reality are as effectively deferred by becoming absorbed in a television program as by going on a "trip" induced by drugs or alcohol. And just as alcoholics are only inchoately aware of their addiction, feeling that they control their drinking more than they really do ("I can cut it out any time I want—I just like to have three or four drinks before dinner"), people similarly overestimate their control over television watching. Even as they put off other activities to spend hour after hour watching television, they feel they could easily resume living in a different, less passive style. But somehow or other while the television set is present in their homes, the click doesn't sound. With

television pleasures available, those other experiences seem less attractive, more difficult somehow.

8   A heavy viewer (a college English instructor) observes:

9   "I find television almost irresistible. When the set is on, I cannot ignore it. I can't turn it off. I feel sapped, will-less, enervated. As I reach out to turn off the set, the strength goes out of my arms. So I sit there for hours and hours."

10   The self-confessed television addict often feels he "ought" to do other things—but the fact that he doesn't read and doesn't plant his garden or sew or crochet or play games or have conversations means that those activities are no longer as desirable as television viewing. In a way a heavy viewer's life is as imbalanced by his television "habit" as a drug addict's or an alcoholic's. He is living in a holding pattern, as it were, passing up the activities that lead to growth or development or a sense of accomplishment. This is one reason people talk about their television viewing so ruefully, so apologetically. They are aware that it is an unproductive experience, that almost any other endeavor is more worthwhile by any human measure.

11   Finally it is the adverse effect of television viewing on the lives of so many people that defines it as a serious addiction. The television habit distorts the sense of time. It renders other experiences vague and curiously unreal while taking on a greater reality for itself. It weakens relationships by reducing and sometimes eliminating normal opportunities for talking, for communicating.

12   And yet television does not satisfy, else why would the viewer continue to watch hour after hour, day after day? "The measure of health," writes Lawrence Kubie, "is flexibility . . . and especially the freedom to cease when sated."[1] But the television viewer can never be sated with his television experiences—they do not provide the true nourishment that satiation requires—and thus he finds that he cannot stop watching.

WHAT DID THE WRITER SAY AND WHAT DID YOU THINK? _____

1. How does the author define *addiction?*
2. To what other addicts does Winn compare the heavy television viewer?
3. What distinctions does the author draw between "lighthearted" and serious addictions?

---

[1] Lawrence Kubie, *Neurotic Distortion and the Creative Process* (Lawrence: University of Kansas Press, 1958). [Winn's note.]

4. Why does Winn feel that television does not really satisfy?
5. How does too much television cause harm?
6. Why does Winn acknowledge the pleasures of addiction?

HOW DID THE WRITER SAY IT? ―――――――――

1. Why does the author spend so much time defining addiction in general?
2. What is the purpose of the one-sentence paragraph 6?
3. Winn writes, "he doesn't read and doesn't plant his garden or sew or crochet or play games or have conversations. . ." Why is this phrasing more effective than writing, "he doesn't do anything?"

═══════════WHAT ABOUT *YOUR* WRITING?═══════

Just because writers of short essays usually present their theses by the end of their first paragraphs doesn't mean they always do. Or always should. Marie Winn lets us wait until the next-to-last paragraph before directly presenting her thesis that television watching, for some people, does fit the definition of a serious addiction. Had she presented the thesis in the first paragraph, much of the sense of shared intellectual exploration that fills this essay would have been lost. If the formula that usually works doesn't turn out to work this time, it's too bad for the formula.

10

ARGUMENTATION

*I*n this chapter, argumentation does not refer to fighting or bickering. It refers to providing logical reasons in support of a particular point of view. In that sense, of course, this whole book has been about argumentation. It has urged you from the start to form a thesis and devote your primary energies to proving or supporting it.

The readings in argumentation in this chapter have two outstanding characteristics. First, they employ no particular pattern of development consistently; a paragraph that describes may be followed by a paragraph that compares and contrasts and another that explores cause-and-effect relationships. To that extent, the readings here can be viewed simply as readings that refuse to fit neatly into one of the patterns dealt with in previous chapters. This mixture of patterns is a healthy antidote to excessive rigidity of thought; not all subjects lend themselves to only one pattern, and in such cases it's as absurd to write in only one pattern as it would be to play a round of golf with only one club.

The second characteristic of these readings in argumentation is that they rely, to a far greater extent than any others studied so far, on the techniques of formal logic. Formal logic generally combines two ways of thinking: induction and deduction.

Induction is the process of arriving at general conclusions by studying individual cases. All the cats we have seen or read about have whiskers. As far as we can determine, all the cats our friends and acquaintances have seen or read about also have whiskers. We therefore conclude that all cats have whiskers. We haven't come close to surveying all the cats in the world, and to reach our conclusion we must make an *inductive leap.* We work on the unproven assumption that what is true of some or many is true of all. Induction is often the only possible way to approach certain subjects, and it can be extremely convincing. Ultimately, however, the final step in the inductive process must be a leap, an intelligent guess, not proof in the strictest sense of the word.

Doctors use induction when, seeing a child with a fever and a particular kind of rash, they conclude that the child has chicken pox, since all the other children the doctors have known with those symptoms have turned out to have chicken pox. (The same symptoms could be those of an obscure tropical disease—just as some cats somewhere may have no whiskers—but the doctors are justified in making their inductive leap.) Customers in a supermarket use induction when they no longer buy milk there. The three most recent times they bought milk it was sour, and by induction they conclude that milk supplies in that store are likely to be of poor quality. Readers use induction when, having been bored by three of a novelist's books, they conclude that the novelist is a boring writer.

Skillful induction is mostly a matter of seeing to it that conclusions about a group are drawn only from a study of well-chosen members of that group. Chapter 4 on examples discusses this issue at length (pp. 87–114).

Deduction is the process of arriving at a conclusion by starting with a general premise or assumption instead of with a specific instance. The primary tool in deductive reasoning is the *syllogism,* a three-part argument consisting of two premises and a conclusion.

All Rembrandt paintings are great works of art.

The Night Watch is a Rembrandt painting.

Therefore, *The Night Watch* is a great work of art.

All doctors are quacks.

Smith is a doctor.

Therefore, Smith is a quack.

The syllogism is a tool for analyzing the validity of an argument. You'll rarely find a formal syllogism outside of textbooks on logic. Mostly, you'll find *enthymemes,* abbreviated syllogisms with one or more of the parts unstated.

The Night Watch is by Rembrandt, isn't it? And Rembrandt is a great painter, isn't he?

Look, Smith is a doctor. He must be a quack.

Translating such statements into a syllogism enables the logic to be examined more coolly and clearly than it otherwise could be.

If both premises in a syllogism are true and the reasoning process from one part of the syllogism to the other is valid, the conclusions will be proven. No leap or intelligent guess will be required; the conclusion will be inescapable.

Few arguments worth going into, of course, are open-and-shut cases. The premises are often debatable, to mention just one possible source of difficulty. (*Are* all doctors quacks? Didn't Rembrandt ever have *any* off days?) Argumentation, therefore, usually combines deduction and induction. A deductive argument, for example, will often have to call upon induction to establish the soundness of its premises. A reader has been bored by three books a particular novelist has written and inductively arrives at a conclusion about that novelist's work. That inductive conclusion can now serve, in turn, as the first premise of a syllogism:

Books by Irwin Shaw are likely to bore me.

Rich Man, Poor Man is a book by Irwin Shaw.

Therefore, *Rich Man, Poor Man* is likely to bore me.

In addition to relying on formal logic, good argumentation, though it usually does not limit itself to one special rhetorical pattern, usually does require a special pattern of manners. The readers have not yet, in theory, made up their minds and need to be convinced not only that the writer's argument is logical but also that the writer is a reasonable, fair-minded person.

Go Easy on Universals. Qualify when Appropriate.   Reasonable people can disagree. Logic beats chaos any day, but logic can not create total uniformity of opinions. Be moderate with sweeping generalizations that use—or imply—terms like *all, every, always, never, nobody.* Qualifying terms like *usually, often, perhaps, it seems likely, probably, seldom, rarely, almost* can be helpful in establishing a climate of reason, a sense that the writer is fully aware of the complexities and ambiguities of human experience. Don't assume from these comments that you should not express strongly held views in a strong way or that obvious truths should be expressed with mealy-mouthed hypocrisy. Assume only that most writers are sometimes tempted to be carried away by enthusiasm for their own ideas into making gross overstatements—and the good writer successfully resists the temptation.

Give Consideration to Differing Opinions.   After starting with a cool, impartial presentation of the issue and your way of dealing with it, present any opposition to your ideas fairly. Sometimes you may even wish to begin by outlining your opponents' point of view. Refute the opposition when you can. When you can't, concede that the opposition has a good point. Argumentation that shows awareness of only one viewpoint will rarely gain a reader's respect.

Be Cautious with Abuse and Ridicule.   You may consider some of the opposition's arguments foolish or even dangerous. Moreover, one of the hazards built into any piece of argumentation is that it may commit itself so completely to the precision of logic that it reads as if it were written by a computer instead of by a human being. Still, though there's no law against introducing humor or even passion into argumentation, be careful that such elements do not sabotage the essential logical strengths of your paper. Be particularly careful that any irrestible abuse or ridicule is directed against the ideas of your opponents, not the opponents themselves.

Devote Most of Your Attention Toward Supporting Your View, Not Advocating It.   You're trying to show that your opinion is logical. You're not trying, except in a minor way, to preach or to inspire. The introduction and conclusion will express your basic opinion. By and large, the rest of the paper will discuss your reasons for holding that opinion or for disagreeing with arguments against it.

SOME COMMON LOGICAL FALLACIES

Very briefly, here are some of the most common logical fallacies. Good argumentation depends on sound logic, and it may be valuable to have a handy guide to possible pitfalls.

Hasty Generalization.   Not enough examples or untypical examples. (See pp. 88–89.)

Post Hoc, Ergo Propter Hoc.   "After this, therefore because of this."

> I failed the test after I walked under the ladder; therefore I failed the test because I walked under the ladder.

For further discussion, see page 189.

Either/Or.   A writer presents a case as if there were only two alternatives and tries to force the reader to choose between them. Life usually offers more options than that.

Either you're for me or against me.

Either we abolish automobiles or we destroy our planet through pollution.

Non Sequitur.   "It does not follow"—often the result of omitting a necessary step in the thought process or of taking wild emotional flights in which no thought process ever existed.

I despise Professor Jones; so I'm never going to read another book as long as I live.

We all hate war and poverty and racism. How could we possibly care who wins the football game?

Ignoring the Question.   Instead of dealing with the topic under discussion, the writer or speaker becomes unintentionally sidetracked or deliberately creates a diversion. The question can be ignored in a number of ways. Among them are

"Ad hominem" argument—arguing "to the man," attacking the person who raised the issue rather than dealing with the issue itself.

How dare Congressman Arnold advocate population control when she herself has six children?

Congressman Arnold's failure to practice what she preaches has nothing to do with the merits of population control.

Setting up a straw man—accusing one's opponents of saying something they never said or intended to say and then attacking them for saying it.

You allege this movie has too much sex and violence, but people like you who want censorship are a menace to the basic constitutional rights of free American citizens.

Question begging—assuming the truth of a debatable point and basing the rest of the argument on that shaky assumption.

What prison sentence shall be given the medical murderers who perform abortions?

Before deciding on prison terms for the doctors, the writer must first offer convincing evidence that abortion is a criminal act of murder.

Shifting the burden of proof—as in law, "He who asserts must prove." It is not logical argument to declare

> I believe the government is run by secret Martian agents, and nobody can prove that I'm wrong.

Argument by Analogy. An analogy is an extended comparison. It can be valuable in clarifying a difficult point or dramatizing an abstract idea. *It can never prove anything.* No matter how many suggestive similarities there may be, they can never be more than suggestive since there must also be differences.

Analogy used to clarify or dramatize

> Finding a cure for cancer is much like finding a cure for inflation. The exact causes of the diseases are shrouded in mystery; medication carries the risk of unpredictable side effects, but without medication the illnesses grow beyond control; cures are increasingly difficult the longer they are delayed; and the experts always—but always—disagree.

Argument by analogy: analogy used to prove

> The Chairman has been unjustly criticized in this country for executing his political opponents in order to create a better society. Surely, one of the oldest truths is that you can't make an omelet without breaking a few eggs. It's too bad the beautiful shells have to be cracked open. There's a terrible mess for a little while. But the final result is well worth the effort, and only fools would waste tears over the sad fate of the poor little eggs. The Chairman has the right recipe for a greater tomorrow, and those who don't understand his techniques should stay out of the kitchen.

The second analogy assumes that a few similarities between breaking eggs and killing political opponents mean that the two actions are alike in all other respects. The writer thus attempts to prove that because one action is justified the other must be justified, too. Argument by analogy ignores all differences. Here, for example, nonhuman things are being compared to humans, nonliving things to living, breaking to killing, and so forth.

Faultily Constructed Syllogisms. *Introduction of a new term in the conclusion*—the two terms in the conclusion must have appeared previously in the premises. Note how the following syllogism introduces a new term in the conclusion and destroys all pretense at logic:

All teachers are cruel.

Mr. Jones is a teacher.

Therefore, Mr. Jones should be fired.

Reasoning from negative premises—*two* negative premises can never lead to any valid conclusion.

No human being is free from prejudice.

Fido is not a human being.

Therefore . . .

Shift in meaning of a term —some syllogisms are rendered invalid because a word has changed in meaning from one part of the syllogism to another.

Indian leaders live in India.

Sitting Bull is an Indian leader.

Therefore, Sitting Bull lives in India.

In the first premise *Indian leaders* referred to leaders of the nation in Asia. In the second premise, the same term shifted meaning and referred to a leader of Native Americans.

Improper relationship between terms —a well-constructed syllogism establishes relationships that make a particular conclusion inevitable. The following syllogism does not:

Sexists refuse to hire women.

Jones refuses to hire women.

Therefore, Jones is a sexist.

The first premise does not establish that sexists are the *only* ones who refuse to hire women. Jones could theoretically be an ardent supporter of women's rights but be under strict orders—orders he despises—to hire only men. He could be the manager of a men's professional basketball team. Jones could also be the name of a six-week-old puppy. *All* syllogisms constructed with the same relationship between terms as this one will be logically invalid. Even if the conclusion is "true," it will be true by accident, not by logic. (Jones *could* be a sexist, after all.)

Politicians are corrupt.

Simmons is corrupt.

Therefore, Simmons is a politician.

Baptists are not Methodists.

She is not a Methodist.

Therefore, she is a Baptist.

WRITING SUGGESTIONS FOR ARGUMENTATION ESSAYS

Employing the techniques of formal argumentation, attack or defend one of the numbered statements below.

1. American drivers will never renounce their cars for mass transit systems.
2. The celibacy requirement for the Roman Catholic priesthood should be eliminated.
3. Most people get married (or *divorced*) for foolish reasons.
4. The world's worst bore is _____.
5. Parents who try to impose their values on young people are the only ones young people respect.
6. The *F* grade should be abolished.
7. The greatest baseball (or *other sport*) player of all time is _____.
8. Elderly people should be required to take road tests before having their driving licenses renewed.
9. The greatest holiday of all is _____.
10. Life is a constant process of discovering that older people have been idiots.
11. The worst show on television is _____.
12. Required English courses should be abolished.
13. Students should have a voice in the hiring and firing of teachers.
14. Married couples should not be allowed to have more than two children.
15. Renting an apartment makes better financial sense than buying a house.
16. Cats make better pets than dogs.
17. The manufacture of cigarettes should be prohibited.
18. Automatic advancement to the next grade level must be eliminated from our schools.

Why Try Computers?

Elizabeth J. Langley (student)

Thesis: Everyone should learn to use computers.

    I.   Arguments against
         A. Fear of unfamiliar language
         B. Fear of general difficulty

    II. Arguments for
         A. Ease of operation
            1. hard only for uninformed
            2. easy for knowledgeable
         B. Productivity
            1. banks
            2. libraries
            3. business writing
         C. No real choice
            1. computers here to stay
            2. danger of falling behind
            3. danger of being trapped by ignorance

Conclusion: Fear should not stop you from learning vital computer skills.

Computers are, I will admit, pretty scary. They and their users often speak a language which barely resembles English, filled with bizarre terms like "mother board" and "high density 60MB hard drive" and "modem port." For the uninitiated, computers look like a mystery that they will never solve. This sense of terror and incomprehension leads to the occasional computer-phobe who refuses to use a bank machine, insists on going to a library without a computerized book index, and trembles when anyone mentions word processing. I have a good deal of sympathy for these folks, but I also believe that they must learn to use computers, despite their fears.

Before I begin to convince you that you should all learn to use computers, I must strike down the major argument against computer use. Almost everyone thinks that computers are incredibly difficult, and almost everyone is wrong. Computers are easy. It's true. For most minor computer tasks—using a bank machine; finding a book, magazine, or tape at the library; even using a simple word-processing program—hardly any computer-speak is necessary. In fact, more and more computers are being programmed to respond to more "human-sounding" commands. So, instead of needing to learn a whole new language, all that is really necessary is learning to use familiar words in a slightly different way. Those who have had bad experiences with incomprehensible computers have probably either been working with an old and inferior model of machine or have tried to learn too much too fast. If you have an up-to-date, user-friendly machine, and if you only concentrate on remembering the bare essentials, you will finish your computer tasks more quickly, pleasantly, and free of stress.

The most important reason to learn to use computers is to increase the efficiency of the machines. A computer can't do its job if its users can't do theirs, and that's just the way it is. In fact, those times when the bank machine ate your card, when the library computer claimed never to have heard of Mark Twain, and when that almost-finished letter completely disappeared from the computer screen may well have been caused by some computer-phobe—perhaps you—who confused the machine so severely that it just shut down. Learning to use a computer with competence will eliminate problems like these and allow computers to assist humans as much as possible.

Learning to use computers will also make people more productive. Instead of having to wait in line for hours at the bank, they can go to the bank machine and be done in moments. Instead of hunting laboriously through a card catalog, they can use a computer to scan an eight-million-volume index in seconds. Instead of re-typing each form letter just to change the name of the addressee, they can use a computer to replace Mr. Smith with Mrs. Jones and be done in no time. Learning to use a computer makes people faster, helping them to finish potentially dull and time-consuming tasks more quickly than ever.

The last reason to learn to use a computer is that, like it or not, they are here to stay. Every day, computers are adding to or replacing some older method of doing a job, and every day they are becoming easier to use and faster at their tasks. And every day, those who don't know how to cope with computers fall farther and farther behind, trapped in their ignorance.

So, why not sign up for a computer literacy class at your community college? Then you can deposit checks, find library books, and even word process with ease and with the latest technology. Don't let your fears keep you from learning. Give computers a chance.

IN DEFENSE OF GENDER

CYRA MCFADDEN

Cyra McFadden who once taught English at her alma mater, San Francisco State University, became a professional writer in 1976. Aside from her satiric novel *The Serial* (1977) and the autobiographical *Rain or Shine: A Family Memoir* (1986), McFadden has written numerous magazine articles appearing in *McCall's*, the *New York Times Magazine*, the *Nation*, and *Smithsonian*. In her essay "In Defense of Gender," written in 1981, the author argues against the effects that feminist linguists have had on English.

Words to check:

archaic (paragraph 1)	redress (9)
scourging (2)	ideologically (13)
aspirant (3)	suffuses (14)
generic (4)	gentility (16)
liturgy (6)	lethargic (18)
replete (8)	

1   So pervasive is the neutering of the English language on the progressive West Coast, we no longer have people here, only persons: male persons and female persons, chairpersons and doorpersons, waitpersons, mailpersons—who may be either male or female mailpersons—and refuse-collection persons. In the classified ads, working mothers seek childcare persons, though one wonders how many men (archaic for "male person") take care of child persons as a full-time occupation. One such ad, fusing nonsexist language and the most popular word in the California growth movement, solicits a "nurtureperson."

2   Dear gents and ladies, as I might have addressed you in less troubled times, this female person knows firsthand the reasons for scourging sexist

bias from the language. God knows what damage was done me, at fifteen, when I worked in my first job—as what is now known as a newspaper copy-person—and came running to the voices of men barking, "Boy!"

3   No aspirant to the job of refuse-collection person myself, I nonetheless take off my hat (a little feathered number, with a veil) to those of my own sex who may want both the job and a genderless title with it. I argue only that there must be a better way, and I wish person or persons unknown would come up with one.

4   Defend it on any grounds you choose; the neutering of spoken and written English, with its attendant self-consciousness, remains ludicrous. In print, those "person" suffixes and "he/she's" jump out from the page, as distracting as a cloud of gnats, demanding that the reader note the writer's virtue. "Look what a nonsexist writer-person I am, voiding the use of masculine forms for the generic."

5   Spoken, they leave conversation fit only for the Coneheads on "Saturday Night Live." "They have a daily special," a woman at the next table told her male companion in Perry's, a San Francisco restaurant. "Ask your waitperson." In a Steig cartoon, the words would have marched from her mouth in the form of a computer printout.

6   In Berkeley, Calif., the church to which a friend belongs is busy stripping its liturgy of sexist references. "They've gone berserk," she writes, citing a reading from the pulpit of a verse from 1 Corinthians. Neutered, the once glorious passage becomes "Though I speak with the tongues of persons and of angels. . . ." So much for sounding brass and tinkling cymbals.

7   The parson person of the same church is now referring to God as "He/She" and changing all references accordingly—no easy undertaking if he intends to be consistent. In the following, the first pronoun would remain because at this primitive stage of human evolution, male persons do not give birth to babies: "And she brought forth her firstborn son/daughter, and wrapped him/her in swaddling clothes, and laid him/her in a manger; because there was no room for them in the inn. . . ."

8   As the after-dinner speaker at a recent professional conference, I heard a text replete with "he/she's" and "his/her's" read aloud for the first time. The hapless program female chairperson stuck with the job chose to render these orally as "he-slash-she" and "his-slash-her," turning the following day's schedule for conference participants into what sounded like a replay of the Manson killings.

9   Redress may be due those of us who, though female, have answered to masculine referents all these years, but slashing is not the answer; violence never is. Perhaps we could right matters by using feminine forms as the generic for a few centuries, or simply agree on a per-woman lump-sum payment.

10   Still, we would be left with the problem of referring, without bias, to transpersons. These are not bus drivers or Amtrak conductors but persons in transit from one gender to the other—or so I interpret a fund-drive appeal asking me to defend their civil rights, along with those of female and male homosexuals.

11   Without wishing to step on anyone's civil rights, I hope transpersons are not the next politically significant pressure group. If they are, count on it, they will soon want their own pronouns.

12   In the tradition of the West, meanwhile, feminists out here wrestle the language to the ground, plant a foot on its neck and remove its masculine appendages. Take the local art critic Beverly Terwoman.

13   She is married to a man surnamed Terman. She writes under "Terwoman," presumably in the spirit of *vive la différence.* As a letter to the editor of the paper for which she writes noted, however, "Terwoman" is not ideologically pure. It still contains "man," a syllable reeking of all that is piggy and hairy-chested.

14   Why not Beverly Terperson? Or better, since "Terperson" contains "son," "Terdaughter"? Or a final refinement, Beverly Ter?

15   Beverly Terwoman did not dignify this sexist assault with a reply. The writer of the letter was a male person, after all, probably the kind who leaves his smelly sweat socks scattered around the bedroom floor.

16   No one wins these battles anyway. In another letter to the same local weekly, J. Seibert, female, lets fire at the printing of an interview with Phyllis Schlafly. Not only was the piece "an offense to everything that Marin County stands for," but "it is even more amusing that your interview was conducted by a male."

17   "This indicates your obvious assumption that men understand women's issues better than women since men are obviously more intelligent (as no doubt Phyllis would agree)."

18   A sigh suffuses the editor's note that follows: "The author of the article, Sydney Weisman, is a female."

19   So the war of the pronouns and suffixes rages, taking no prisoners except writers. Neuter your prose with all those clanking "he/she's," and no one will read you except Alan Alda. Use masculine forms as the generic, and you have joined the ranks of the oppressor. None of this does much to encourage friendly relations between persons, transpersons or—if there are any left—people.

20   I also have little patience with the hyphenated names more and more California female persons adopt when they marry, in the interests of retaining their own personhood. These accomplish their intention of declaring the husband separate but equal. They are hell on those of us who have trouble

remembering one name, much less two. They defeat answering machines, which can't handle, "Please call Gwendolyn Grunt-Messerschmidt." And in this culture, they retain overtones of false gentility.

21   Two surnames, to me, still bring to mind the female writers of bad romances and Julia Ward Howe.

22   It's a mug's game, friends, this neutering of a language already fat, bland and lethargic, and it's time we decide not to play it. This female person is currently writing a book about rodeo. I'll be dragged behind a saddle bronc before I will neuter the text with "cowpersons."

WHAT DID THE WRITER SAY AND WHAT DID YOU THINK?

1.   What is McFadden's thesis?
2.   What bothers McFadden about the "neutering" of English? Does she believe it is a passing fad? Why or why not?
3.   Why do you think that the author finds "person" suffixes and the "he/she" use ridiculous? Do you agree? Why or why not?
4.   Why does McFadden include the religious references in paragraphs 6 and 7? How do they support her argument against change?
5.   The author also points out her objection to hyphenated names. Does her example in this instance support her major argument? Why or why not?
6.   After reading McFadden's essay, do you agree with her theory that "the war of the pronouns and suffixes rages, taking no prisoners except writers"? Why or why not?
7.   Does the author offer any solution to the problems associated with neutering English? If so, what?

HOW DID THE WRITER SAY IT?

1.   What does McFadden's title imply?
2.   Aside from the numerous examples, including some narrative ones, what other modes does McFadden use?
3.   Why did the author choose the word "neuter" to indicate the elimination of sexism from the language? What are some of its connotations?

4. The author uses figures of speech throughout the essay. Select at least one metaphor and one simile and explain how each aids McFadden's purpose. (See What About *Your* Writing, pp. 107–108.)

=========================**WHAT ABOUT *YOUR* WRITING?**=========================

Cyra McFadden's "In Defense of Gender" is an attack on the neutering of English, a change which has produced a new jargon. Indirectly, the essay is an attack on jargon of any kind. Jargon is the specialized language and trade talk—the technical vocabulary—that insiders use to communicate with each other. Psychology, sociology, education, government, economics, the armed forces—virtually every area of human activity has its own jargon, even the feminist movement. Jargon is sometimes necessary, of course. Nobody can logically object when nuclear physicists or brain surgeons, addressing themselves to their colleagues, use the restricted vocabulary of their own field. There isn't any synonym in everyday English for the medulla oblongata. So much material, however, allegedly written for general audiences, has been filled with jargon that in addition to its original meaning the word has now come to refer to pompous double-talk, offensive to outsiders and insiders alike. Jargon of this kind gives the impression that the author is unable to tolerate simplicity, or gender, according to McFadden. Sometimes it gives the even more objectionable sense of being deliberately designed to give commonplace ideas a bogus air of dignity, presumably to impress all the ignorant peasants—like us. As McFadden notes, unisex jargon demands "that the reader note the writer's virtue. 'Look what a nonsexist writer-person I am, voiding the use of masculine forms for the generic.'"

You will be writing for a general audience in your composition course. It's almost always possible to turn the high-sounding mumbo jumbo of jargon into everyday English. Be extremely careful about picking subjects in which it is not possible: tuning an engine, programming a computer, performing a chemical analysis, or operating a fork lift. If you decide to go ahead anyway, be sure to provide simple definitions for all the unfamiliar terms.

Offensive Jargon	**Everyday English**
Maximum utilization of vehicular resources . . .	Making the best use of transportation . . .
Furtherance of interpersonal communications between disparate socioeconomic units . . .	Getting people of different backgrounds to talk more with each other . . .

Offensive Jargon	Everyday English
Bilateral accommodation is imperative.	Both sides will have to compromise.
The classroom situation is geared to the fostering of meaningful, democratic decision-making opportunities by the student person population.	Students have a voice in determining what happens in class.

WHAT'S WRONG WITH BLACK ENGLISH?

RACHEL L. JONES

Rachel L. Jones wrote this essay for *Newsweek* magazine in 1982 when she was a student at Southern Illinois University. Ms. Jones has written for *The Chicago Reporter* and is now a feature writer for the *Detroit Free Press.* Her frequently anthologized essay is one of the important documents in the ongoing debate over black English.

Words to check:

patois (paragraph 1)   rabid (5)
doggedly (4)

1   William Labov, a noted linguist, once said about the use of black English, "It is the goal of most black Americans to acquire full control of the standard language without giving up their own culture." He also suggested that there are certain advantages to having two ways to express one's feelings. I wonder if the good doctor might also consider the goals of those black Americans who have full control of standard English but who are every now and then troubled by that colorful, grammar-to-the-winds patois that is black English. Case in point—me.

2   I'm a 21-year-old black born to a family that would probably be considered lower-middle class—which in my mind is a polite way of describing a condition only slightly better than poverty. Let's just say we rarely if ever did the winter-vacation thing in the Caribbean. I've often had to defend my humble beginnings to a most unlikely group of people for an even less likely reason. Because of the way I talk, some of my black peers look at me sideways and ask, "Why do you talk like you're white?"

3   The first time it happened to me I was nine years old. Cornered in the school bathroom by the class bully and her sidekick, I was offered the opportunity to swallow a few of my teeth unless I satisfactorily explained why I always got good grades, why I talked "proper" or "white." I had no ready answer for her, save the fact that my mother had from the time I was old enough to talk stressed the importance of reading and learning, or that L. Frank Baum and Ray Bradbury were my closest companions. I read all my older brothers' and sisters' literature textbooks more faithfully than they did, and even lightweights like the Bobbsey Twins and Trixie Belden were allowed into my bookish inner circle. I don't remember exactly what I told those girls, but I somehow talked my way out of a beating.

4   I was reminded once again of my "white pipes" problem while apartment hunting in Evanston, Illinois, last winter. I doggedly made out lists of available places and called all around. I would immediately be invited over—and immediately turned down. The thinly concealed looks of shock when the front door opened clued me in, along with the flustered instances of "just getting off the phone with the girl who was ahead of you and she wants the rooms." When I finally found a place to live, my roommate stirred up old memories when she remarked a few months later, "You know, I was surprised when I first saw you. You sounded white over the phone." Tell me another one, sister.

5   I should've asked her a question I've wanted an answer to for years: how does one "talk white"? The silly side of me pictures a rabid white foam spewing forth when I speak. I don't use Valley Girl jargon, so that's not what's meant in my case. Actually, I've pretty much deduced what people mean when they say that to me, and the implications are really frightening.

6   It means that I'm articulate and well-versed. It means that I can talk as freely about John Steinbeck as I can about Rick James. It means that "ain't" and "he be" are not staples of my vocabulary and are only used around family and friends. (It is almost Jekyll and Hyde-ish the way I can slip out of academic abstractions into a long, lean, double-negative-filled dialogue, but I've come to terms with that aspect of my personality.) As a child, I found it hard to believe that's what people meant by "talking proper"; that would've meant that good grades and standard English were equated with white skin, and that went against everything I'd ever been taught. Running into the same type of mentality as an adult has confirmed the depressing reality that for many blacks, standard English is not only unfamiliar, it is socially unacceptable.

7   James Baldwin once defended black English by saying it had added "vitality to the language," and even went so far as to label it a language in its

own right, saying, "Language [i.e., black English] is a political instrument" and a "vivid and crucial key to identity." But did Malcolm X urge blacks to take power in this country "any way y'all can"? Did Martin Luther King Jr. say to blacks, "I has been to the mountaintop, and I done seed the Promised Land"? Toni Morrison, Alice Walker and James Baldwin did not achieve their eloquence, grace and stature by using only black English in their writing. Andrew Young, Tom Bradley and Barbara Jordan did not acquire political power by saying, "Y'all crazy if you ain't gon vote for me." They all have full command of standard English, and I don't think that knowledge takes away from their blackness or commitment to black people.

8   I know from experience that it's important for black people, stripped of culture and heritage, to have something they can point to and say, "This is ours, *we* can comprehend it, *we* alone can speak it with a soulful flourish." I'd be lying if I said that the rhythms of my people caught up in "some serious rap" don't sound natural and right to me sometimes. But how heartwarming is it for those same brothers when they hit the pavement searching for employment? Studies have proven that the use of ethnic dialects decreases power in the marketplace. "I be" is acceptable on the corner, but not with the boss.

9   Am I letting capitalistic, European-oriented thinking fog the issue? Am I selling out blacks to an ideal of assimilating, being as much like white as possible? I have not formed a personal political ideology, but I do know this: it hurts me to hear black children use black English, knowing that they will be at yet another disadvantage in an educational system already full of stumbling blocks. It hurts me to sit in lecture halls and hear fellow black students complain that the professor "be tripping dem out using big words dey can't understand." And what hurts most is to be stripped of my own blackness simply because I know my way around the English language.

10   I would have to disagree with Labov in one respect. My goal is not so much to acquire full control of both standard and black English, but to one day see more black people less dependent on a dialect that excludes them from full participation in the world we live in. I don't think I talk white, I think I talk right.

WHAT DID THE WRITER SAY AND WHAT DID YOU THINK?

1. What is the thesis?
2. What specific problems has the author experienced because of her "white pipes"?
3. What problems does the author see black English causing for other blacks?
4. Does the author see any value to black English?

HOW DID THE WRITER SAY IT?

1. What is the significance of the story about searching for an apartment?
2. Why does the author quote James Baldwin directly instead of merely summarizing his statements?
3. Explain the rhyming last sentence.

WHAT ABOUT *YOUR* WRITING?

Aware that her support of standard English is likely to arouse hostility, Rachel L. Jones tries to turn the tables on her opponents by showing that they support standard English too. If James Baldwin thinks black English is so fine, how come he is such a master of standard English and shows that mastery in everything he writes? Different readers will assess the validity of Jones's argument differently. As writing strategy, though, her approach can lead to interesting and effective papers.

Anticipate the strongest argument of your opponents, and try to turn it against them. If they contend that your stand against a new highway is holding back progress, show how they are holding back progress in mass transit systems, ecology, and so forth. If they maintain that grades in school are artificial and should be abolished, try to show that nothing is more artificial than an environment in which good work is not rewarded and bad work is not penalized. These approaches won't prove in themselves that your own position is correct, but they put your opponents on the defensive, and that's where you want them to be.

A SCIENTIST: I AM THE ENEMY

RON KARPATI

A graduate of UCLA medical school, Ron Karpati is a fellow at the University of California, San Francisco, specializing in bone-marrow transplants and the treatment of cancer in children. This essay was first printed in *Newsweek* in 1989 as a response to an attack on animal experimentation.

Words to check:

vilified (paragraph 1)   alleviate (4)
apathetic (2)   expedient (6)
unconscionably (3)   placate (6)

1   I am the enemy! One of those vilified, inhumane physician-scientists involved in animal research. How strange, for I have never thought of myself as an evil person. I became a pediatrician because of my love for children and my desire to keep them healthy. During medical school and residency, however, I saw many children die of leukemia, prematurity and traumatic injury—circumstances against which medicine has made tremendous progress, but still has far to go. More important, I also saw children, alive and healthy, thanks to advances in medical science such an infant respirators, potent antibiotics, new surgical techniques and the entire field of organ transplantation. My desire to tip the scales in favor of the healthy, happy children drew me to medical research.

2   My accusers claim that I inflict torture on animals for the sole purpose of career advancement. My experiments supposedly have no relevance to medicine and are easily replaced by computer simulation. Meanwhile, an apathetic public barely watches, convinced that the issue has no significance, and publicity-conscious politicians increasingly give way to the demands of the activists.

3   We in medical research have also been unconscionably apathetic. We have allowed the most extreme animal-rights protesters to seize the initiative and frame the issue as one of "animal fraud." We have been complacent in our belief that a knowledgeable public would sense the importance of animal research on the public health. Perhaps we have been mistaken in not responding to the emotional tone of the argument created by those sad posters of animals by waving equally sad posters of children dying of leukemia or cystic fibrosis.

4   Much is made of the pain inflicted on these animals in the name of medical science. The animal-rights activists contend that this is evidence of our malevolent and sadistic nature. A more reasonable argument, however, can be advanced in our defense. Life is often cruel, both to animals and human beings. Teenagers get thrown from the back of a pickup truck and suffer severe head injuries. Toddlers, barely able to walk, find themselves at the bottom of a swimming pool while a parent checks the mail. Physicians hoping to alleviate the pain and suffering these tragedies cause have but three choices: create an animal model of the injury or disease and use that model to understand the process and test new therapies; experiment on human beings—some experiments will succeed, most will fail—or finally, leave medical knowledge static, hoping that accidental discoveries will lead us to the advances.

5   Some animal-rights activists would suggest a fourth choice, claiming that computer models can simulate animal experiments, thus making the actual experiments unnecessary. Computers can simulate, reasonably well, the effects of well-understood principles on complex systems, as in the application of the laws of physics to airplane and automobile design. However, when the principles themselves are in question, as is the case with the complex biological systems under study, computer modeling alone is of little value.

6   One of the terrifying effects of the effort to restrict the use of animals in medical research is that the impact will not be felt for years and decades: drugs that might have been discovered will not be; surgical techniques that might have been developed will not be, and fundamental biological processes that might have been understood will remain mysteries. There is the danger that politically expedient solutions will be found to placate a vocal minority, while the consequences of those decisions will not be apparent until long after the decisions are made and the decision making forgotten.

7   Fortunately, most of us enjoy good health, and the trauma of watching one's child die has become a rare experience. Yet our good fortune should not make us unappreciative of the health we enjoy or the advances that make it possible. Vaccines, antibiotics, insulin and drugs to treat heart disease, hypertension and stoke are all based on animal research. Most complex surgical procedures, such as coronary-artery bypass and organ transplantation, are initially developed in animals. Presently undergoing animal studies are techniques to insert genes in humans in order to replace the defective ones found to be the cause of so much disease. These studies will effectively end if animal research is severely restricted.

8   In America today, death has become an event isolated from our daily existence—out of the sight and thoughts of most of us. As a doctor who has watched many children die, and their parents grieve, I am particularly

angered by people capable of so much compassion for a dog or a cat, but with seemingly so little for a dying human being. These people seem so insulated from the reality of human life and death and what it means.

9   Make no mistake, however: I am not advocating the needlessly cruel treatment of animals. To the extent that the animal-rights movement has made us more aware of the needs of these animals, and made us search harder for suitable alternatives, they have made a significant contribution. But if the more radical members of this movement are successful in limiting further research, their efforts will bring about a tragedy that will cost many lives. The real question is whether an apathetic majority can be aroused to protect its future against a vocal, but misdirected, minority.

WHAT DID THE WRITER SAY AND WHAT DID YOU THINK?

1. What is the thesis?
2. Explain the author's account of when computer models work well and when they don't.
3. Why does the author feel that he and his fellow researchers are partially to blame for the rise in public opinion against animal research?
4. What argument does Karpati use to refute the idea that animal researchers are "malevolent and sadistic"?
5. What negative effect of restricted animal research does Karpati fear most?

HOW DID THE WRITER SAY IT?

1. An effective technique is to turn the arguments of one's opponents against them. How does the author attempt to do this with the argument that we should have more compassion for animals?
2. The first paragraph seems to contradict its own topic sentence. Explain. What is the real topic sentence?
3. What is the purpose of the author's description of his student days in medical school?

================**WHAT ABOUT *YOUR* WRITING?**================

Especially when you feel your opponents have been carried away by their emotions, it is important to establish your own credentials as a reasonable, solid sort of person who can be relied on for good sense and fairmindedness. One of the last comments Karpati makes in this essay is the acknowledgement that "the animal-rights movement has made us more aware of the needs of these animals, and made us search harder for suitable alternatives." Karpati concedes that his opponents are not all bad, and as a result we feel more inclined to trust him—and his arguments.

The more controversial or potentially obnoxious your own views might be to a particular audience, the more important it is to establish at the start your credentials for rationality. Express your awareness of both sides. Grant your opponents any strong points they have. If you're complaining about unfounded accusations of "police brutality," concede that some policemen *have* acted terribly and that you're all for punishing them. If you're protesting against police brutality, admit that some hardened criminals habitually holler "brutality" no matter what the cause and that you're not interested in sticking up for them. Demonstrate your thoughtful recognition of the complexities of life. Then, and only then, will your own case get your reader's full and respectful consideration.

THE CASE FOR TORTURE

MICHAEL LEVIN

Some readers will be horrified when they read Levin's "The Case for Torture." Some readers will sense that they have always agreed with Levin but never realized they did. Few readers will be indifferent.

Words to check:

regime (paragraph 1)

arraign (3)

electrodes (4)

irrevocably (7)

extant (7)

extort (10)

disingenuous (11)

1   It is generally assumed that torture is impermissible, a throwback to a more brutal age. Enlightened societies reject it outright, and regimes suspected of using it risk the wrath of the United States.

2   I believe this attitude is unwise. There are situations in which torture is not merely permissible but morally mandatory. Moreover, these situations are moving from the realm of imagination to fact.

3   Suppose a terrorist has hidden an atomic bomb on Manhattan Island which will detonate at noon on July 4 unless . . . (here follow the usual demands for money and release of his friends from jail). Suppose, further, that he is caught at 10 A.M. on the fateful day, but—preferring death to failure— won't disclose where the bomb is. What do we do? If we follow due process—wait for his lawyer, arraign him—millions of people will die. If the only way to save those lives is to subject the terrorist to the most excruciating possible pain, what grounds can there be for not doing so? I suggest there are none. In any case, I ask you to face the question with an open mind.

4   Torturing the terrorist is unconstitutional? Probably. But millions of lives surely outweigh constitutionality. Torture is barbaric? Mass murder is far more barbaric. Indeed, letting millions of innocents die in deference to one who flaunts his guilt is moral cowardice, an unwillingness to dirty one's hands. If *you* caught the terrorist, could you sleep nights knowing that millions died because you couldn't bring yourself to apply the electrodes?

5   Once you concede that torture is justified in extreme cases, you have admitted that the decision to use torture is a matter of balancing innocent lives against the means needed to save them. You must now face more realistic cases involving more modest numbers. Someone plants a bomb on a jumbo jet. He alone can disarm it, and his demands cannot be met (or if they can, we refuse to set a precedent by yielding to his threats). Surely we can, we must, do anything to the extortionist to save the passengers. How can we tell 300, or 100, or 10 people who never asked to be put in danger, "I'm sorry, you'll have to die in agony, we just couldn't bring ourselves to. . . ."

6   Here are the results of an informal poll about a third, hypothetical, case. Suppose a terrorist group kidnapped a newborn baby from a hospital. I asked four mothers if they would approve of torturing kidnappers if that were necessary to get their own newborns back. All said yes, the most "liberal" adding that she would administer it herself.

7   I am not advocating torture as punishment. Punishment is addressed to deeds irrevocably past. Rather, I am advocating torture as an acceptable measure for preventing future evils. So understood, it is far less objectionable than many extant punishments. Opponents of the death penalty, for example, are

forever insisting that executing a murderer will not bring back his victim (as if the purpose of capital punishment were supposed to be resurrection, not deterrence or retribution). But torture, in the cases described, is intended not to bring anyone back but to keep innocents from being dispatched. The most powerful argument against using torture as a punishment or to secure confessions is that such practices disregard the rights of the individual. Well, if the individual is all that important—and he is—it is correspondingly important to protect the rights of individuals threatened by terrorists. If life is so valuable that it must never be taken, the lives of the innocents must be saved even at the price of hurting the one who endangers them.

8   Better precedents for torture are assassination and preemptive attack. No Allied leader would have flinched at assassinating Hitler, had that been possible. (The Allies did assassinate Heydrich.) Americans would be angered to learn that Roosevelt could have had Hitler killed in 1943—thereby shortening the war and saving millions of lives—but refused on moral grounds. Similarly, if nation A learns that nation B is about to launch an unprovoked attack, A has a right to save itself by destroying B's military capability first. In the same way, if the police can by torture save those who would otherwise die at the hands of kidnappers or terrorists, they must.

9   There is an important difference between terrorists and their victims that should mute talk of the terrorists' "rights." The terrorist's victims are at risk unintentionally, not having asked to be endangered. But the terrorist knowingly initiated his actions. Unlike his victims, he volunteered for the risks of his deed. By threatening to kill for profit or idealism, he renounces civilized standards, and he can have no complaint if civilization tries to thwart him by whatever means necessary.

10   Just as torture is justified only to save lives (not extort confessions or recantations), it is justifiably administered only to those *known* to hold innocent lives in their hands. Ah, but how can the authorities ever be sure they have the right malefactor? Isn't there a danger of error and abuse? Won't We turn into Them?

11   Questions like these are disingenuous in a world in which terrorists proclaim themselves and perform for television. The name of their game is public recognition. After all, you can't very well intimidate a government into releasing your freedom fighters unless you announce that it is your group that has seized its embassy. "Clear guilt" is difficult to define, but when 40 million people see a group of masked gunmen seize an airplane on the evening news, there is not much question about who the perpetrators are. There will be hard cases where the situation is murkier. Nonetheless, a line

demarcating the legitimate use of torture can be drawn. Torture only the obviously guilty, and only for the sake of saving innocents, and the line between Us and Them will remain clear.

12   There is little danger that the Western democracies will lose their way if they choose to inflict pain as one way of preserving order. Paralysis in the face of evil is the greater danger. Some day soon a terrorist will threaten tens of thousands of lives, and torture will be the only way to save them. We had better start thinking about this.

WHAT DID THE WRITER SAY AND WHAT DID YOU THINK?

1. What is the thesis?
2. What examples support the thesis? Does it matter that the examples are hypothetical rather than factual?
3. Why does the author not advocate torture as punishment?
4. Why does the author believe that terrorists have no right to complain about torture?
5. How does the author respond to the argument that the use of torture will turn "Us into Them?"
6. Does the survey of four mothers in paragraph 6 provide logical support for the thesis?

HOW DID THE WRITER SAY IT?

1. Why are only three examples enough to support the author's highly controversial thesis? Would additional examples have strengthened the author's case?
2. What organizing principle determines the order in which the examples are presented?
3. What is the purpose of the quotation marks around *liberal* in paragraph 6?
4. The specific phrase "apply the electrodes" brings the horror of torture much more vividly to mind than would an abstract phrase like "inflict pain." Does the author's brutal honesty interfere with his chances of convincing the readers that his thesis is valid?

=========WHAT ABOUT *YOUR* WRITING?=========

Inseparable from Levin's presentation of his own point of view about torture is his attack on what he considers conventional attitudes. His scorn for those attitudes gives his thesis a dimension that it would not otherwise have had.

Getting started is a problem for many writers, and Levin here demonstrates one of the most effective ways of dealing with the problem: *Many people think such and such, but.* . . . Instead of opening with a direct and sometimes flat statement of your thesis, let your thesis emerge as a response to some other people's ignorance or superstition or sentimentality or general wrongheadedness. Your thesis will then exist in a dramatic context, not an intellectual vacuum, and will have built right into it the appeal of a lively argument.

Most people think such and such about torture, says Levin, *but.* . . . With a thesis that spanking small children is often the best method of handling certain difficulties, you might begin with a few satirical references to the belief that three-year-olds appreciate the fine points of logic and that the ideal family is a loosely organized debating society. With a thesis that country music is fun, you might begin by observing that respectable people traditionally are supposed to scorn country music as trivial and commercialized nonsense. Then, perhaps, you declare that you guess you're just not respectable, *but.* . . .

For other suggestions on getting started, consult pp. 126–127 and 264–265.

THE AUSTRALIA-SIBERIA SOLUTION

RUTH LIMMER

"The Australia-Siberia Solution" can be read as a contemporary "modest proposal," though readers may disagree about how seriously the proposal is meant to be taken (see page 310 for Jonathan Swift's original modest proposal). Former director of publications at Hunter College in New York City, Ruth Limmer wrote this essay for the *New York Times* as part of a series called "Anarchy in the Streets."

Words to check:

sensibilities (paragraph 2)   heinous (11)
perpetrators (2)   feasibility (16)
geriatric (5)

1   Enough statistics, O.K.? Let's just agree that crime, justice, jails, rehabilitation all present mind-boggling problems. Fine, now let's move ahead.

2   We can define crime as something that offends community attitudes and sensibilities. (If it didn't offend, we wouldn't want to punish it.) So what offends? Murder? Rape? Insider trading? Crack? Double parking? Cheating on SATs? The answer must surely be that different communities have different sensibilities, but that some forms of behavior offend all communities—and we all wish the perpetrators gone from us.

3   That's important. Communities should be able to say: You have passed beyond any behavior we can condone or explain or permit.

4   Society should be able to say to the "wilding" rapists in Central Park,[1] for example, and to every other criminal who violates another human being in similarly monstrous ways: You terrify us. We fear you and we are right to fear you. We don't want you around.

5   What we can't agree on is whether, when found guilty, these offenders should be awarded scholarships to graduate schools of criminality and despair or be put to death. I'll not argue for either. I'll merely note that life sentences, including eventual geriatric care, cost more money than I enjoy coughing up.

6   Moreover, although I'm not philosophically opposed to the death penalty, it seems always to be carried out years after I've forgotten why I thought the perpetrator especially deserved it. Revenge is small beer when you can't remember why you wanted it.

7   There is, however, a solution we haven't considered: the Australia-Siberia solution. Devil's Island. Exile.

8   Isn't it time to think about sending the murderously violent away—not to a cell in a shockingly expensive, grimly run hotel for criminals but to a place (island? territory?) where they can apply surplus energy to building shelter, finding and growing food and managing their own lives?

9   Perhaps we could turn one or more of the Aleutian Islands[2] over to criminal colonies. The location matters not, so long as it is truly unpleasant: cold, distant, uninhabited.

10 Lawless, violent people are obviously our own product. We reap what we have sown. Having proved we are incapable of establishing a just, humane, crime-free society, we'd do well to step out of the way of a new society in the creation.

---

[1] The reference is to rampaging young men in New York City who raped and almost killed a jogger in April, 1989.

[2] A remote group of small islands in Alaska.

11   The potential colonists have committed crimes so heinous that the stain and shame must necessarily infect those we might ask to live and work in contact with them.

12   Moreover, if we leave the colonists to their own devices, those who conquer the elements and survive may (or may not, it's up to them) become prideful, coping, independent men and women.

13   Our job, and perhaps the only one that we can be sure to do well, is to supply items like lumber, nails, tools, copies of "Robinson Crusoe," technical manuals, vegetable seeds and perhaps a couple of pairs of rabbits.

14   In other words, raw materials but no luxuries: no generators, no TV sets, no branch post offices, and no jailers, no wardens, no doctors, no chaplains.

15   Better we apply their wages to mending ourselves. Better that we turn the money we spend operating death rows and isolation cells over to the innocent needful—to babies who need better nutrition, to toddlers who need day care, to youngsters who need good education.

16   Anyone who thinks I'm not serious deserves to read the feasibility and environmental-impact studies that would be required before the plan was put into effect.

17   You can guess the contents: complaints that the Aleutians are "strategic" (so, in a far more meaningful way, is Central Park); that the climate is too fierce (American soldiers served there during World War II); that prisoners would escape because friends could get them out via plane, helicopter, boat (possibly, but few prisoners would); that without jailers, they might kill each other (better each other than us), and, that as a punishment, exile is cruel and unusual (what is more cruel than prison or more traditional—think of Adam and Eve—than exile?).

WHAT DID THE WRITER SAY AND WHAT DID YOU THINK?

1. What is the thesis? How does the introduction prepare the audience for it?
2. What characteristics should a perfect place for exile possess?
3. Why does Limmer suggest giving exiled criminals a copy of *Robinson Crusoe?*
4. How does the author feel we should spend the money currently used to pay for prison expenses?
5. What is Limmer's stated objection to the death penalty? To prisons?
6. Is Limmer's proposed method of punishment too harsh? Too mild?

HOW DID THE WRITER SAY IT? ─────────────────────────

1. Explain the meaning of the title.
2. Why does the author make so much use of slang and humor in dealing with a topic viewed with almost universal seriousness?
3. To what extent is this essay a serious proposal? To what extent is it meant as an amusing intellectual exercise?

═══════════WHAT ABOUT *YOUR* WRITING?═══════════

"The Australia-Siberia Solution" ends with an attempt to refute arguments against the author's proposal. Many readers and instructors may feel that the essay should have had an additional paragraph, a normal concluding paragraph designed in one way or another to remind readers of the main point.

Ordinarily, your paper needs a concluding paragraph. Without one, your paper usually ends with the last small detail of supporting evidence, and your reader is all too likely to forget about or neglect your main point.

Your conclusion must be related to, must grow out of, what has come before. It is your last chance to remind your reader of your thesis and to drive home its importance. It is not the place to introduce irrelevant or trivial new topics. It is not the place to worry about being under or over any assigned number of words. The words of your conclusion are the last ones your reader will see, and they ought to be good words.

Beyond these observations, unfortunately, there are no tidy rules governing the writing of conclusions. Too many different kinds of conclusions exist to be wrapped into one neat package. Your best bet for writing a good conclusion is to keep the various choices in mind so they'll be available when you need them—and then to trust your instincts and common sense.

The following list suggests a few of the most useful kinds of conclusions:

Summary

We can see, then, that for many people divorce has become the preferred method of settling marital problems. Liberalized grounds for divorce, the increased social acceptance of those who have been divorced, and the loosening of religious taboos have all contributed to the dramatic increase in the divorce rate.

> *Note:* Summaries run the risk of dullness. If your conclusion is a summary, try at least not to make it a word-for-word repetition of language used earlier in the paper. Summaries work best in long papers.

The shorter the paper, the more you should consider another kind of conclusion.

Call for Action

As this paper has shown, the divorced man gets sympathy and attention and lots of dinner invitations. The divorced woman generally just gets propositioned. It's time she got some sympathy, too. She's not asking for special favors, but it's time to stop treating her like a social outcast.

Prediction

And so it goes. Divorce becomes more common every day. Eventually it may become so common that it will stop mattering much. Then, perhaps, we will find people boasting about their former marriages the way our quaint old grandparents used to boast about shipping on a tramp steamer, or winning first prize for apple pie at the county fair, or—their voices soft with pride and joy and love—staying happily married for forty or fifty years.

Question

The increasing divorce rate is not merely a colorful statistic. It raises disturbing questions. How great is the damage done to children? Does divorce solve a problem or only run away from it? Is marriage itself a dying institution? Can a society of broken homes be a healthy society? These and other questions will trouble this nation for years to come.

Quotation

All in all, there seems little any one person or group can do about the increasing number of broken marriages except to start taking seriously the century-old wisecrack of *Punch* magazine: "Advice to those about to marry: Don't."

Anecdote

Yes, everybody's doing it. The tragedy has gone from divorce. It's now an official part of the natural cycle. Last week one of the churches in my town had a divorce service. It was a big dress-up occasion. Friends and relatives got invited. Music. Prayers. Lots of lofty sentiments about change and growth and stages. It was just like getting married. It was just like dying.

Restatement of Importance of the Topic

At a time when newsmagazines and television specials go into weekly panics about gas mileage and electric bills, about the balance of payments and inflation, about deficits and dictatorships, it may seem almost frivolous to start brooding about how many people are getting divorced. In an age of revolution, it may seem almost irresponsible to create a new panic by studying statistics at the county courthouse. In the long run, however, nothing may be less frivolous or more thoroughly revolutionary for American civilization than the frightening basic truths revealed by the divorce figures of our turbulent society.

A MODEST PROPOSAL

JONATHAN SWIFT

Jonathan Swift (1667–1745) still has the power to inspire, to shock, and to offend. Active in politics, dean of St. Patrick's Cathedral (Church of England) in Dublin, Swift is the master of satire in English literature, as seen in *A Tale of A Tub* (1704), *The Battle of the Books* (1704), "An Argument Against Abolishing Christianity in England" (1708), *Gulliver's Travels* (1726), and, in the majesty of its full title, "A Modest Proposal for Preventing the Children of Poor People in Ireland from Being a Burden to Their Parents or Country, and for Making Them Beneficial to the Public" (1729). The fury, hatred, and cruelty in much of Swift's satire often make readers overlook his passionate and idealistic commitment to human welfare. Also too often overlooked is his spare and muscular prose style, especially remarkable in an age sometimes given to forced elegance.

"A Modest Proposal" is an attack on British oppression and exploitation of Ireland. As you read, distinguish between what is said and what is meant.

Words to check:

importuning (paragraph 1)	desponding (18)
alms (1)	tithes (20)
prodigious (2)	curate (20)
dam (4)	emulation (25)
raiment (4)	brevity (26)
proficiency (6)	parsimony (28)
nutriment (7)	animosities (28)
collateral (12)	factions (28)
repine (13)	effectual (31)
mandarins (17)	sustenance (31)

1   It is a melancholy object to those who walk through this great town[1] or travel in the country, when they see the street, the roads, and cabin doors, crowded

---

[1] Dublin.

with beggars of the female sex, followed by three, four, or six children, all in rags, and importuning every passenger for an alms. These mothers, instead of being able to work for their honest livelihood, are forced to employ all their time in strolling to beg sustenance for their helpless infants, who, as they grow up, either turn thieves for want of work or leave their dear native country, to fight for the Pretender in Spain, or sell themselves to the Barbadoes.[2]

2   I think it is agreed by all parties that this prodigious number of children in the arms, or on the backs, or at the heels of their mothers, and frequently of their fathers, is in the present deplorable state of the kingdom a very great additional grievance; and therefore whoever could find out a fair, cheap, and easy method of making these children sound and useful members of the common-wealth, would deserve so well of the public as to have his statue up for a preserver of the nation.

3   But my intention is very far from being confined to provide only for the children of professed beggars; it is of much greater extent, and shall take in the whole number of infants at a certain age, who are born of parents in effect as little able to support them, as those who demand our charity in the streets.

4   As to my own part, having turned my thoughts, for many years, upon this important subject, and maturely weighed the several schemes of other projectors, I have always found them grossly mistaken in their computation. It is true, a child just dropt from its dam, may be supported by her milk for a solar year with little other nourishment, at most not above the value of two shillings, which the mother may certainly get, or the value in scraps, by her lawful occupation of begging; and it is exactly at one year old that I propose to provide for them in such a manner, as, instead of being a charge upon their parents, or the parish, or wanting food and raiment for the rest of their lives, they shall, on the contrary, contribute to the feeding and partly to the clothing of many thousands.

5   There is likewise another great advantage in my scheme, that it will prevent those voluntary abortions, and that horrid practice of women murdering their bastard children, alas! too frequent among us—sacrificing the poor innocent babes, I doubt,[3] more to avoid the expense than the shame—which would move tears and pity in the most savage and inhuman breast.

6   The number of souls in this kingdom being usually reckoned one million and a half, of these I calculate there may be about two hundred thousand

---

[2] The Pretender was James Francis Edward Stuart (1688-1766), son of the deposed Catholic king of England, James II. He claimed the British throne and was supported by most of Catholic Ireland. Many Irishmen tried to escape from their poverty by hiring themselves out as indentured servants in the Barbadoes and other West Indies islands.

[3] I think.

couples whose wives are breeders; from which number I subtract thirty thousand couples, who are able to maintain their own children, although I apprehend there cannot be so many, under the present distresses of the kingdom; but this being granted, there will remain an hundred and seventy thousand breeders. I again subtract fifty thousand, for those women who miscarry, or whose children die by accident or disease within the year. There only remain an hundred and twenty thousand children of poor parents annually born: The question therefore is, How this number shall be reared, and provided for: which, as I have already said, under the present situation of affairs, is utterly impossible by all the methods hitherto proposed; for we can neither employ them in handicraft or agriculture; we neither build houses (I mean in the country) nor cultivate land: They can very seldom pick up a livelihood by stealing till they arrive at six years old, except where they are of towardly parts,[4] although, I confess, they learn the rudiments much earlier; during which time they can however be properly looked upon only as probationers; as I have been informed by a principal gentleman in the country of Cavan,[5] who protested to me, that he never knew above one or two instances under the age of six, even in a part of the kingdom so renowed for the quickest proficiency in that art.

7   I am assured by our merchants, that a boy or a girl before twelve years old, is no saleable commodity, and even when they come to this age, they will not yield above three pounds, or three pounds and a half crown at most, on the exchange; which cannot turn to account either to the parents or kingdom, the charge of nutriment and rags having been at least four times that value.

8   I shall now therefore humbly propose my own thoughts, which I hope will not be liable to the least objection.

9   I have been assured by a very knowing American of my acquaintance in London, that a young healthy child well nursed is at a year old a most delicious nourishing and wholesome food, whether stewed, roasted, baked, or boiled; and I make no doubt that it will equally serve in a fricassee, or a ragout.

10   I do therefore humbly offer it to publick consideration, that of the hundred and twenty thousand children, already computed, twenty thousand may be reserved for breed, whereof only one fourth part to be males; which is more than we allow to sheep, black cattle, or swine; and my reason is that these children are seldom the fruits of marriage, a circumstance not much regarded by our savages; therefore one male will be sufficient to serve four

---

[4] Advanced talents.

[5] An especially poor district of Ireland.

females. That the remaining hundred thousand may, at a year old, be offered in the sale to the persons of quality and fortune through the kingdom; always advising the mother to let them suck plentifully in the last month, so as to render them plump and fat for a good table. A child will make two dishes at an entertainment for friends; and when the family dines alone, the fore or hind quarter will make a reasonable dish, and seasoned with a little pepper or salt will be very good boiled on the fourth day, especially in winter.

11   I have reckoned upon a medium that a child just born will weigh 12 pounds, and in a solar year, if tolerably nursed, increaseth to 28 pounds. I grant this food will be somewhat dear,[6] and therefore very proper for landlords, who, as they have already devoured most of the parents, seem to have the best title to the children.

12   Infant's flesh will be in season throughout the year, but more plentiful in March, and a little before and after; for we are told by a grave author, and eminent French physician,[7] that fish being a prolific diet, there are more children born in Roman Catholic countries about nine months after Lent than at any other season; therefore, reckoning a year after Lent, the markets will be more glutted than usual, because the number of popish infants is at least three to one in this kingdom: and therefore, it will have one other collateral advantage, by lessening the number of papists among us.

13   I have already computed the charge of nursing a beggar's child (in which list I reckon all cottagers, laborers, and four-fifths of the farmers) to be about two shillings per annum, rags included; and I believe no gentlemen would repine to give ten shillings for the carcass of a good fat child, which, as I have said, will make four dishes of excellent nutritive meat, when he hath only some particular friend or his own family to dine with him. Thus the squire will learn to be a good landlord, and grow popular among his tenants; the mother will have eight shillings net profit, and be fit for work till she produces another child.

14   Those who are more thrifty (as I must confess the times require) may flay the carcass, the skin of which artificially dressed will make admirable gloves for ladies, and summer boots for fine gentlemen.

15   As to our city of Dublin, shambles[8] may be appointed for this purpose in the most convenient parts of it, and butchers we may be assured will not be wanting; although I rather recommend buying children alive and dressing them hot from the knife, as we do roasting pigs.

---

[6] Expensive.
[7] Francois Rabelais (c. 1494–1553) in *Gargantua and Pantagruel.*
[8] Slaughterhouses.

16   A very worthy person, a true lover of his country, and whose virtues I highly esteem, was lately pleased in discoursing on this matter to offer a refinement upon my scheme. He said that many gentlemen of this kingdom, having of late destroyed their deer, he conceived that the want of venison might be well supplied by the bodies of young lads and maidens, not exceeding fourteen years of age nor under twelve; so great a number of both sexes in every country being now ready to starve for want of work and service; and there to be disposed of by their parents if alive, or otherwise by their nearest relations. But with due deference to so excellent a friend, and so deserving a patriot, I cannot be altogether in his sentiments; for as to the males, my American acquaintance assured me from frequent experience, that their flesh was generally tough and lean, like that of our schoolboys, by continual exercise, and their taste disagreeable, and to fatten them would not answer the charge. Then as to the females, it would, I think with humble submission, be a loss to the publick, because they soon would be breeders themselves: And besides it is not improbable that some scrupulous people might be apt to censure such a practice (although indeed very unjustly) as a little bordering upon cruelty, which, I confess, hath always been with me the strongest objection against any project, how well soever intended.

17   But in order to justify my friend, he confessed, that this expedient was put into his head by the famous Psalmanazar,[9] a native of the island Formosa, who came from thence to London, about twenty years ago, and in conversation told my friend, that in his country when any young person happened to be put to death, the executioner sold the carcass to persons of quality, as prime dainty, and that, in his time, the body of a plump girl of fifteen, who was crucified for an attempt to poison the Emperor, was sold to his Imperial Majesty's prime minister of state, and other great mandarins of the court, in joints from the gibbet, at four hundred crowns. Neither indeed can I deny, that if the same use were made of several plump young girls in this town, who, without one single groat to their fortunes, cannot stir abroad without a chair, and appear at a play-house and assemblies in foreign fineries which they never will pay for, the kingdom would not be the worse.

18   Some persons of a desponding spirit are in great concern about that vast number of poor people, who are aged, diseased, or maimed, and I have been desired to employ my thoughts what course may be taken, to ease the nation of so grievous an encumbrance. But I am not in the least pain upon that matter, because it is very well known, that they are every day dying, and rotting, by

---

[9] George Psalmanazar (c. 1679–1763) was a Frenchman who pretended to be a Formosan and wrote a popular, completely fictional account of the supposed customs of his native land.

cold, and famine, and filth, and vermin, as fast as can be reasonably expected. And as to the young labourers, they are now in almost as hopeful a condition. They cannot get work, and consequently pine away for want of nourishment, to a degree, that if at any time they are accidentally hired to common labour, they have not strength to perform it, and thus the country and themselves are happily delivered from the evils to come.

19   I have too long digressed, and therefore shall return to my subject. I think the advantages by the proposal which I have made are obvious and many, as well as of the highest importance.

20   For *first*, as I have already observed, it would greatly lessen the number of papists, with whom we are yearly over-run, being the principal breeders of the nation, as well as our most dangerous enemies, and who stay at home on purpose with a design to deliver the kingdom to the Pretender, hoping to take their advantage by the absence of so many good Protestants, who have chosen rather to leave their country, than stay at home, and pay tithes against their conscience to an Episcopal curate.

21   Secondly, the poorer tenants will have something valuable of their own, which by law may be made liable to distress and help to pay their landlord's rent, their corn and cattle being already seized, and money a thing unknown.

22   Thirdly, whereas the maintenance of an hundred thousand children, from two years old and upward, cannot be computed at less than ten shillings apiece per annum, the nation's stock will be thereby increased fifty thousand pounds per annum, besides the profit of a new dish introduced to the tables of all gentlemen of fortune in the kingdom who have any refinement in taste. And the money will circulate among our selves, the goods being entirely of our own growth and manufacture.

23   Fourthly, the constant breeders, beside the gain of eight shillings sterling per annum by the sale of their children will be rid of the charge of maintaining them after the first year.

24   Fifthly, this food would likewise bring great custom[10] to taverns, where the vintners will certainly be so prudent as to procure the best receipts[11] for dressing it to perfection, and consequently have their houses frequented by all the fine gentlemen who justly value themselves upon their knowledge in good eating; and a skillful cook, who understands how to oblige his guests, will contrive to make it as expensive as they please.

25   Sixthly, this would be a great inducement to marriage, which all wise nations have either encouraged by rewards or enforced by laws and penalties.

[10] Trade.
[11] Recipes.

It would increase the care and the tenderness of mothers toward their children, when they were sure of a settlement for life to the poor babes, provided in some sort by the public, to their annual profit instead of expense. We should soon see an honest emulation among the married women, which of them could bring the fattest child to the market. Men would become as fond of their wives during the time of their pregnancy as they are now of their mares in foal, their cows in calf, their sows when they are ready to farrow; nor offer to beat or kick them (as is too frequent a practice) for fear of a miscarriage.

26   Many other advantages might be enumerated. For instance, the addition of some thousand carcasses in our exportation of barreled beef, the propagation of swine's flesh, and improvement in the art of making good bacon, so much wanted among us by the great destruction of pigs, too frequent at our table; which are no way comparable in taste or magnificence to a well-grown, fat, yearling child, which roasted whole will make a considerable figure at a lord mayor's feast or any other public entertainment. But this and many others I omit, being studious of[12] brevity.

27   Supposing that one thousand families in this city would be constant customers for infants' flesh, besides others who might have it at merry-meetings, particularly at weddings and christenings, I compute that Dublin would take off annually about twenty thousand carcasses; and the rest of the kingdom (where probably they will be sold somewhat cheaper) the remaining eighty thousand.

28   I can think of no one objection that will possibly be raised against this proposal, unless it should be urged that the number of people will be thereby much lessened in the kingdom. This I freely own, and 'twas indeed one principal design in offering it to the world. I desire the reader will observe that I calculate my remedy for this one individual kingdom of Ireland, and for no other that ever was, is, or, I think, ever can be upon earth. Therefore let no man talk to me of other expedients: of taxing our absentees at five shillings a pound: of using neither clothes, nor household furniture, except what is of our own growth and manufacture: of utterly rejecting the materials and instruments that promote foreign luxury: of curing the expensiveness of pride, vanity, idleness, and gaming in our women: of introducing a vein of parsimony, prudence and temperance: of learning to love our country, wherein we differ even from Laplanders, and the inhabitants of Topinamboo:[13] of quitting our animosities, and factions, nor act any

[12] Concerned with.

[13] Jungle region of Brazil.

longer like the Jews, who were murdering one another at the very moment their city was taken:[14] of being a little cautious not to sell our country and consciences for nothing: of teaching landlords to have at least one degree of mercy towards their tenants. Lastly, of putting a spirit of honesty, industry, and skill into our shop-keepers, who, if a resolution could now be taken to buy only our native goods, would immediately unite to cheat and exact[15] upon us in the price, the measure, and the goodness, nor could ever yet be brought to make one fair proposal of just dealing, though often and earnestly invited to it.

29   Therefore I repeat, let no man talk to me of these and the like expedients, till he hath at least some glimpse of hope, that there will ever be some hearty and sincere attempt to put them in practice.

30   But as to myself, having been wearied out for many years with offering vain, idle, visionary thoughts, and at length utterly despairing of success, I fortunately fell upon this proposal, which as it is wholly new, so it hath something solid and real, of no expense and little trouble, full in our own power, and whereby we can incur no danger in disobliging England. For this kind of commodity will not bear exportation, the flesh being of too tender a consistence, to admit a long continuance in salt, although perhaps I could name a country, which would be glad to eat up our whole nation without it.

31   After all, I am not so violently bent upon my own opinion, as to reject any offer, proposed by wise men, which shall be found equally innocent, cheap, easy, and effectual. But before something of that kind shall be advanced in contradiction to my scheme, and offering a better, I desire the author or authors, will be pleased maturely to consider two points. *First,* as things now stand, how they will be able to find food and raiment for a hundred thousand useless mouths and backs. And *Secondly,* there being a round million of creatures in human figure throughout this kingdom, whose whole subsistence put into a common stock would leave them in debt two millions of pounds sterling, adding those who are beggars by profession, to the bulk of farmers, cottagers and labourers, with their wives and children, who are beggars in effect; I desire those politicians, who dislike my overture, and may perhaps be so bold to attempt an answer, that they will first ask the parents of these mortals, whether they would not at this day think it a great happiness to have been sold for food at a year old, in the manner I prescribe, and thereby have avoided such a perpetual scene of misfortunes as they have since gone through, by the

---

[14] Reference to the fall of Jerusalem, as described in the Bible.
[15] Impose.

oppression of landlords, the impossibility of paying rent without money or trade, the want of common sustenance, with neither house nor clothes to cover them from the inclemencies of the weather, and the most inevitable prospect of entailing the like or greater miseries upon their breed for ever.

32   I profess, in the sincerity of my heart, that I have not the least personal interest in endeavoring to promote this necessary work, having no other motive than the public good of my country, by advancing our trade, providing for infants, relieving the poor, and giving some pleasure to the rich. I have no children by which I can propose to get a single penny; the youngest being nine years old, and my wife past childbearing.

WHAT DID THE WRITER SAY AND WHAT DID YOU THINK? _____

1. "A Modest Proposal" is an ironic essay: The author deliberately writes what he does not mean. What is the real thesis? Is there more than one?
2. Is the essay only an attack on something? Does Swift ever present any serious proposals for improving conditions? If so, where?
3. What is the character of the "projector" of the proposal? Don't confuse him with Swift.
4. Are there any flaws in the logic? Could you refute the proposal by using logic? What assumptions about life and morality does the projector make before the logical argument begins?
5. What people or groups are singled out as special targets for Swift's attack?
6. Are the Irish presented completely as innocent victims, or are they also to blame?
7. Where does Swift's own sense of bitterness and rage come closest to emerging from beneath the cool irony?
8. Would it be possible to read this essay as a seriously intended proposal?

HOW DID THE WRITER SAY IT? _____

1. When does the reader start to realize that the essay is ironic? Before or after the actual proposal is made in paragraph 10?
2. Comment on the word choice in "a child just dropt from its dam" (par. 4), "two hundred thousand couples whose wives are breeders"

(par. 6), "a boy or a girl before twelve years old, is no saleable commodity" (par. 7).

3. Comment on the word choice in "people might be apt to censure such a practice . . . as a little bordering on cruelty," (par. 16) and "they are every day dying, and rotting, by cold, and famine, and filth, and vermin, as fast as can be reasonably expected," (par. 18).
4. What is the purpose of the last paragraph?
5. Which parts of the essay are *not* ironic?

══════════════════WHAT ABOUT *YOUR* WRITING?══════════════

Verbal irony in its simplest form is saying the opposite, or near opposite, of what is meant. It can be seen at a primitive level when someone says, "Nice weather we're having," during a thunderstorm, and at the level of genius in "A Modest Proposal."

Nearly any subject can lend itself to the ironic approach, and you may want to consider trying your hand at an ironic paper. Successful irony has structured into it a strong element of humor and dramatic tension—tension between the surface statement and the underlying reality. With its special slant, it can also break through an audience's resistance toward reading another piece on a frequently discussed subject. It can often present familiar ideas in a fresh and exciting way.

A writer opposing capital punishment, for example, may be concerned about being perceived as a shallow idealist who thinks that all murderers are poor misunderstood victims of society. Using irony, the writer might be able to avoid the problem by pretending to be a bloodthirsty advocate of capital punishment, urging public executions, death by torture, and any other hideous ideas that come to mind. A writer supporting capital punishment, on the other hand, concerned about being perceived as an unfeeling brute, might pretend to be a simple-minded idealist, arguing ironically that if only society had provided more playgrounds and Boy Scout troops, the murderer would have become a priest or ecologist.

In writing an ironic essay, watch out for two pitfalls:

Don't Let the Reader Misunderstand.   Exaggerate enough so that the reader knows what side you're really on.

Don't Lose the Ironic Tone.   Don't let your true feelings enter directly. The worst enemy of an effective ironic paper is sincerity. Beware, in particular, of the last paragraph that introduces a "but seriously, folks," or "what I really mean to say" element. If the irony isn't clear long before that, the whole paper probably needs to be reworked.

Critics often distinguish between verbal irony and two other kinds. *Irony of fate* refers to events that turn out differently from a normal person's expectations. A man compulsively afraid of germs has his whole house sterilized, fills his medicine chest with every known drug, and dies before he's thirty by tripping over a discarded bottle of medicine and breaking his neck. Most short stories with surprise endings employ irony of fate. *Dramatic irony* occurs when a literary character says or does something without realizing its significance, but the audience or reader does realize it. The hero of a melodrama beats up some villains, turns to the audience, says "Virtue triumphs again," and does not see another villain sneaking up behind him with a club.

Sarcasm is verbal irony used in an extremely bitter and personal fashion: "You really have a big heart, don't you?"

CREDITS AND ACKNOWLEDGMENTS

INDEX